MANIFEST LIKE A GODDESS

SARA DAVES

Dear Erika,

Divine blessings on your
manifesting journey

♥
Sara

KWE
PUBLISHING, LLC

MANIFEST LIKE A GODDESS

Daves, Sara. *Manifest Like a Goddess.*

Copyright © 2022 by Sara Daves

ISBNs: 979-8-9860475-0-8 (print), 979-8-9860475-1-5 (ebook)

Library of Congress Catalog Number: 2022911657

Cover photography by Melody Smith

Cover graphics by Laurie Baines

Cover art by Michelle Fairbanks | Fresh Design

Published by KWE Publishing https://kwepub.com

Daves, Sara. Manifest Like a Goddess.
1. BODY, MIND & SPIRIT: Inspiration and Personal Growth. 2. BODY, MIND & SPIRIT: Goddess Worship

REVIEWS FOR MANIFEST LIKE A GODDESS

In her debut book, my dear friend, Sara Daves reminds readers that although humans typically express in physical form as either masculine or feminine, it requires embracing both energies to create or manifest our dreams. Sara invites us to introduce the archetypal male and female genders inherent to each of us, then establish a space within us for them to rise in love. When they openly declare their love for one another, a sacred union ritual is held. From this wedding, the honoring of authentic love-making occurs. In the afterglow, the entire community patiently perseveres, nurturing the lovers' dreams until they are born into the world of form where the celebration of life continues. Sara delivers a dream worthy of our nurturing.

—Albert C. Moore, author of *Eyes In The Mirror: Everything Changed When He met His Soul*

Manifest Like a Goddess is an all-inclusive one-stop read that provides readers with proven insights and diverse wisdom practices that would otherwise require a lifetime of research and years of practice to embody. For those committed to making a meaningful difference in your life, Sara Daves cut out the guesswork, but not the fun for you to manifest!

—Denise Dolan, Thought Leader, Medium, & Inner Wisdom Development Coach

Sara has a huge heart and wants the whole world to shine. She taught me how to be a true Goddess and manifest my dreams. Thank you Sara for being such a calming light in this world. This book will teach people how to really show up for themselves and become the human they are meant to be.

—Honesty Liller, CPRS, *Best-Selling Author of Scattered Pink*

This book takes the mystery of manifestation and reveals the essential elements and practices with which any individual can engage to create the life they know to be possible for them. Grounded in research, timeless wisdom, and a wealth of life experience, Sara Daves invites us to wake up to our potential and join her on a journey of conscious living. Her insights inspire the imagination, and her strategies catalyze the potential that we each innately carry. She artfully brings balance to the polarities of life, acknowledging the wide variety of experiences we have each had. Sara invites us to live within the natural rhythms and flow of life and leads us to discover our own creative potential. Whether this finds you simply curious, feeling stuck, or celebrating success, this book will guide you in taking your life to the next level.

—Sharon Addilynn, Coach Practitioner

CONTENTS

NEXT STEPS AFTER READING
THE BOOK

This book is dedicated to the feminine essence, for without her, life would not only be without wonder, it simply could not be.

FOREWORD

Authentic. Honest. Inspirational.

These are just a few words to describe my fellow author, trail-blazer, changemaker, and dear friend, Sara Daves. As a lifelong student and teacher, Sara has spent decades seeking truth, both in the 3-D world we live in, as well as in the inner spiritual world where anything you can imagine can manifest.

As a workshop facilitator and purpose coach, Sara empowers individuals, families, organizations, and entire communities to seek and fearlessly pursue a path towards personal transformation and enlightenment. I've heard her say many times, "What we fear most often turns out to be paper tigers." So many of our deepest worries are a byproduct of our programming and fabrication of our mind. When we learn to see the landscape of our lives and the cast of characters who coexist with us in this reality with a curious and open heart, everything changes in the blink of an eye.

In her highly anticipated and masterfully written book *Manifest Like a Goddess,* Sara's poetic yet pragmatic words inform, encourage, and delight. As she takes you on an interpersonal journey from separation to oneness, Sara shares practical tips and a wide variety of methods for understanding and working with energy. These techniques are used to achieve the ultimate goals of self-acceptance, self-love, and manifesting the life, the love, and the happiness that is our divine right to experience.

Sara incorporates the best master teachings from some of the greats such as Carl Jung, Eckhart Tolle, Sir Isaac Newton, Deepak Chopra, and Joe Dispenza to name a few. From soul contracts to tarot, and from moon cycles to runes... Sara reveals how these systems are all interconnected and point us to the same truth. We are one. We are connected to each other and to the divine.

In the words of Tony Robbins, "Where your focus goes, energy flows." Whether you are a seasoned manifestor or just beginning your manifesting journey, *Manifest Like A Goddess* is guaranteed to awaken your inner goddess. And with her, you will unlock ancient memories and timeless mysteries.

Hang on to your chariot, dear goddess... life as you know it is on the precipice of change.

Are you ready? Then turn the page...

—Delanea Davis, *International Best-Selling Author, CEO of Cloud9 Online and Partner/Co-Founder of Experience Design International*

PREFACE

"Manifesting: To reveal the presence of."

My business coach (and self-professed word nerd—a woman after my own heart) discovered this definition of manifesting. When she shared it with me, I knew immediately that I would add this definition to my book. This one tiny sentence represents the core of everything you are about to read. It is a simple, yet profound truth. We are expansive, spiritual beings having a human experience. It is imperative that we understand this and that what we desire is already here, waiting to be discovered.

The ability to manifest is a gift all humans possess, regardless of age, religion, ethnicity, life circumstances, cultural background, or socio-economic status. The barrier to accessing and utilizing this divine gift lies in social conditioning. We've been conditioned to believe that in order to get what we desire, we must either fall in line with societal standards, or take full control and make everything happen on our own. Both of these options are oppressive. Accepting the fate of your conditioning is a relinquishment of your personal power. Yet, ironically, I consider this to be the higher path of the two, because the latter—trying to control outcomes—cuts you off from your divine right to co-create with the universe and represents resistance to the acceptance of what is. Acceptance is necessary while you're waiting for your manifestations to arrive.

You've surely heard the saying, "If you want something done, you have to do it yourself." While this is true on some level, this belief ignores the fundamental component to conscious manifesting: co-creation.

We co-create using both masculine and feminine energy. We all possess both masculine and feminine energy within. Every person leads with one or the other, but everyone has access to both. Conscious manifesting requires the use of both masculine and feminine energy, however, society has devalued the feminine for centuries. As a result, we've lost access to half our manifesting power. This book is for those who already know how to use their masculine energy to make stuff happen and wish to understand the powerful energy of the feminine that can help you co-create with the universe.

Being goal-oriented, driven, and competitive takes an enormous amount of energy, which represents the pure masculine essence. It requires intense focus and planning to confidently achieve your goals. If masculine energy is the only energy you're using to create your reality, you will end up walking through life feeling as if you have the weight of the world on your shoulders. Overusing masculine energy creates controlling behaviors, which can bring forth toxicity, regardless of whether you lead with the masculine or feminine essence. The focus becomes solely about obligation—what you should do—regardless of whether or not you're happy.

I spent a long time attempting to control everything around me. I ended up settling for what "should" make me happy. I knew I wanted more out of life, but I was not sure what that was. I was in too deep—and change felt incredibly frightening. It was only when I was forced to surrender the control I thought I had that I could step into the unknown and see the unlimited possibilities all around me.

In the space of the unknown, I learned that time is not linear—and there is much more to our existence than meets the untrained eye. As I opened up to self-understanding, my awareness of the intricate connection of everything expanded. I took responsibility for my own healing by resting my mind and feeling my way through. I did not turn away from my pain—I offered love to all the parts of myself that hurt and that is how I discovered that true happiness comes from within.

From this experience, I recognized that the world is my mirror and everything that was "happening to me" was a direct reflection of what was "happening within me." Then, I watched as grief transformed into purpose and confusion into clarity. This awareness gave me the strength to embrace my unique gifts, and I watched my external world transform in amazing ways. I began to experience joy on a level that was once unfathomable to me. I found love, purpose, and my powerful inner Goddess.

My pain could have buried me, but instead, it became the catalyst for realizing my life's purpose. It doesn't have to take a traumatic experience that shakes you to your core in order to awaken. Anyone can discover their inner power and emerge with this divine knowledge.

I invite you to take the fascinating journey of exploring your beautiful inner self—the parts that maybe you can't yet see, which will make your true desires crystal clear, so you can begin Manifesting Like a Goddess.

INTRODUCTION

As human beings, we seek both joy and purpose.

Discovering your authentic self is essential to living a joyful and purposeful life. When you understand and accept your true self and your reason for being alive, your entire life changes for the better, and so does the world. Purpose is a masculine-oriented concept, yet we all have a purpose.

Equally important is understanding how to manifest your joyful life into being, which is feminine-oriented. The feminine represents the full expression of life and the joy that derives from that full expression. We all have access to joy.

Joy is the natural state of our beingness—it is non-dualistic, which is why when we drop the body (and the dualistic nature of our human experience), there is nothing left but joy.

My journey of learning how to embrace my joyful feminine essence and live into my purposeful masculine essence has been simultaneously beautiful and heartbreaking. When my son was 18 years old, he was forced to plead guilty to a crime he did not commit. There was no evidence to prove his guilt, however, his court-appointed attorney told us that if he did not plead guilty, he could potentially face up to 25 years in prison, simply because the jury was not that of his peers. He was offered a two year sentence if he took the plea. We had an impossible decision to make as a family. He chose to not take the chance of spending more than two decades in prison, and pleaded guilty. After spending a year in jail waiting for his court hearing, that two years turned into five. He spent five years doing his best to maintain his sanity while dealing with physical and emotional violence. When it was finally over, we thought the nightmare had finally come to an end. After only six weeks of Trey being home, he died of an overdose.

I fell into a deep, dark pit of grief. There, I experienced the most debilitating pain I had ever felt. The grief pit was a terrifying place for me and became unbearable, so I climbed out. I felt if I allowed myself to exist in that space for too long, I would have died myself.

So I left the grief pit prematurely, putting my heart and soul at risk. I was only in the preemie stages of grieving. Think of a premature infant who desperately needs comfort and love to survive. On a deep level, that is what I needed. Infants are naturally co-dependent. Grief-stricken adults are too. As an adult, I thought there was in fact something I could do about this need. I began manufacturing happiness. I married a man who was in the Navy and about to be stationed clear across the country, so we went for it. Soon after we married, he received an honorable discharge after three years of service. The outcome was a relief.

My then-new husband and I decided to plan our wedding for the following year, and I spent most of my savings to pay for it. While we were on our honeymoon, I wondered if I had made a terrible mistake. But it was too late. I was not going to give up, no matter what. Six grueling years went by—he left 13 times. As he came and went, the grief compounded, and I felt like I was living inside a psychological thriller novel. Our blended energy created toxicity. I felt I had danced with the devil, and he danced me into oblivion. I had no idea my co-dependent energy had attracted this.

Our marriage was born out of a series of traumatic events that included the death of my son and my father. The marriage represented a trauma bond, which was incredibly difficult to break. Slowly, I became controlled through gaslighting and intermittent reinforcement while I grieved the death of my son and my father. Gradually, I experienced isolation, triangulation, and severe confusion. I didn't realize what was happening until I became completely immobilized. I felt like my soul had been sucked out of my body.

I walked away from that experience feeling completely worthless. I felt under attack in many areas—my finances, gender, body, sexuality, mental capacity, and emotional health.

For safety, I hid from the world. I was trying to grow my business, but it got nowhere. All of my life energy seemed to have left my body. I became an empty shell of myself.

Today, I'm grateful for the experience. For without it, I would have never discovered the hidden wounds that were buried deep within the crevices of my heart. I thought I had cleaned them up a long time ago. Yet there they were, challenging me to go even deeper for healing.

There was nothing left to do but face my wounds and move through every ounce of the pain. I learned that the world is my mirror and it reflected back to me all of the buried pain I was carrying. Visibility is sometimes still a challenge for me. I still feel afraid, which is why I must show up. It has become part of my healing journey. We all have challenges to meet, fear to dance with, and growing to do. We must feel it all because the only way out is through.

Today, I have a very close relationship with Trey. We communicate through synchronicities, dreams, and spiritual nudges. While he is no longer my son in the flesh, he is still with me; he's become my teacher. He taught me that death is destiny; when it's time to leave the body, you will. He also taught me that time is irrelevant. Twenty years or 120 years on this planet is nothing more than a blink of an eye. Through my own healing, I learned that the universe loves us more than we can possibly imagine. We are just getting started on our new work together, with Trey in the spiritual realm and me in the earthly realm.

His guidance has helped to heal my broken heart and show up for love in ways I never could before. I learned to embrace my authentic self, which led me to discover my purpose: to anchor the consciousness of Oneness on the planet. I do my small part to fulfill this purpose in three ways: I empower people to discover their own unique purpose, heal their inner wounds (by learning to resolve their conflicts), and to manifest consciously. This work allows me to joyfully serve in ways that uplift the collective vibration of humanity.

What I've learned from my own life and through working with clients is that many of us have struggled with allowing ourselves to feel too much of anything, and therefore, we become blocked from experiencing joy. We all have the capacity to feel, yet we've been trained to shrink ourselves to fit into the mold of oppressive cultural norms, believing that emotional health means stuffing feelings and the most vulnerable parts of ourselves, which blocks authentic expression. Celebrating our true, authentic self is something we don't often do as a collective, even though it is our divine right. The collective wounds of humanity have formed the widespread belief that we are either too much or not enough.

You are more than enough, and if others can't handle all of you, that is their problem.

You are a divine being, and you are here to share your soul's unique expression as you move through the world in your beautiful and magical human body.

I invite you to embrace all the beautifully vulnerable aspects of yourself. As you read this book, give yourself permission to connect with both your feminine and masculine energies, which are your divine right to experience and share. When we appropriately blend these energies, we gain the ability to powerfully manifest. The masculine aspect of self supports taking action in the world, and the feminine aspect of self opens the door to allowing and receiving. As I mentioned, most of us already know how to use our masculine energy to create, which is why the primary focus of this book is how to access and work with feminine energy.

A powerful mantra that helped me to embrace my feminine essence and manifest my new reality is:

I am open to allowing and receiving.

I use it daily. I make it a daily practice to ask for what I desire and then remain open and curious about the unseen possibilities that are all around me, just waiting to enter into my reality.

For the men reading this book, know that you have a feminine aspect of self. You may or may not lead with it. If you are attracted to the feminine, then it is fairly safe to say that you lead with masculine energy. The inclination to lead with masculine energy does not mean that your own feminine energy is not valuable. If you have been cut off from your feminine aspect, you may also be cut off from your emotions and creativity and have not allowed yourself to experience joy or imagine a better life situation. It may feel like you are walking around in a robotic fog and just getting stuff done. This book can help you change that.

You may also learn something new about the challenges that those who lead with feminine energy face and will be able to use what you learn to more deeply support the feminine beings you love. What I especially wish for you is that you allow yourself to explore the creative possibilities that the feminine essence offers every human being.

Like many women I know, I spent the first half of my adult life trying to manifest my desires by forcing my way through, controlling outcomes, and manufacturing happiness. I was still manifesting, as we all do—it just was not the things, people, and situations I wanted. It wasn't until I turned inward and got honest with myself about what I really wanted that I was able to manifest my deepest and truest desires. It was only after I peeled back the layers of everything that wasn't me that I was able to uncover the powerful feminine essence that was in hiding. I learned how to tap into the sensual, creative, and vulnerable parts of myself. From there, I discovered that there was a big difference between what I actually wanted to manifest versus what I had been told I "should" want out of life.

You know what happens when you "should" on yourself? You end up living the life someone else expects of you.

Today, I fully honor my divine feminine Goddess power. I learned to manifest exactly what I want—spiritual understanding, joy, love, passion, purpose, and a life that is so worth living.

In this book, you will learn what it takes to merge the energies of the masculine and feminine to create the alchemical marriage within...this is your Goddess power. Forming an intimate bond with these polarities will help you master the art of working with universal energy and trusting yourself to do it.

No matter what has happened in your life thus far, know that the Goddess resides within you, and you have the power to access her at will. Once you become intimate with the inner workings of yourself and universal consciousness, you will gain profound insight into who you are, discover your true desires, and be able to manifest them.

Thank you for allowing me to be your guide on your manifesting journey.

MANIFESTING MANIFESTO

We are always manifesting, whether we like it or not. And sometimes, we discover that what we end up manifesting is not even close to what we actually wanted. In order to manifest on purpose, you must have a healthy sense of self-worth so you can get closer to the vibration of joy, which is the vibration of universal consciousness.[1] Otherwise, you'll keep creating a reality that will never be able to satisfy you.

Your journey toward conscious manifesting begins with having compassion for yourself.

Think of the word compassion...(come, passion).

Practicing self-compassion helps you learn about yourself and raise your self-worth, which makes it so much easier to attract your true heart's desires. Passion is the energetic pull toward your heart's true desires. When I decided to follow my passion, I found my purpose. I was only able to do this after I developed compassion for myself and lovingly embraced all the parts of me. When you are clear about who you really are deep down, you recognize your true worth and your purpose finds you. Then, there are no more decisions to make, only actions to take.

We must know when to take action and also when to patiently allow and receive. This knowing aligns you with the universal law of Oneness that is comprised of the dichotomy of seemingly two opposing ideas:

1. Everything you need is within you. (Action/masculine)
2. We are all connected in a vast sea of Oneness. (Non-action/feminine)

These two concepts are not mutually exclusive nor hypocritical. Both statements are valid, similar to the push and pull of the opposing energies of the masculine and feminine.

Once you understand these concepts, you will be able to manifest rapidly.

AUTHOR'S NOTE

Masculine and feminine essence are not solely defined by sex or sexual orientation. Both polarities exist in us all. We tend to lean toward one or the other, which is an innate preference that no one can define for us. In order to manifest, both polarities must be embraced; yet still, we lead with one or the other. Over centuries, our social structures have devalued the feminine essence, which you will learn more about as you move through the chapters of this book. For the sake of clarity and expediency on this subject, I will sometimes refer to women when I'm talking about the feminine energy or essence, and I'll sometimes refer to men when I talk about the masculine energy or essence.

HOW I LEARNED TO MANIFEST

When I first began studying the art of manifesting, I made a lot of mistakes. I wanted to be a master manifestor and the sole designer of my life—and I wanted it all immediately. So I rushed to get married, quickly started a small communications business, and began making plans to move out of the country. [2]

That was until everything blew up in my face. My new business slowed to a crawl. My new marriage was on the verge of being over. Yet I kept pushing, forcing, and controlling because I thought I had to do it all on my own. I was firmly anchored in the toxic aspect of masculine energy because I did not believe that the universe was working for me, and I felt I had to overcompensate for my former husband's lack of direction. I thought I had to do it all by myself like I had always done.

I grew weary. Eventually, I let go and surrendered my fate to the universe. I was tired and had no drive left in me. When I finally let go, seemingly random events started to occur. The act of letting go created the space for the universe to bring me something different. Two weeks after my former husband walked out the door (for the first time), leaving me without a car, I got a really nice car with a friend's help. A week later, I was randomly gifted a free trip to Monterey, California, to attend a women's business workshop, where I learned how to start my coaching business. When I came home from that trip, I was able to take some time off and just rest.

It seemed counterintuitive to not get back to work immediately. I came home with a wealth of information and the drive to implement it all. But I learned at that workshop to listen to what my body needed, and it needed rest. So I listened. I was able to catch up on sleep, spend time with friends, read, journal, and just simply be quiet. It was a practice in radical self-care, and it helped me open up to the energy of receiving. Then, I received the greatest gift of all: clarity on my purpose.

My purpose is to anchor the consciousness of Oneness on the planet in any way I feel inspired to do so. Today, I'm living into my purpose in a few ways. I teach conflict resolution facilitation based on the theory of Unitive Justice, which describes lovingkindness in action. This work was created by my mentor and friend, Sylvia Clute, president of the Alliance for Unitive Justice. It brings the concept of Oneness into conscious awareness—our forever connection to everything.

Understanding this concept was critical in developing my own understanding of the importance of purpose as well as how to consciously manifest. I'm also an Intuitive Purpose Coach, helping clients clarify their life's purpose so they can design the magnificent life that is waiting for them. When we live into our purpose, we fulfill our soul's design by being of service to the world, and we recognize our connection to everything.

That work led to the creation of my four manifesting programs in the *Manifest Like a Goddess Experience*. And from those programs, I was inspired to write this book. Learning how to co-create with the universe requires an understanding that we are an integral part of something bigger than ourselves.

None of this happened overnight, nor was it supposed to. There were some important lessons I needed to learn first. When I felt inspired to take action, I began the creation process by first setting my intention—to build a comprehensive learning experience for those who were just beginning to get serious about their manifesting journey and also for those who had been on the journey for a while but were feeling stuck.

I had some ideas about what it would look like.

My initial vision was a self-guided, eight-week online course that would help people eliminate common blocks that keep them from creating the life of their dreams and provide some tools to manifest those dreams into reality.

Today, it is so much more than that.

Over several months, that idea blossomed into a bigger one—a twelve-month full-immersion experience with four distinct programs. It includes everything I've learned along my own journey—most of the time, the hard way.

While I logically understood the concepts I wanted to share, it wasn't until I fully lived out certain life experiences around manifesting that I was able to anchor these concepts within the fibers of my own being.

In order to teach this sacred work, I needed to learn each lesson first-hand. It took me years of trial and error and lesson-learning before I was ready to offer something this special. As I initially began creating the foundation of this experience some years back, I was immediately stopped in my tracks. I learned that my former husband had just ended a months-long affair, while we were in the midst of reconciliation. My work came to an abrupt halt.

My heart was crushed. I ended up in bed for weeks in horrific physical and emotional pain. After weeks of feeling debilitated, I remembered that my happiness was my own responsibility. With the conflict resolution tools that I learned, I looked within for the original wound. I asked myself, "What do I need to know about how I'm feeling right now?" The answer didn't come right away. Eventually, the answer came to the surface, revealing an old wound. Because I had spent the last few years immersed in Inner Child work, I was surprised at what I found. It was my original wound, which I realized had impacted my entire life in myriad ways.

I was born a preemie, so I essentially lived inside of an incubator for the first weeks of my life. I spent a lot of time alone, except when I was being fed or when it was safe for others to hold me. Judging from the way I was feeling—utterly alone and like I was going to die—it now all made perfect sense.

This wound was revealing itself to me because it was time to let it go so I could step into a new paradigm and manifest a different life experience. For my entire life thus far, this wound had convinced me that the world is a lonely place to be and that love was painful. I knew the only way out of this false reality was to move right through the pain. So I embraced every ounce of that pain and gave my Inner Child all the love I could muster. My programs would not have been born without that experience. I am eternally grateful for all of it.

Six weeks later, I felt lighter and began working again.

"Take all my pain and turn it into white light." –Twiddle, "Out in the Cold"

The process of building the *Manifest Like a Goddess Experience* taught me so much about manifesting. As I built it, I learned some important lessons that I needed to understand before my work was ready to be shared with the world.

LESSON #1: HEAL YOUR WOUNDS

During that dark night of the soul experience that lasted for six weeks, seemingly, nothing of any importance was accomplished during this time. I didn't recognize the full value of this experience until it was over.

In those six weeks, I allowed myself to rest and follow my intuition, which told me that "right now is not the time for creating." I had to first release the pain of the buried wounds that would inevitably get in my way and quite possibly keep me spinning my wheels and prevent me from moving my life in the direction I wanted it to go. I felt my way through all of it and got to the other side—as I always do.

Pain is a part of life. Suffering is a choice. Moving through your own pain is the greatest gift you can give yourself. I did not pull up my big girl pants and put a fake smile on my face. I instead stopped everything and allowed myself to feel every single ounce of it.

Stuffing pain creates thick walls that you only have to break down later by doing the inevitable: moving through it.

Once that phase was completed, the space opened up again for me to create. I became inspired and had so much more of myself to give. While you cannot force inspiration, you can absolutely create the space for it to arrive on its own.

LESSON #2: RELEASE WHAT NO LONGER SERVES YOU

I had to get very brave and release the people, places, and things that were not serving my highest good. I had to settle the indecision within myself by accepting all the parts of me that wanted different things. I had to honor those parts of me so I could come into wholeness.

Once you're whole, there are no more decisions to make, only actions to take. I began divorce proceedings. I ended all the toxic relationships in my life. I witnessed karmic cycles come to completion. I cleared the space and raised my vibration in preparation for the next inspired action. I chose my own happiness. When you make room for all the things you've asked for and become a match to them, the universe will bring them swiftly into your reality.

The act of releasing is a powerful practice. When you release what no longer serves you—negative beliefs, a bad habit, negative self-talk, goals you may have outgrown, or situations that are not serving your highest good—you create room for the universe to fill the empty spaces with people, places, and things that light you up.

LESSON #3: TRUST THAT THE UNIVERSE HAS YOUR BACK

Even if you think you've screwed up the manifesting process in the past, know that you received exactly what you needed in order to grow in whatever way that was necessary to heal your wounds and be ready to receive your desires.

We are in a time-space reality based on polarity and contrast. We learn what we *do* want based on experiencing what we *don't* want. All of your experiences have been necessary in order for you to become very clear about what you truly want to manifest in your life, and you can't get it wrong. Having clarity around your true desires is necessary for you to manifest them into reality.

We are always co-creating with the universe because we are a part of the whole, part of All That Is. We cannot create alone, because nothing is created alone. The universe will always have your back because you are an extension of Source consciousness. It is you, and you are it.

This does not mean you sit back and do nothing to set your goals in motion. The universe cannot do it all. You have to work as hard as you would like the universe to work for you. But don't try to control the process.

Instead, get curious and take inspired action. You do not need to have it all figured out. You cannot know all of the wonderful treats the universe has in store for you, nor would you want to!

You must choose over and over again to trust that the universe has your back, even when it doesn't appear to be true because you have evidence showing you otherwise. Sometimes we will experience pain. This is not a punishment; pain is part of the dualistic nature of life. As I mentioned in Lesson #2, it can feel like a loss when we are forced to let go of people, places, and things. But sometimes it is necessary to achieve our destiny. Your energy and environment must be in alignment with what you're asking for in order to achieve it, and since you are destined to achieve it, the universe will move the puzzle pieces in your world around so that you can get there. As you get closer, not everyone will be able to come along with you.

And when humans drop the body, it means they are ready for their new destiny, which is beyond our understanding and it is not personal—it is destiny.

LESSON #4: LINEAR TIME IS IRRELEVANT

I was reminded over and over again that linear time means nothing in the manifesting process. Oftentimes, the universe knows your true desires better than you do and exactly when to give them to you. Amazing creations do not happen overnight, and if they did, we would most likely not be ready for them when they arrive.

I continued to open myself up to the flow of inspiration. Sometimes I have to patiently wait for it and sometimes it comes in a wave. I had to learn to become fully present in order to recognize this. I learned to trust the process and move in unison with divine timing. This helped me learn how to bend time.

In our third-dimensional (3-D) reality, we experience linear time. But in all other realities, time is not linear; it is fluid. If I had taken complete control of the process of building the *Manifest Like a Goddess Experience*, I would have beaten myself up through the creation process and ended up with an eight-week online course, which was my original plan. And while it may have served clients on some level, it would not be the comprehensive experience it is today, with the ability to reprogram the subconscious mind and transform lives.

LESSON #5: JUST BEGIN

It doesn't matter where you begin, as long as you begin. It does not matter if you cannot envision how your desires will unfold, or how to reach your end goal. You only need to take one step, and then another—and know "what" it is that you want and "why" you want it.

The "how" and "when" are none of your business.

Allow what you want and why you want it to inspire you. The more you can practice non-attachment from the outcome, the better. Human beings cannot predict exactly how the future will unfold. All of life is a journey, and when the journey is over, you go back to being the pure, joyful divine spirit you are with the full recognition of your connection to everything.

So go ahead and play with the universe. If you are willing to play with it, it will play with you. You can begin to flex your imagination by remembering how it felt to play when you were a child.

"Imagination and faith are the secrets of creation." –Neville Goddard

LESSON #6: LOVE YOUR SHITTY WORK

The eight-week course I initially began creating might have ended up being pretty damn good. But it would have been nothing close to what it is now. Next to what it is today, that course I had originally envisioned would have looked shitty.

Loving your shitty work can feel hard to do. However, I highly encourage you to love all of it, because without it, you never would have begun. Think of all your creations from childhood to adulthood—your first art project, that time you changed your hair color by yourself, when you fumbled over your words on stage, or when an important relationship fell apart—all the times you set out to create something beautiful, and it didn't turn out the way you wanted. You have to start somewhere, and rarely is it perfect the first time around.

As my dad would say—it's all relative. I can look back at all my past creations and see how they could somehow be better, and I bet you could do the same. Looking back at your old creations and feeling embarrassed about them means you've grown.

When I say, "love your shitty work," I mean that it's important to appreciate where you are in the creative process and what you have created so far. Your best work cannot come to life until you begin. Love your shitty work for getting you to a place where you can see something even better beyond it. Then, be willing to let go of your original idea instead of creating an attachment to it. If I had been attached to what I originally created, I wouldn't have been able to let it go for something better. And it kept getting better and better—and better.

This is also true for my choices in clothing, hairstyles, careers, and relationships.

Keep an open mind and allow your imagination to soar as you read this book. There is a lot of information here that will help you step outside of your uncomfortable comfort zone and masterfully co-create with the universe, so long as you're willing.

Together, we've got this.

INNER MASCULINE-FEMININE DYNAMIC

I SPENT THE FIRST HALF OF MY LIFE TRYING TO MANIFEST BY pushing, forcing, and controlling outcomes. Looking back over this time in my life, I can see clearly how all that energy I expended did not get me far. I grew up with an angel of a grandmother who worked full-time as an executive secretary at the Department of Agriculture. She came from a small town in Southwest Virginia that boasted one stoplight. She grew up on a farm with many siblings, including one brother. There was work to be done on the farm, and she and her sisters had a lot of responsibility as a result. As a young woman, she moved to Richmond, Virginia, a very small capital city, and became part of the first generation of American working women. I watched her handle her work and home responsibilities seemingly with ease. Dinner was on the table at the same time every night. My grandfather worked long hours as a manager of the public university's bookstore. On the weekends, they would take care of their modest home. It seemed to work for them.

As a single mom, I decided I could also do everything. I was taking care of my son, working full-time, and attending college—all of which I did seemingly effortlessly. I got promoted often, made As and Bs, carried my son to his sports practices, helped him with his school projects, and dinner was on the table at the same time every night. I did not want to admit that I was exhausted. I learned how to do more in one day than most people do in a week. My son Trey would often say, "You're my hero." That was music to my ears. I thought I was doing everything right. I did not need a man to help me. I could do it all myself and even do it better. I guess I thought I had something to prove. But that left me overwhelmed, too busy for fun, and quite lonely.

My crazy schedule was strict with zero downtime to play or dream. I was so wrapped up in "doing" that I lost track of why I was even doing it.

My grandmother used to say, "Hindsight is 20/20." If I could go back and do it all over again, I would not have stayed so busy. I would have accepted more help. I would have had more fun. I would have been a more relaxed mom. Maybe I would have stepped into my purpose sooner. But it took all that overdoing and spending years leading with my masculine energy for me to eventually burn out and question everything. Today, I still use my masculine energy, but I have learned to embrace my femininity and lead from that space. Today, I actually do much less. I spend more time being than doing, and my life is richer for it.

I had to undo years of cultural conditioning before I could embrace my feminine essence. Once you understand how the structures we are born into create our belief systems, you can choose something different. You don't know what you don't know, but when you find out, it becomes your responsibility to make the necessary changes.

MASCULINE AND FEMININE ENERGY

Masculine energy is about DOING: it represents taking action in the world. It is logical, goal-oriented, proactive, protective, driven, courageous, and externally focused. The power of the divine masculine is rooted in raw power, assertiveness, and taking action in the world.

Feminine energy is about BEING: it is receptive, intuitive, nurturing, sensual, and inner-focused. The power of the divine feminine lies in the mysterious and is rooted in sensuality, allowing, and receiving. It manifests through inspiration, feeling, and knowing.

THE UNANSWERABLE QUESTION

My dad often used to ask me to explain the unexplainable.

"Sara, tell me about women's knowledge."

How do you describe the mysterious depths of the ocean? I was not old enough to answer the question to his satisfaction, and it irritated him to no end.

Today, my answer to him would be, "It's not necessary to completely understand the feminine essence in order to nurture it and benefit from it."

And I would have left it there.

The feminine essence is a magical mystery. It cannot be fully articulated, because it is the energy of creation. The totality of the universe cannot be explained or understood through words.

DUALITY

We are constantly playing and working with duality on this plane of existence, and herein lies the ultimate duality—the push and pull between masculine and feminine energies. It is the union of these two energies that supports the recognition of wholeness, and there is great power to be found when we learn how to harmonize them.

The societal systems that are ingrained in the collective consciousness do not make it easy for us to find harmony in this way. The great power of the feminine has been long forgotten. Society still tends to look at women who embody masculine roles and give them props for being strong and put-together, while looking down at women who embody more feminine roles; those who own and express their sensuality, accept help when needed, and vulnerably express emotion. It wasn't always this way. Our conditioning is responsible for what we believe and how we move through the world.

RELIGION AND SCIENCE DEFINES OUR REALITY

In his Gaia series, Inner Evolution, stem cell biologist Bruce Lipton speaks about how our social conditioning (based on religion and science) has redefined our reality. When we understand how we arrived at a place in time where collective fear-based beliefs have shaped our experiences, we can shift our perception of how life works and choose a different way of moving through the world. Let's take a brief look at the history of the beliefs of mankind.

Ten thousand years ago, humans practiced Animism, which is the belief in a supernatural power that organizes and animates the material universe. Animism recognized and honored the souls of plants and everything in nature. Spirit and matter were considered one and the same, and both the material and spiritual realms were honored.

This ideal began to fade away with polytheism, which is the belief in many gods. The Egyptians, Greeks, and Romans took the spirit out of the people and nature and created gods of water, crops, stars, and the sun—there was a god to represent everything in nature. Our direct access to spirituality was cut off and given to the gods.

Later came monotheism, the belief in one god, which essentially collected the spirit of the entire planet, put it into one god, and then sent that god off the planet. This is when the church began to run the world. We left the time where everything was spiritual to a time where nothing was spiritual except God, who existed in a faraway place.

Then came scientific materialism, brought to us by Isaac Newton, who taught us that matter is our fundamental, ultimate reality. Newton was considered a heretic because his data did not fit with the knowledge offered by the church. To appease the church, scientists eventually agreed to study only the physical realm of the universe and leave the invisible stuff to religion. This marked the separation of physics (the material) and metaphysics (the spiritual) and anchored the belief in separation. These beliefs are responsible for creating an entire civilization—based on incorrect information. While the Newtonian laws of matter apply at the gross physical level, we now know a more fundamental reality exists beyond matter—an all-encompassing field of energy where separation does not exist.

The idea that competition is a necessary part of life is due to the "Survival of the Fittest theory," explained by Charles Darwin, who took the research of Alfred Russel Wallace and changed it, and then published it as his own. Darwin's idea that only the strong survive was a very different idea than Wallace's—that the weakest become eliminated in nature. It is much easier to not be the weakest than it is to be the strongest. To be the strongest, you would have to constantly compete for that title, which is not the case with Wallace's original theory.

Science also created the belief of random evolution, which describes our evolution as nothing more than a series of random accidents, and therefore, our existence has no purpose. We now know that the idea of random chance being responsible for evolution is incorrect. All living things are adaptable and conform to their environment so all living organisms can live in harmony. When one organism is out of control, another organism will come in and neutralize it to maintain harmony. This proves that everything has purpose.

When science redefines our reality, we adapt in ways that reflect our new understanding of that reality. Through quantum physics, we now recognize that it is cooperation that drives evolution, not competition. Quantum physics came into being in 1925 and debunked the idea that there is a duality of matter and energy because it was discovered that the entire universe is made of one thing: energy. Quantum physics proves that there is a spiritual component that exists within everything, including us. This revelation in science is responsible for giving us our power back. Quantum physics is aligned with the ancient knowledge and sacred practices of achieving balance through harmony, as seen in many spiritual traditions, which is very different from what science teaches us is true.

Put simply, there is more to us than our material existence. We are incredibly powerful beings.

But because separation appears to be confirmed by our everyday physical existence, we tend to believe we are separate from our environment. Humanity has upended the environment to seek out material wealth without regard for the consequences, which has created mass destruction of natural resources. We can be sure that nature will correct this imbalance, even if it means that humans get tossed off the planet. Mother nature has suffered due to the belief in separation but still is a powerful representation of the feminine and a powerful creator. She creates harmony by eliminating the weakest link.

COLONIZATION

With the rise of the patriarchy came the colonization of the Goddess. This is what all colonization is: the desire to make the feminine like the masculine. Colonization was designed to perpetuate obedience, but like nature, the wild, divine feminine essence cannot be suppressed indefinitely. Under the thumb of oppression, women have embraced their masculine essence in order to fight for equality. This is what we have seen in recent generations.

The oppression of the mysterious feminine eventually evoked a collective uprising of women against the masculine. In the quest for equal rights, the feminine collective became socialized to disown their innate sense of being and embraced the feminine shadow, which has served as a mirror to the shadow aspect of the masculine. Our generation and past generations have been so busy trying to prove that women can do everything that men can do, women have lost sight of the unique qualities that set us apart. Our divinely unique way of being does not support the idea that women can and should do everything men can do. Women were created to do everything a man cannot do.

Over time, we learned to believe that the feminine essence was not valuable—and for men, it was off-limits. Men had to be stoic and strong and were told to "suck it up, shake it off," and all kinds of other emotionally invalidating commands. Boys are taught that their own sexuality is perverse, and therefore there is a collective tendency toward perverseness, proven by a $97 billion global pornography industry, which continues to grow.

What you resist persists.

Today, many men are not the decision-makers when it comes to finances or plans for the family. Culturally, it seems normal for the "women to wear the pants." This is all in the name of creating equality between the sexes. As a result, we are bearing witness to generations of men who have lost their drive and sense of direction. They give up their natural inclination to lead in their relationships because they may have come to believe that their masculine desire to lead in relationship is somehow wrong. We have created a culture that has devalued the healthy masculine essence in the name of equality, and therefore suppressed the healthier aspects of both the masculine and feminine to the point of being put to sleep.

The definition of equality through the lens of punitive or duality consciousness means each individual or group is given the same resources or opportunities. Who gets to decide what constitutes the exact resources and opportunities needed to reach an equal outcome? What is an equal outcome when circumstances and people are so different? This definition supports defining equality through the lens of separation, and the need to treat everyone the same. But our needs are not the same. Especially in the context of the masculine/feminine dynamic.

According to Unitive Justice Theory, equality is defined through the lens of unity consciousness as inclusiveness without exception; the condition of being accorded the same value, respect, dignity, connection, and humanity as all others, without exception. Such equality honors the likeness of God or living spirit that dwells within each one of us. True equality supports roles that are differentiated based on skills and knowledge, but these roles do not have entitlement, privilege, or superiority attached to them.

Our social structures have created an imbalance of the masculine and feminine in order to control the masses through fear-based, punitive measures, creating a punitive culture entirely based on fear by pitting one group against another. This way of being has become part of the collective consciousness.

THE SLEEPING FEMININE

The message to women has been that we not only must do everything men can do, but we have to do it all and do it better. Instead of resting in the flow of allowing and receiving, we decided that we must use force in order to control outcomes. The outcome of all that effort looks like women who are completely drained and exhausted from trying to do everything themselves. This issue has perpetuated through generations, as I witnessed in my own family.

Women claimed the masculine role, taking over family, household, financial, and many other decisions, and essentially became the leader in the family dynamic, while the masculine found themselves caught in a Catch-22; feeling damned no matter what energy they embody, and many men have given up, only to walk through life as empty shells.

When the masculine is empty of light, he cannot shine his light on the feminine, like the sun does with the moon. And she cannot add her love to that light and reflect it out into the world. When women cannot reflect the light back and be witnessed doing so, they also become empty shells.

Many women secretly dream of a knight in shining armor who will come along on a white horse and whisk her away, make passionate love to her, and take care of her every need. Yet, women have taken over many of the masculine roles by leading their relationship. Do you see the irony here?

We've all learned on some level that the feminine essence is not valuable, and in rejecting femininity, women began to embody the feminine's shadow side. We see the shadow side of the feminine surface as a controlling nature through manipulation, helplessness, criticism, trickery, gossip, catastrophizing, depression, and silence.

When the feminine essence goes unacknowledged, so does intuition, collaboration, community, awareness, receptivity, connection—these are all the parts of ourselves we are expected to abandon in order to succeed in a masculine-oriented world. This conditioning puts the feminine at risk of losing touch with her inner power and becoming an empty shell.

As our values shifted toward the masculine, we removed feelings from the equation, increasing surface-level efficiency and effectiveness, which were the two primary objectives of the Industrial Revolution. We are still under this spell. For example, the belief exists that the less feminine you present in a corporate environment, the more valuable you are. We have become adept at using masculine energy to manifest through exercising control and competing with one another.

THERE IS ANOTHER WAY—THE WAY OF THE GODDESS

The Goddess essence consists of the communion of the masculine and feminine. Goddess energy is created when the divine masculine and divine feminine meet. When both energies are activated, we blend strength, determination, and courage with receptivity, spirituality, and tenderness. This is the sacred space where creation occurs. This knowledge is not something we need to learn; it is instead what we need to remember. We know it innately.

On many levels, we've all been conditioned to deny our feminine power, which includes connection, our innate sensuality, and the art of collaboration. While the masculine component is crucial for creation, in the absence of the feminine, it creates disharmony within humanity as it moves into the masculine shadow. Humanity has learned to push, fight, and force desires into manifestation. As the masculine shadow grows, we begin to see the after-effects: the Earth's destruction, enslavement, food insecurity, oppression, war—the list goes on.

The feminine aspect of Goddess energy is accessed through tapping into her senses or her beingness. The most obvious feminine expression of beingness is sensuality. Women have been taught that their sensuality is unacceptable. Society generally brands women who are comfortable with their sensuality as promiscuous. This is a shame tactic that has been used for millennia. One of the surest ways to silence the feminine essence and strip her of her power is to attack her sexuality, either physically or emotionally. Entire cultures have been wiped out using this tactic.

Sensuality allows you to access your sensing intelligence, which is the superpower of the Goddess. Sensing intelligence opens the gates to the magic of the feminine.

SENSING INTELLIGENCE

My favorite example of sensing intelligence is the genius of the ancient Polynesians, who navigated the ocean without modern-day tools. The Polynesians used their intuition to travel hundreds of miles in canoes and were intricately connected to nature—the waves, currents, clouds, wind, and stars. They could predict land nearby without even being able to see it because they were at one with natural forces. They passed down this gift through generations until it became part of their collective consciousness. This ability represents the mastery of the divine feminine within.

The healthy feminine essence is wild, free, mysterious, and powerful—representing sensuality, receptivity, and intuition. The feminine essence has a direct connection to the moon phases and to Mother Earth. We are innately flowing with the current of universal law, and we have a direct influence on everything, including the health of the planet.

We are also emotional beings, which means we have the power to direct energy using "E-motion" (energy in motion). Emotions are connected to our physical senses. Our sensual energy is the most powerful tool we have to create in the world and manifest in the physical.

AWAKENING THE GODDESS

To awaken the Goddess within, you must reclaim your feminine essence.

Goddess energy is the omnipotent force derived from the merging of the divine masculine and feminine energies within. It has been said that the closest humans can come to knowing to God is when the masculine and feminine essence comes together in the physical through the act of sex. Since we possess both energies, we have the ability to merge them which helps us to co-create with Source. This is the alchemical marriage—the union of duality and a primal force that is the foundation of self-mastery and ultimately perfection of the soul. The pure harmonic flow of these blended energies supports creation, which includes all manifestations in the material world. When we can bring both energies together, we have the ability to manifest anything.

We are now waking up to the ancient ways of the Goddess, and she is rising.

She asks you to stop ignoring your intuition and embrace your innate wisdom. She asks you to use your breath, imagination, and feelings to discover the hidden depths of your connection to everything—to step into the unknown and courageously receive.

In order to receive, we must surrender, which takes faith in ourselves and the universe at large—it is the ultimate spiritual practice. When you release resistance and allow, you will receive the messages you need to hear that will guide you toward alignment for the highest good of all.

Surrendering is mastery of the art of allowing, receiving, and working with what we can't see. The feminine possesses the natural ability to work with the darkness, with what cannot be seen. In the darkness, there is seemingly nothing, yet out of the darkness came everything.

The feminine is the embodiment of the darkness and of love. And love serves as a mirror for light—with light representing the masculine essence. This innate ability of the feminine to serve as a reflection of the masculine brings light (or enlightenment) into conscious awareness.

You have the magic of the divine feminine and masculine at your fingertips. All the knowledge you need to manifest is already within you.

MANIFESTING USING FEMININE ENERGY

Creating the space for allowing and receiving is a natural way to manifest using divine feminine expression. We are in constant duality regarding which energy we should embody, and this creates confusion about how to manifest desires with ease.

Many of us were taught that we have to push, fight, and force what we desire into manifestation, which represents the overusing of masculine energy. Our masculine energy is not wrong or bad; but actually most women long to rest in their feminine energy, which is always at our disposal, and yet we don't utilize its power.

THE MASCULINE-FEMININE RELATIONSHIP

For an intimate, romantic relationship to exist, both polarities must be present or there is not enough energetic charge to keep it going. All romantic relationships include one partner who leads with the feminine and one partner who leads with the masculine.

Like the ocean, the healthy feminine essence represents love, openness, beauty, mystery, and magic. And at times, she is unpredictable.

The healthy masculine aspect represents taking action in the world. He is logical, goal-oriented, proactive, protective, driven, assertive, and externally focused, like the ship that must sail through the ocean's unpredictable waters.

If one energy is absent, there is an imbalance. This imbalance becomes most obvious within the context of romantic relationships. Humanity has devalued the feminine, and therefore, the solution is often reintroducing the feminine back into relationship. To those who lead with the feminine essence: if polarity imbalance is a problem you're experiencing in your relationship, you actually can change this dynamic by yourself. I highly recommend reading *The Empowered Wife* by Laura Doyle. She explains in her book the importance of the feminine learning to let go and allow her desires to come to fruition by doing less. For men who would like to better understand their feminine partners, I highly recommend Bryan Reeves' book, *Choose Her Every Day (or Leave Her)*. The link to these books are located in the References section in the back of this book.

✾ 2 ✾

GODDESS ARCHETYPES

"Who is She? She is your power, your Feminine source. Big Mama. The Goddess. The Great Mystery. The web-weaver. The life force. The first time, the twentieth time, you may not recognize her. Or pretend not to hear. As she fills your body with ripples of terror and delight.

But when she calls you will know you've been called. Then it is up to you to decide if you will answer." –Lucy H. Pearce, *Burning Woman*

WHETHER WOMEN ARE WILLING TO ADMIT IT OR NOT, WE ALL dream about a life where we can relax into our beingness and simply ask for what we want and need and experience the joy of receiving it. I once thought this was not a possibility for me. A life of peace, contentment, and joyous anticipation simply was not in the cards. Well, that was true because I believed it. I created a self-fulfilling prophecy of living the life of a struggling single mom trying to show her son how to take the reins of responsibility and create a fulfilling life. I had no idea I was spinning us in circles. I was showing my son by example how to be a survivor instead of a thriver.

We can certainly have whatever life experience we desire, and we can begin manifesting those experiences at any time. But first, you have to make sure that you really want what you're asking for. It requires the practice of self-awareness to achieve an understanding of the difference between our desires that are based in love and those that are based in fear.

Only when you slow down and become familiar with the intricacies of your core self can you know what you actually want and then consciously manifest it. I was manifesting out of fear because I didn't want to be poor and I didn't want my son to go without. I didn't want to fail him. I was focusing on everything I did not want instead of what I actually did want. I was manifesting, but not consciously, and therefore, I was not manifesting the best possible life experience for us.

I also did not understand the power of my own feminine essence. I actually thought women were pretty horrible. I thought they were silly, dramatic, overly emotional, and gossipers who cause unnecessary drama. Who needs that? I was busy and clearly did not have time for any of it. I had no idea how wrong I was. I was living in the shadow aspect of the feminine and therefore that was all I saw—the shadow aspects of other women. It was my reality because I had created it.

I had no idea I was a powerful Goddess who could manifest an amazing life experience. We all have this ability. To access the Goddess within requires radical self-awareness. When you understand yourself, only then are you able to celebrate the magical, mystical feminine being that lives within you. You are already a Goddess. You just have to acknowledge this fact.

"Goddesses get what they ask for. It's not about whether you deserve it; it's that you are it." –Sherrill Burroughs

What does it mean to live like a Goddess? We know of the magical powers of Goddesses in mythology, but what does it mean to be a modern-day Goddess in the flesh?

Owning your inner Goddess requires two things: standing in your authenticity and learning how to tap into your awe-inspiring feminine power. Goddesses are powerful because they know when to use their masculine and feminine energies, and they know what they truly want deep down.

Every great story since the beginning of time includes archetypes. We can, on some level, relate to each and every one because we embody certain elements of each archetypal trait. They exist within every one of us. This is why the dynamics that we see play out in legendary stories are recognized and felt on a collective level.

Using Goddess Archetypes is an empowering way to learn to embrace the beautiful feminine aspects of yourself. The Goddess Archetypes will help you understand your light and dark aspects and release any judgment. You will begin to develop a relationship with the Goddesses you resonate with most. Their energies can help you manifest what you most desire.

In this chapter, you will read descriptions of twelve Goddess archetypes from around the world, organized by the elements of Earth, Water, Air, and Fire. These twelve Goddesses described here were carefully chosen to represent the full range of innate personality types, along with the defense mechanisms that we play out in our lives. Give yourself plenty of time to read each description and feel their energy. Then, choose the Goddess that most closely resonates with you.

If you strongly identify with more than one, you can choose more than one to work with. You may find that once you move deeper into this work, other Goddess descriptions will resonate more, and you can choose to work with the others as you see fit.

Each Goddess archetype possesses both positive and negative traits—they represent the light and the shadow sides of human consciousness. You may even notice aspects of yourself in many of them, which is the nature of the archetype concept. In my purpose coaching work, I test personality preferences and defense mechanisms to determine light and shadow aspects of clients I work with. The reason for this is so they can let go of self-judgment and come into authentic wholeness. I used what I've discovered from my experience to create the Goddess archetypes.

You will notice both the light and shadow sides of some of these Goddesses in yourself. You may also notice in the descriptions certain aspects that remind you of the people in your life. If you or someone you know is playing out the shadow aspect of any archetype, then rest assured that the positive aspects are present as well. We all embody light and dark, and we cannot have one without the other.

The shadow aspect is the most important element to understand in order to fully embody your Goddess essence because it contains clues about ways you might be living through your fear-based defense mechanisms instead of acknowledging your true nature or innate preference, which was born from love.

These Goddess archetypes will serve three purposes as you begin learning to manifest like a Goddess. These archetypes will help you to:

- Understand yourself and others more clearly and release any judgment as you learn about the dualistic nature of yourself and others;
- Make love-based decisions so you can move through the world in a way that is more in line with your authentic truth; and
- Develop a relationship with the Goddess archetypes you resonate with most, so their powerful energy can help you manifest.

The Goddess archetypes are categorized by the elements (Earth, Water, Air and Fire). You will notice some of the historical descriptions of the Goddesses include some elements beyond their categories. Don't let this confuse you. Each Goddess not only embodies both light and dark aspects, but they also contain all of the elements, just like us.

Once you read the archetype descriptions, if you are still unsure of which archetype represents you at this phase in your life, you can take my Goddess Archetype Quiz here: https://saradaves.com/goddess-quiz/.

EARTH GODDESSES

Isis: Egyptian Mother Goddess

Isis represents the force of love that can create new life out of the old. She is a timeless expression of the Divine Feminine. She supports the awakening of humanity as we move toward the concept of Oneness. She brings value and respect to the roles of wife and mother. Isis is the patron of magic, nature, and healing, and is the protector of the dead.

Isis can reconnect us with our innate healing powers. She supports everyone's quest to reclaim their individual power and take responsibility for their own healing journey. She reveals our ability to heal ourselves and others. Isis can help to awaken your healing abilities and intuition and communicate with the physical body in order to intuit any need you may have for healing. She empowers others to use the healing power of love and gratitude and to raise the energy level of the physical body by connecting to Source.

Isis represents the archetypal feminine being who has healed all the fragmented parts of herself and has finally come into wholeness. After her healing journey, she discovered her natural talents and became inspired to use them courageously. She teaches others how to awaken to their truth and walk through their own shadows, which is necessary for wholeness and soul connection.

The shadow aspect of this archetype looks like one who embarks upon a healing journey only to become stuck there because she is looking outside of herself for healing, rather than moving into the dark depths of her own pain in order to gain an understanding of her wounds and truly heal.

Historical description of Isis – From 3,000 BC to the 2nd century AD, Isis was worshipped in Egypt as the Great Mother Goddess of the Universe. She was present every day at sunrise and with every new and full moon. She married Osiris, who was murdered by Set in a jealous rage. Eventually, Set scattered pieces of Osiris in all directions. Isis traveled up and down the Nile, searching for lost pieces of her husband. This represents the fragmentation of the masculine essence. Eventually, she was able to put his pieces back together and create wholeness within him, and they conceived a child.

As the protector of women, Isis helps women in childbirth and comforts them when their loved ones die. Compassionate and loving, she shows us that women have great reservoirs of strength and inspiration.

Sophia: Goddess of Truth

As a biblical figure, Sophia has been described as the co-partner of God and sometimes as the female God. She is your guide to finding your own truth and sense of personal justice. She leads her followers down the path of inner wisdom, because when self is known, all is known. There are many traits associated with Sophia: righteousness, wisdom, lovingkindness, communication, knowledge, creation, protection, life giving, and the truth.

Sophia represents the archetypal feminine being with unwavering faith in her spiritual practice—it comes before all else. She understands the reason she has incarnated and will not rest until she has fulfilled her purpose.

She has experienced her own personal calling toward her faith and enlightenment and understands that her true allegiance is to Source consciousness. She walks her talk, taking the path of inner guidance, and she refuses to be pulled off track. She sees it and tells it as it is; she has no fear of the truth.

The shadow aspect of this archetype is one who has a tendency to practice blind faith at the expense of other aspects of her life. Her family or work life may suffer as a result of her spiritual pursuits.

Historical description of Sophia – The early Christians sometimes used her as a metaphor for Christ. Her origins are almost impossible to trace, yet she can be traced to every era, culture, and society. She is the original manifestation of the Divine Feminine and can be linked with practically every Goddess.

Her sacred shrine is in Istanbul, and she is symbolized by the dove, crescent moon, stars, a cup, or a tree. Sophia is also known as the Grail Goddess. The Grail legend can be traced back to pre-Christianity, and Sophia guards the Grail in the interest of Earth's consciousness.

When the Knights Templar were arrested and tortured in October 1307, they were convicted of heresy, which included worshipping BAPHOMET, which is thought to be Sophia. The Templars were believed to be the protectors of the Grail, which many say is the lineage of Jesus Christ and Mary Magdalene. It is believed that Sophia came to Earth in the body of Mary Magdalene, who is often considered to have been the teacher of Jesus.

Gwenhwyfar: Welsh Goddess of the Islands

Gwenhwyfar is the eternal feminine principle of strength and peace in the universe. She is listed along with the weapons of another world that Arthur received as a gift, suggesting her divine origin and reinforcing her power and sovereignty. This representation suggests that she is fully balanced in the masculine and feminine energies and can rule from either energy. She is a powerful and influential queen and is complete and whole by herself.

This Goddess represents the archetypal feminine being who is equally balanced in masculine and feminine energies, signifying the symbol of Oneness. She is self-made and highly influential. She can easily enhance the lives of others if they heed her wisdom.

The shadow aspect of this archetype is separation—one who believes she doesn't need a masculine counterpart for anything and therefore loses out on the union with the masculine, as she easily provides everything she needs for herself. This ultimately leaves her feeling lonely and unfulfilled.

Historical description of Gwenhwyfar – She is the first lady of the Welsh Islands and the sea. She is known as the daughter of the first Welsh bard, a giant named Ogyrvan. She is known in Germany as the symbol of female wisdom but is most recognized as Queen Guinevere, wife of King Arthur.

When they married, she gave her husband a round oak table that could seat 150 knights. The table was a symbol of equality since none could sit higher or lower than any other. The table promoted peace among warring knights and became the emblem of the golden age of Camelot, the castle of King Arthur.

Gwenhwyfar is the symbol of the throne of Wales, and no one could rule without her. For this reason, she was in constant danger of being abducted. Legend has it that, after Arthur's death, she went to live in her own castle called Joyous Gard, where earthly paradise still exists.

AIR GODDESSES

Freya: Norse Goddess of Beauty and Love

Freya is the sensual bringer of feminine knowledge and is famous for her fondness of love, fertility, beauty, and fine material possessions. She's considered to be the party girl of the Aesir, one of the two main tribes of deities in the Norse tradition. She's a seeker of passion, pleasure, and thrills, and she is a powerful bringer of magic.

This Goddess represents the feminine archetype who is independent, has a heart of gold, and falls in love easily. She has had many partners while in search of the right one, which has created quite a reputation for her, but she knows exactly the type of partner she wants as a result.

She would rather exist in a state of love above all else and will do what-ever it takes to maintain peace, except at the expense of herself. She is smarter than most of the people she is surrounded by and understands spirituality on a profound level. She has an uncanny ability in the practice of magic.

The shadow aspect of this archetype is one who feels largely misunderstood and suffers from loneliness because she is unable to communicate her knowledge to those around her for fear she will be further misunderstood and ultimately abandoned.

Historical description of Freya – She is the archetype of the völva, a practitioner of the most organized form of Norse magic. Given her expertise in controlling and manipulating the desires, health, and prosperity of others, she's a being whose knowledge and power are almost without equal.

Freya's husband, Od, God of Ecstasy, mysteriously disappeared after the birth of their daughter, Nos, whose name means delight. Freya wept tears of gold as she rode through the sky on her golden chariot in search of him. This story represents unrequited love and the pain associated with being abandoned.

Sarasvati: Indian Goddess of Knowledge

Sarasvati is the Goddess of all knowledge and is held in special esteem by students, writers, and musicians. She is said to represent the powerful, pure light of education that destroys the darkness of ignorance.

This Goddess represents the highly educated feminine archetype with an all-knowing nature who can intuitively see through facades and knows the truth about people. She may often be asked, "How in the world did you know that?" or hear, "You are always right!" She has a wide range of knowledge in many areas, including the occult. She has a warm heart but will not allow others to take advantage of her good nature.

She has learned how to master her own masculine energy. She is an unstoppable force in business, rarely loses a battle and can outwit anyone in the boardroom. She is logical and inventive, able to come up with ideas that no one else has considered. She may also be a mother or wife who everyone relies on to save the day, but she is sure to provide lessons on how those she loves can learn to be self-sufficient.

The shadow aspect of this archetype can surface as a lack of compassion for others. There is a tendency to focus on logical facts and ignore the feelings of others. This archetype has the ability to cut off her emotions in order to form logical deductions, which can sometimes manifest in the appearance of cold-heartedness, paranoia, or extreme selfishness.

Historical description of Sarasvati – She is credited in India with the creation of the first fruits of civilization, such as the first alphabet, the arts, mathematics, music, and magic. She is beautiful, graceful, and wears brilliant clothing.

It is believed that Sarasvati and her consort, Brahma, were born from a golden egg that came from the sea. They created all the knowledge and creatures in the world. Many consider Sarasvati the mother of all life since it was her divine energy that was united with the awareness of Brahma, which brought everything into being.

She is depicted with four arms, showing that her power extends in all directions. In one hand, she holds a book, and in the other, a strand of beads. The book represents learning, while the beads indicate spiritual knowledge. With her other hands, she plays the vina, an Indian lute, representing the art of music.

Xochiquetzal: Mexican Flower Goddess

Xochiquetzal (*Show-chee-ket-zal*), or Xochi for short, is the Mexican Flower Goddess who is worshipped by the Aztecs who ruled over a vast empire in Mexico during the Middle Ages. She is one of the merriest of the Aztec deities and is also considered the Goddess of dance, music, crafts, and love.

This Goddess represents the free-flowing feminine artist archetype who is in love with beauty and all the pleasures of life. Her creativity is unmatched. She is the creator of life, yet she is not necessarily family-oriented. She accepts herself for exactly who she is and remains unapologetic for the way she creatively moves through the world.

The shadow aspect of this archetype is one who feels like she is not up to the task of caring for others or her creations because she is not enough. This belief comes from deeply-rooted shame. She cannot help but destroy everything she creates—including her relationships—in fear that they may destroy her identity.

Historical description of Xochiquetzal – She lives on top of a mountain above the nine heavens. This flowery garden paradise was populated by merry dwarves, dancing maidens, and musicians. The Aztecs believed that anyone who was faithful to Xochiquetzal would spend eternity in paradise in the afterlife.

The legend associated with her is the story of infidelity. Though many men fell in love with her due to her beauty and happy nature, she remained loyal to her husband, Tlaloc, for many years. But there was another god, Texacatlipoca, who was mischievous, manipulative, and persistent, and eventually won her away from her husband.

FIRE GODDESSES

Kali: Warrior Goddess

Kali represents the undomesticated feminist warrior Goddess. She is considered extremely unpredictable to those who try to control her. Devout Hindus were even wary of her wrath. In the seventeenth century, Kali was depicted as voluptuous, motherly, young, and beautiful, with a gentle smile. She wears attractive ornaments and has a pleasing, blue complexion.

This Goddess represents the archetype of the carnal nature of sexuality. She is grounded in the earthly reality and cannot be controlled by man or faith. Her mantra is that life is for living and should be lived to the fullest. She is sexy and independent and will not hesitate to cut someone out of her life if they try to press her to change. She has no desire for children and is happiest with multiple sexual partners. She is not inclined to settle down with just one partner until much later in life. She is non-judgmental and expects the same in return.

The shadow aspect of this archetype is a lack of spiritual pursuit, which can eventually create feelings of emptiness and loneliness because she is disconnected from Source consciousness. She is also at risk of having many acquaintances but few true friends since she never stays around long enough to build lasting memories with others.

Historical description of Kali – Although she brandishes weaponry and severs heads, two of her right hands are depicted as making soothing gestures—known as the mudras of fearlessness and blessing.

Today, her image reflects her duality. Kali is often depicted in the act of killing but smiles engagingly. Her protruding red tongue signals both modesty (a Bengali tradition) and her thirst for blood. Her disheveled hair hints at unrestrained blood lust and alternatively the metaphysical mystery of death that encircles life. Her three eyes represent omniscience. Her voluptuous breasts represent both sexual lust and nurturance.

Oya: African Goddess of the Niger River

Oya is praised for her persuasive, charming speech and is considered the patroness of female leadership.

This Goddess represents the feminine archetype who has an unrelenting free spirit and a wild love of nature. She is not afraid of change—she inspires it and is inspired by it. Her animalistic nature is seductive, and she can charm anyone with her beauty and her words. She knows her own power and uses it wisely, as she understands that her actions can create irreversible consequences.

The shadow aspect of this archetype represents unpredictability. Her feminine essence is often expressed through chaotic emotions and she is prone to act before she thinks. This archetype wants what she wants and doesn't consider how her actions impact others.

Historical description of Oya – She rules the Niger River and is known as the Goddess of the wind, the primeval mother of chaos. Since spoken words are made of the air we breathe, you can ask Oya to help you choose the right words to ease conflicts and gain power in situations, which is very different from control.

When Oya is happy, the river flows smoothly, bringing clear water to nurture the families who depend on it. But when she is angered by the deeds of humans, she makes the river overflow or run dry. She sends warnings of tumultuous winds to warn the people that her husband, Shango, the thunder god, is near.

Considered a free spirit, Oya was originally an antelope and wore the animal's skin to transform into her natural state. She hid her antelope coat from Shango before they married. Shango eventually found it and threw it away. Oya was furious. Shango begged for her forgiveness and offered Oya her favorite food, bean cakes, so she would stay with him. She eventually agreed to stay married to him and help him fight his battles against those who vexed him.

Oya cannot be contained but relies on her husband to provide her with a firm foundation and stability. This union represents the highest order of the masculine and feminine union.

Yemana: Cuban Santeria Goddess

Since Yemana is the Goddess of the waters, she is often called the Holy Queen of the Sea. She owns all the riches of the ocean: seashells, pearls, oysters, coral reefs, and every sea creature. Yemana is revered as the great mother of all since the sea is like the waters of the womb, from which all humans are born.

This Goddess represents the archetype of a fiercely protective mother who says what she means. She is truthful, direct, and frank and will make the tough decisions necessary for her children. All of them have a huge amount of respect for her. She can always be counted on in any situation and lives in her integrity, always fulfilling her promises.

The shadow aspect of this archetype is one who is brutal in her honesty. Delivering the truth in brutality is equivalent to telling sweet lies as it relates to the harm it can cause. She is usually oblivious to the fact that her fiery nature can burn others and cause irreparable harm.

Historical description of Yemana – She is the daughter of the Earth Goddess, Oddudua, who is considered the divine mother of the fourteen gods and Goddesses who make up the sacred pantheon. She occupies an exalted position in the Santeria religion.

Santeria developed from the Yoruba religion, which was practiced by enslaved Africans who were brought to Cuba to work on sugar plantations during the nineteenth century. Santeria spread from Cuba throughout the Caribbean as well as North and South America and is still widely practiced today.

Women who wish for children can ask her for assistance. The number "7" is sacred to Yemana, and those who steadfastly worship her wear seven bracelets on their arms to represent the power of the number.

WATER GODDESSES

Persephone: Goddess of Innocence

Persephone represents the youthful, innocent, and joyous maiden aspect of a woman, as well as the more womanly self whose innocence was lost and family attachments loosened—she can begin to consciously decide for herself. Her challenge is to stand in her own power and direct her life as she chooses.

This Goddess represents the feminine archetype who maintains a youthful dream about what she's going to do when she grows up and is open to transformation. Once she has decided her direction in life, she has the highest potential for growth.

The shadow aspect of this archetype represents an innate malleability that unconsciously reflects what others expect of her. She may lack a core identity and remains childlike, even in her later years. Her sexuality has not awoken in her, and she remains passive and compliant, preferring to follow the lead of others. She is unaware of who she really is and of her own strengths and desires.

Historical description of Persephone – In Greek mythology, Persephone is the possessor of the soul's dark wisdom. She is also considered the harbinger of spring and represents the growth and hope that it brings. She was abducted into the underworld and later returned to it willingly, and became unseen.

Persephone can move between the world of the ego and the spiritual unconscious. She easily connects with all things psychic and mystical and has a great potential for spiritual growth.

Her passivity and dependency were fostered by her mother, who tried to make choices for Persephone because she believed she knew best. Persephone is the most naturally compliant of all the Goddesses but is resentful as a result.

Lakshmi: Indian Goddess of Prosperity

Lakshmi is the Hindu Goddess of good fortune, prosperity, and beauty. She is believed to be all that is feminine. She is seen as the personification of abundance, prosperity, well-being, and harmony.

This Goddess represents the feminine archetype who has an unwavering romantic nature that can inspire her romantic partner and family in amazing ways. She is a wise woman and stands in her full loving feminine essence. She is the feminine power behind the successful masculine, but also successful in her own right. When times get tough, her loyalty serves as the catalyst for renewed strength to overcome any obstacle and achieve any goal.

The shadow aspect of this archetype is the one who cares for so many, yet does not see the value in caring for herself. Her lack of self-care creates stagnation for herself as well as those around her. She feels busy all the time but she is only running in circles, unable to make any headway.

Historical description of Lakshmi – Legend has it that her consort, Vishnu, the conqueror of the darkness, created Lakshmi by churning the Ocean of Milk while attempting to create a potion that would give him eternal life. She arose from the Ocean of Milk, standing on a lotus flower. They fell in love and married.

Lakshmi brings comfort, healing, and great fortune, even in the darkest moments. She offers a sense of courage, hope, and power. Lakshmi is attracted to sparkling jewels, like the riches she bestows on her worshippers. She lives in the sky with the most beautiful jewels of all, the stars.

Tara: Tibetan Goddess of Mercy

The most important deity for Tibetan Buddhists is the compassionate mother Goddess Tara. Tibetans believe that she has the power to heal all sorrows and grant all wishes. This Goddess represents the feminine archetype whose heart is wide open and extends compassion to anyone in need. She has exactly the right answers or piece of advice for anyone who is afraid to take action.

The shadow aspect of this archetype represents enmeshment—one who confuses the emotions of others with her own and cannot differentiate between when it is beneficial to offer help to others and when she must allow others to help themselves. Her tendency to help others out of precarious situations can sometimes hinder the personal growth of those she loves. This shadow signifies co-dependency and martyrdom.

Historical description of Tara – Tara is Tibet's most popular deity. She is honored as the protector against the many fears that block men and women from living in happiness and harmony. She protects her followers and saves all those who cry out her name at the moment of their suffering.

It is believed that Tara eventually reached enlightenment and became the first female Buddha. She worked and prayed for the welfare of humans everywhere for more than ten million years before she reached her goal. Then, she was transformed into a Goddess whose only wish was to ease the world's pain.

Give yourself some space to consider which Goddess archetype resonates with you the most so you can carry her energy with you throughout your manifesting journey.

3

SELF-AWARENESS

What is self-awareness? It is the knowledge of your inner self—why you think what you think, feel how you feel, what your needs are in any given moment, and why you move through the world the way you do. This includes understanding the origin of the many beliefs you've picked up along your journey.

Creating awareness of these aspects of self without judgment allows you to explore your inner depths so you can learn to pinpoint certain beliefs or habits that may not be serving you any longer. When you become aware of the shadow aspects of your inner self, you can begin to see how your external environment began to influence your beliefs and action patterns long ago.

Once you create this awareness (without judgment) and love all the parts of you, it becomes much easier to make decisions based on what actually serves you, rather than operating out of the conditioned beliefs and expectations that have been placed upon you. This requires you to go within for answers, instead of looking outward for validation. Essentially, you have to re-learn how to listen to your inner voice.

We have all been trained on some level to ignore our inner voice, usually because our hunches or gut feelings were consistently dismissed, beginning at a very young age, by the authority figures in our lives. Most of us have been pulled so far out of ourselves as a result of becoming socialized within the systems we grew up in (and still exist within) that oftentimes, we have no idea what parts are us and what parts are system programming.

If the system is rigged for you to abandon yourself, how do you reverse it?

By developing a relationship with all the parts of yourself, without judgment.

Self-awareness is actually a practice in self-worth. The more you honor yourself, the closer you are to self-understanding.

Growing your self-awareness helps to strengthen your intuition—the voice of your inner self—which is your direct access to your true essence, or the messages from your soul. In the conflict resolution work that I offer in support of Unitive Justice Theory, the practice of self-awareness is rooted in self-governance. When you learn to access and listen to your inner voice, you learn to trust yourself, and your self-worth increases because you are living into your personal integrity and doing what is right for you.

You will be better able to use your inner voice to make decisions with ease and be at peace with your decisions, and they will serve you well.

The most typical way people abandon themselves is by not honoring how they truly feel and taking action based on what is expected of them instead of what is good for them. So, the first step in gaining self-awareness is to create an intimate relationship with all of your feelings, especially the uncomfortable ones.

When you ignore your feelings, they often show up in the physical body as disease (literally dis-ease), manifesting as physical injury or illness. The practice of self-awareness includes paying attention to and checking in with how your body is doing in any given moment.

When you notice that you're feeling stressed, take a moment to remove all of your attention from the external world and focus your awareness on what is happening within. Get curious. Pay attention to every physical and emotional sensation that you're experiencing, and allow yourself to feel all of it. Sitting with uncomfortable emotions is a necessary part of this process; it's the only way to truly understand why uncomfortable emotions exist within you. It is only after you develop this understanding that you can do anything to change it. The defense mechanisms that are created in childhood can block your ability to access certain emotions and understand them fully. Uncomfortable emotions have important information for you, and we will delve into this later on in your reading journey. But for now, we'll explore defense mechanisms—what they are and why they exist.

DEFENSE MECHANISMS

Our innate power can sometimes feel obscure. Perhaps you have experienced glimpses of your personal power only to watch it slip away again. This is what happens when you identify with the persona created by your defense mechanisms.

All children develop a set of defense mechanisms in order to emotionally survive, which are out of sync with the core self. Some of us have been hiding in the shadows of our defense mechanisms for so long that we are unaware that our core selves have long been buried. I call these defense mechanisms The Mask.

During childhood, the talents, gifts, and abilities we were born with were still maturing, which left us essentially powerless in a world full of expectations. We were given massive amounts of information that we absorbed as true because we did not yet have the ability to analyze data and make logical deductions about the world around us. Taking in information at face value is how faulty beliefs are created. Those beliefs began forming our ideas about what we needed to do and how we needed to act in order to be accepted and survive. As children, we felt the need to be accepted so we could get our needs met. Looking for ways to receive love and acceptance is a survival mechanism that we all possess, and we developed these defense mechanisms to stay alive. The defense mechanisms created the masks we wear—the aspect of the conditioned self.

As children, we designed a very special mask that we could wear for protection. We wore the mask so often that we broke it in quite nicely and became really comfortable with wearing it. Eventually, we forgot to take it off. In doing so, we also forgot about our superpowers (aka innate talents, gifts, and abilities), and so they ended up buried deep inside of us.

Many people do not understand that they have been relying on the mask they created to achieve safety and security in the world as they know it.

"Everybody wears the mask, but how long will it last?" –Lauryn Hill, The Fugees

Operating through the mask instead of your authentic self is like climbing barefoot over a mountain of glass while carrying a 100-pound weight on your back—when you could have instead bypassed the mountain altogether and taken the soft, cool, grassy path with a wheelbarrow at your disposal. But if you've never walked the grassy path or used a wheelbarrow, then the pain that the mask brings feels completely normal. Like fish in water, they do not know that they are actually always swimming in water—you also don't know what you don't know—that you are wearing a mask.

The sole purpose of the mask's existence is to protect you, but it does not operate with logic. It is fear-based and exists in the reptilian brain, and it triggers our fight, flight, and freeze responses.

Your mask has sometimes been incredibly helpful when you needed to move through a painful situation, and maybe you have often worn it to help you achieve success. It has most likely given you the fortitude to plow through life's challenges and it may have seemed to protect you during times of stress. The mask is excellent at reactionary problem solving, but it only offers Band-Aid solutions. One quick fix simply creates more hurdles to overcome and does not allow you to achieve inner peace and fulfillment.

Achieving life goals for the sake of the mask's persona is a fear-based way of living and provides only short-term satisfaction.

The mask affects the choices we make in all aspects of our lives— dictating the systems we adopt, the careers we choose, and the types of relationships we keep. Perhaps the most debilitating aspect is the negative impact on relationships with the people we care about the most.

The mask is simply a way to cope; it's the tool we use unconsciously to protect ourselves. The personal life stories we identify with derive from the false beliefs that wearing the mask has created. The mask hijacks the subconscious mind and thoughts become fear-based and irrational. In the midst of this experience, it is impossible to show up for ourselves or anyone else.

Many people are wearing their masks every waking hour. The good news is no one has to live this way. By picking up this book, it means that you are looking for more than what your mask can offer you. You know inherently there is another way of moving through the world, and you feel this on some level. You have desires and dreams that are unachievable as long as you wear the mask, and you're not willing to let go of your dreams —you're ready to do something different. That is because your strong desire to experience your full authentic self is your destiny. That is what all your desires are: your destiny revealing itself. This concept is important to understand in order to become a conscious manifestor.

Understanding your defense mechanisms is the first step toward manifesting the magnificent life that is waiting for you.

Many of us were taught that desires are bad or sinful. This means we should not want anything because wanting something means that we are selfish, entitled, or ungrateful. That could not be further from the truth. Your desires are a representation of your passions begging to be revealed and lived out. Every human being deeply desires to show up authentically and be seen, heard, and understood. Giving space to your truest desires will help you achieve this. Wearing the mask will never fulfill this basic human need. Yet, we wear it anyway so we can be accepted by our family, peers, and society at large. If your authentic self is not accepted by the people you spend the most time around, then it may be time to consider finding a new circle.

INFLUENCERS

We are relational beings and therefore are strongly influenced by the people we spend the most time around. An effective way to determine how you are showing up for yourself is by taking a look at the people around you.

Consider the top five people you spend the majority of your time with. These are your influencers. We essentially become influenced by both the positive and negative energetic frequencies of the people we spend the most time around.

Who are your influencers? What are their positive and negative traits?

How do these traits impact your overall well-being on a regular basis? Can you identify any traits of your influencers within you? It's very difficult to see yourself, which is why the universe sets up our world to be our mirror.

If you have influencers who are not serving your highest good, find new ones. I don't mean that you need to abandon the people around you. You don't necessarily have to eliminate people from your life when you notice their negative aspects are impacting you negatively or traits you don't like are rubbing off on you. Just being aware of how you are impacted by your influencers can actually be enough to create a shift in energy, not only in yourself but in them as well. It only takes one person in a relationship dynamic to shift the energy. This is true all the time, and you have the power to do this whenever you choose. You just simply have to choose your authentic truth and live into it.

Being your authentic self is your fundamental right as a human being. If you are shrinking yourself to fit in, you are denying yourself the magnificent life that is meant for you. As you begin to embrace your authenticity, you'll find that the people who do not accept you for who you are will naturally fall away and move out of your life and become replaced with those who celebrate your authenticity alongside you.

What other people think about you is not your business, even if your conditioning tells you that you could suffer if you are not accepted by the people around you. You are not responsible for the way others feel about you. Because the world is our mirror, it's important to allow others to take responsibility for the way they experience the world and allow yourself to take responsibility for the way you experience the world.

This doesn't mean that you're automatically off the hook if there is conflict present in your relationships. Conflicts are gifts that reveal the wounds that come up to be healed on both sides. Then, it becomes important to recognize the impact we have on others. This is different from taking responsibility for the wounds of others.

What I'm referring to is your human right to be you—authentically. You have a right to live your life however you see fit, and if there are people surrounding you who don't approve, that is ultimately their problem. Owning your authentic self is the way of the Goddess, and doing so will help you immensely in the manifesting process.

However, if you find yourself getting triggered by the behaviors of others, there is something else happening entirely. Triggers are clues that there is an aspect present that you don't accept about yourself, and there is an internal wound coming to the surface because it is ready to be healed. Becoming triggered by the actions of other people is a key indicator that there is an inner conflict revealing itself to you. When you are free of inner conflict, all the triggers will disappear.

Managing internal conflict is something we will get into in later chapters. Recognizing and managing conflict within will free you from the limiting beliefs you have about who you are and how you "should" show up in the world.

For now, I want you to question the expectations that you have of others and also the expectations that others have of you. I want you to begin to question everything. The trail on the map of your self-awareness journey begins and ends with more curiosity and less cleverness.

I also encourage you to get curious about how you make decisions. Before you make any decision, practice asking yourself: "Am I coming from a place of love or fear?" Asking this question will help you determine whether you are operating from your defense mechanisms (your mask) or your innate preference for moving through the world.

If you have trouble with this question, you can simply ask, "Why am I taking this action or making this decision?" And if your answer is because you are trying to avoid pain, you are coming from fear and are living through your defense mechanism. If your answer is that you feel inspired and as a result, inspiration fills your heart and moves you to take action, you are coming from a place of love and acting from your innate preference. When you realize that you're taking fear-based actions or making fear-based decisions, you're recognizing the limitations of your mask. You can then choose to take love-based actions and make love-based decisions.

The choice is always yours.

❦ 4 ❧
LIMITING BELIEFS

WHAT ARE LIMITING BELIEFS? LIMITING BELIEFS ARE FEAR-based, personal yet subjective truths that you believe to be true on a conscious or subconscious level, and they dictate all of your life choices and experiences. It doesn't matter what you believe to be true—you are right 100 percent of the time.

Limiting beliefs dictate what we manifest. We humans are powerful beings. We have the ability to manifest anything into existence. We are always manifesting.

"Whether you think you can, or you think you can't—you're right."
–Henry Ford

Whatever beliefs you are using to create your reality are powerful. It doesn't matter what you believe, you will cast forth those beliefs like a plot in a movie and you will get what you expect every single time. You are both the director and star in your own movie.

I spent decades manifesting using my limited belief system. One of those beliefs was that life was difficult and that I had to work extra hard just to survive. And I manifested that reality for myself.

As you can imagine, I didn't like the destination. I worked hard to climb the corporate ladder and the farther up I climbed, the more painful life became. I found myself trapped in a toxic corporate hell-on-Earth. My self-imprisonment was dictated by money and my paycheck was my jailor. I thought, *Well, this is what I have to deal with in order to make this amount of money.* I told myself to suck it up and keep going.

I ended up depressed, completely stressed out, began suffering from health problems, and gained forty pounds. I was posturing each day, wearing a mask to fit into a place where I didn't belong. I eventually lost myself. I didn't know who I was anymore, or what I even wanted out of life.

It took a series of compounding traumatic events to wake me up. Once I became aware that I felt like a victim, I decided it was time to do something about it. Awareness is always the first step. The second step was healing some very old wounds that were responsible for my limiting belief system. My debilitating truth during that time was that I would have to endure these horrible circumstances forever.

I set out on a spiritual journey that opened my eyes to some uncomfortable truths. During that time, I ended up trading a toxic corporate hell-on-Earth for a toxic marital hell-on-Earth. It was clear I had not yet found that wound.

I eventually found it, or rather, it found me. My belief systems that created my reality knocked me down so hard that I hit bottom. I entered the Dark Night of the Soul, and it was excruciating.

The pain was intense. I stayed present with my emotions and refused to judge myself. When my ego began to attach a story about how awful the people in my life had treated me or how awful I was for allowing it to happen, I stopped and focused on the wound that was trying to come up for healing.

I allowed myself to feel all of the emotions tied to those experiences. It required me to stop everything and acknowledge the wounds that were begging for my attention. I journaled my thoughts and feelings daily. I questioned everything. The wound came right to the surface and stared me directly in the face. I learned that my limiting beliefs were many. They included: I wasn't good enough, I didn't matter, I was unlovable, something was fundamentally wrong with me, I was too much, the list goes on. My immediate reaction was to turn away and stuff those awful beliefs back down, so I could get on with life! But this time I didn't turn away. Instead, I loved all the parts of me that I had been hiding from myself. I embraced the very young part of me that had accepted those beliefs as truth, and I asked myself, "Is it true?" And the wounds began to dissolve.

All of the hurtful things that were said to me no longer belonged to me. Empathy and insight replaced judgment, and I found the beauty in the many painful experiences of my life. I took responsibility for all of it.

This self-healing process was the catalyst that moved me out of victimhood and into my own power. Blaming other people and societal systems for my own life situation wasn't getting me anywhere. It was only making me more miserable. It was stealing my power.

We are responsible for the state of our lives. Taking responsibility for every life experience puts you firmly back into a position of power. Taking responsibility is not the same as accepting blame. There is no fault or blame without prior agreement. Casting and accepting blame are disempowering. Blaming others places you in the role of the victim because it means you have to rely on others to change their behavior before you can reach the outcome you desire. In the victimhood role, there are no options. Attempts to control others through blame are temporary at best and rarely ever create the outcome you want. By taking full self-responsibility, you become empowered, and your options become endless.

Power and control are two sides of a coin. I've learned that these two words have nothing in common. There are several definitions out there for the word power, and most of them are actually definitions of control—authority, or influence over others; the ability to act or produce an effect as well as physical might. The true definition of power I am referring here is: "the ability to do something or act in a particular way, especially as a faculty or quality." Essentially, owning your power means standing in your authentic truth and making values-based decisions that serve you (and therefore serve everyone around you). And my favorite definition of power is: "a supernatural being, deity, or force." When you stand in your authentic truth and make decisions that support the highest good for yourself, you become powerful beyond measure.

Sylvia (who I mentioned earlier and will mention throughout the book) taught me that control and power are different concepts entirely. Consider Mahatma Gandhi and his work in the world. He was an incredibly powerful force, and yet he controlled no one; instead, he helped empower a nation. Adolf Hitler, on the other hand, was controlling on the grandest scale. He exerted control by removing the free will of masses of people. The only perceived power Hitler could claim was a short-lived reign, and he empowered no one. In the end, he lost any perceived power he had.

This concept is further explained in Unitive Justice Theory, the Arc: From Control to Self-Governance. Here are Sylvia's definitions of control and self-governance:

"Control: the process of dominating others and restricting their freedom through physical, mental, or emotional coercion; wielding influence using fear tactics, be they blatant or covert. Control is territorial and requires perpetual enforcement."

Fear is needed to maintain control.

"Self-Governance: internal self-control and self-mastery; being one's own master; the ability to exercise the function of regulation upon oneself without the intervention of an external authority."

Love is needed to maintain power.

Your challenge is to create awareness of the fear-based beliefs that aren't serving you. The end goal is to become aware of this limiting belief system and disable it from its origin, and then choose something different. Making a conscious choice to change your awareness puts you back into a place of personal empowerment.

When you cast blame on people or an establishment or when you make negative blanket statements, this is your cue to pay attention. Blanket statements such as "Politicians are corrupt," "Money is the root of all evil, or "Rich people are greedy," are all part of a fear-based belief system that limits your power.

When you hear yourself utter negative statements or talk about all the reasons why you can't do or have this or that, it's time to ask yourself, "Is it true?" Oftentimes, there is no real truth present in these types of statements. Usually, we are just repeating statements we've heard repeatedly. We don't question them because they are so deeply embedded in our psyche.

This also goes for general advice. Many of us in the West grew up hearing: "Don't count your chickens before they're hatched," or "Hope for the best, prepare for the worst, and expect nothing." These are horrible pieces of advice! Now, do you see why we do not allow ourselves to dream?

When a person gives unwarranted advice, usually they are doing nothing more than spreading their limiting beliefs around. And when you heard these types of statements as a child, they became implanted in your own belief system. It's important to note that no one who utters these clichés believes they are spreading negativity. Instead, they believe that they are protecting you, but what is actually happening is they are protecting themselves from having to see the world any differently since they have imprisoned themselves in a very small cage.

As our brains develop into adulthood, the prefrontal cortex is constantly absorbing information that slips into the mind without a filter. The more emotionally charged it is, the more embedded in the subconscious it becomes. This is how we collect the beliefs that become blocks to our happiness. The way to eliminate these beliefs is to create an awareness of them and reprogram something different.

Here is a harsh truth: every negative life circumstance that you have experienced is a direct result of the thoughts you think and the emotions you feel, which are made up of your beliefs. You are the creator of all of your experiences, because behind every experience is a story about that experience. This is true all the time. I am not saying that the bad things that happen to you are your fault. I am saying that you must be willing to take responsibility for the way you feel about them. Once you accept this fact, you are free.

UNHEALTHY BONDING

"It is no measure of health to be well adjusted to a profoundly sick society." –Krishnamurti

Complaining and gossiping are how many people learn to bond with others. This is often unconsciously taught in the family dynamic. Whether it shows up as complaining about others, our own health, or our unhappy lives, unhealthy bonding creates a harmful impact. When the energy of negativity is created, it permeates through the spoken word and becomes part of your belief system, which can manifest all sorts of things you do not want.

Words are spells. The words you speak cast spells, and you become the creator of what you are speaking. When the words you speak are attached to fear-based beliefs, the outcome is a perceived loss of personal power that will eventually be reflected back to you in your external reality.

Maybe you've found yourself trapped in a daily complaint practice—which only attracts more things to complain about. The solution is to become hyper-aware of how you spend your time. Are you mostly worrying or complaining about your life situation? If so, then become curious about how you got here and be willing to choose another way to spend your time.

REMOVE NEGATIVITY

To end this pattern, you must remove all excessive negativity from your life right now. Watching the news, worrying about the future, ruminating over the past, complaining about your current life situation, venting to friends and family, and negative self-talk are all lower vibrational activities that block you from experiencing gratitude and manifesting your desired outcomes.

I don't mean that you must put on a fake smile and go about your day. That is inauthentic and pulls you further away from your authentic self. We are all going to have experiences that we deem negative at certain points in our lives. What I'm saying is that when you catch yourself in a negative pattern, acknowledge the pattern and choose something different.

Any belief that creates separation, fear, anxiety, self-pity, or sadness is internal programming that you did not enter into this life with. You can choose to observe without judgment during the moments when you find yourself complaining.

When do you complain? In the company of certain people? When you get home from work? What types of complaints are you listening to on the news or from the people you know? Why do you feel the need to hear that? Do you feel it's your responsibility to know all the terrible things going on in the world? If so, what are your plans to fix it? If you have no plans to fix the brokenness that you learn of, then direct your attention to things you can do something about. You can begin with self-love.

A beautiful act of self-love is replacing fear-based thoughts with gratitude. It works immediately to move you out of fear-based thinking and into the energy of love. The reason it is immediate is that you can't vent and feel grateful at the same time. The energy of love and the energy of fear cannot exist in the same moment. You are always either coming from a place of love or a place of fear. It's impossible to embody both energies simultaneously.

Your only responsibility to the world is to get yourself to the vibrational level of love, and your light will shine as a beacon of joy, hope, and support for others. When you serve as the example, the world around you shifts into a higher vibration, and life becomes magical. The fastest way to change the world is to be the change.

5

RELEASING AND ALLOWING

I ONCE BELIEVED THAT IN ORDER TO LIVE MY BEST LIFE, I HAD to get rid of everything that was causing me pain, and only then would I find peace. I was looking for peace in all the wrong places. My focus was on the external world—my career and my marriage were two big elements in my life that I believed were holding me back from living the life I wanted.

While it's true that removing toxic elements from your life is necessary in order to make room for the life experience you want, it does not fix the underlying problems. I not only had to release toxic relationships and situations, but I also needed to break the pattern of attracting them. It required a shift in perspective from "these people, places, and things are blocking my happiness" to "something within me is creating every experience I have."

It was only after I released my own limiting beliefs that I could make room for all the goodies waiting to enter my life. I shifted my perception around the grief I was carrying for my child who crossed over and the trauma attached to my failed marriage along with all the emotions tied up in those experiences: guilt, shame, and failure. I wasn't allowing myself to believe that I could have anything better because, deep down, I felt that I didn't deserve it. I spent so much time wrapped up in what other people needed from and expected of me that I could not fathom considering myself even for a second. I was caught in a pattern of devaluing myself, and I was experiencing that devaluation mirrored back to me in my everyday life. I wasn't feeling appreciated, seen, heard, or understood. I was the one who was not appreciating, seeing, hearing, or understanding myself.

Today, the world is showing me a completely different reality.

I shifted my focus toward myself for the first time in my life, and with that shift came a profound sense of self-awareness. This awareness eventually brought me so much clarity around how I repressed self-judgment as well as my own desires. From there, I was able to begin learning what my authentic self really wanted to experience, and I was able to begin manifesting it. I let go of the stories that my ego was feeding me to keep me small and began focusing on what actually made me happy, even if I wasn't experiencing it in that moment. I let my imagination lead.

Before you can release what is no longer serving you and allow new situations and experiences to unfold in your life, you must develop an awareness of your beliefs, emotions, needs, and desires. Getting to know yourself must become a regular practice throughout your life. This means becoming familiar with how you really feel about certain life situations and what it is you really want and need from yourself in order to feel supported and loved. Once you give those things to yourself, you will begin receiving love, support, and understanding from others.

Under the section of this book titled "Tools for Manifesting Like a Goddess," you can reference "How to Work with the Moon's Energies," which will help you choose the right time to set your intentions to release what no longer serves you. The act of releasing is a powerful practice. You can use this practice to release negative beliefs, a bad habit, negative self-talk, any assumptions and goals you may have outgrown, or any life situation that is not serving your highest good.

Before you set your intentions for releasing, you must determine whether your intentions are based in fear or love. Fear-based intention-setting only anchors negative patterns more deeply into the psyche.

ALL EXPERIENCES ARE NECESSARY

We are in a time-space reality based on polarity and contrast. We learn what we want based on experiencing what we don't want. All of your experiences have been necessary in order for you to become very clear about what life experience you actually want to manifest in your life.

Your experiences have also taught you a great deal about yourself, and that's what we're doing here: getting to know ourselves so that life can know itself. You have not wasted any time. Release any judgment or regrets that you may have around feeling like you have tolerated something for too long. The beliefs attached to these types of judgments may be causing you stress and stagnation in your life right now. It's important to accept what is. It's possible that you do not yet understand the importance of everything that's happened in your life thus far. In time, you will.

RELEASING BELIEFS VS. PEOPLE, PLACES, AND THINGS

Often, we think it would be easier to release certain people or situations when what we actually want is a healthier interaction with these people, places, and things. Sometimes, what is needed is a shift in our beliefs about them.

What if you could change the energy around people, places, and things and have a new experience with them?

Give yourself permission to imagine what it would be like to experience different outcomes with the circumstances you are resistant to. Consider your emotions surrounding these situations. Building an awareness of the emotions and beliefs you are carrying can give you clues about how you might be participating in creating the very reality that is not serving you.

Creating space for this understanding will help you learn the difference between circumstances that are not serving you versus beliefs that are not serving you. If you remove the circumstance when the issue is actually a belief you're carrying, you are destined to repeat the cycle.

ALLOWING

The practice of allowing is one of the most significant aspects of creating with feminine energy. The art of allowing includes practicing patience and trust: knowing the universe has your back activates your ability to receive. We have been socialized by a overly masculine-dominant society to push and fight our way through the world in order to get our needs met, which is the opposite of allowing.

Ask yourself what you would like to allow into your life, and then set the intention to receive it without considering how it will show up. Consider why you want this particular thing, circumstance, or experience. What would it feel like to have it? What would it mean to you?

ASK "WHY" AND "WHAT" INSTEAD OF "HOW AND WHEN"

We often worry about the "how" and "when" more than any other aspect of the unknown when it comes to our desires. If we can't see the path toward the desired goal and make plans around when it will arrive, it can sometimes feel difficult to believe that the desire can be achieved.

As a child, were you ever told that what you desired was irresponsible, or even worse, impossible? This programming created the belief that imagination is not valuable. It's likely that you were trained to replace imagination with logic to create. This is how your divinely inspired passions became pipe dreams.

The people who told you your dreams were not valuable only did so out of love. They were coming from their own belief systems rooted in their own conditioned fears because they didn't want you to suffer.

Fear-based thinking is how broken systems are perpetuated. We are asked to shrink our dreams to fit into the mold of what we already know. If we can't see how to get there, then we learn to believe that our dreams are impossible to manifest.

Consider this: when you go on a road trip, you can't see all the roads ahead of you that will get you there. You only see a quarter of a mile or so in front of you. Imagine saying to yourself: "Well, I can't see the entire road, so I guess I can't get there." You would never do that! You also probably don't know "how" the car runs, but you trust it to get you to your destination.

Focus on the "why" and the "what." The "how" and "when" are none of your business. That is for the universe to decide because you don't have all of the information in front of you. Remember, you are not the only one responsible for creating what you desire. The universe has half the responsibility.

❧ 6 ❧
AUTHENTICITY

"Is one devoted to Truth or not? That is what matters in the evolution of consciousness." –Dr. David Hawkins

WHAT DOES IT MEAN TO SHOW UP IN YOUR AUTHENTICITY? IT means to know and be yourself in every situation and circumstance.

You may be thinking, *Well, that's easy, I've been myself my whole life!* However, you would be surprised by how your natural inclinations have shifted over time to fit in with societal expectations. If you find yourself constantly exhausted or stressed in certain situations, this is a key indicator that you are not showing up in your full authenticity. When we can be fully honest about who we are, how we feel, what we think, and what we desire, we experience less pain in our emotional, mental, spiritual, and physical bodies. When you alter your authentic self, you will feel stress that manifests as physical pain, mental or emotional anguish or numbness, or feel cut off from the rest of the world. To deny your authenticity is to create separation which prevents you from truly connecting with others.

If you have been shrinking or altering yourself in some way for the sake of pleasing others, you might be very confused about who you are and what you want. If this behavior goes on for too long, you may end up no longer recognizing who you are or what you're doing and lose touch with your inner self.

While lack of self-worth can make you believe you will never be able to create better circumstances, lack of self-awareness can actually make you forget your deepest desires.

So I will ask you this question: do you really know who you are?

You certainly know all the roles you play; husband, wife, mother, father, brother, sister, [insert role here] at the company you work for, etc. These roles are important and can offer much fulfillment, but do you understand why you think, feel, or react the way you do? (The answer, by the way, has nothing to do with how others make you think, feel, or react.)

Do you know what completely fulfills you? Are you at peace with what your current life situation offers you each day?

When you grow your self-knowledge, your life journey becomes easier. You begin to feel lighter and less bogged down with negative emotions. This does not mean that you will eventually be forever free of negative emotions. Human beings are designed to experience the full range of human emotions—it's how we gain wisdom and learn important lessons. But life isn't supposed to be continuously difficult. You are supposed to have fun along this journey as you contribute your natural talents, gifts, and abilities to the collective.

If you are living anything less than the happiest version of your life that you can imagine, or are not on a joyous path to that destination, chances are, you aren't living in alignment with your authentic self.

"The journey isn't so much about becoming someone. It's about getting rid of everything that isn't really you." –Paulo Coelho

Gaining self-knowledge does not necessarily mean that you will magically have all your desires fulfilled. Our desires and goals are constantly changing and we will never stop desiring. However, it does mean that you are clear about the direction to take to manifest those desires.

True happiness comes from within. This is why it's so important to develop a personal relationship with yourself. When you know who you are and allow yourself to be that and nothing more or less, the path toward fulfillment becomes clear.

Holding onto beliefs like, "Life is hard," or "Living the life I want is impossible because of [fill in the blank]," or "I have to [do this thing I don't want to do] so I can't [do or be what I want]," will only keep you stuck.

These statements represent scarcity consciousness. When you are in alignment with your true desires, all things are possible, because our desires give us clues about our purpose and divine path for this life.

I'll tell you what IS NOT possible: operating in scarcity consciousness when you are fully aligned with your authentic self. You cannot exist in the energy of scarcity and joy at the same time.

SCARCITY CONSCIOUSNESS

Do you feel that you are lacking in money, time, joy, or love? Are your relationships exhausting or unfulfilling? Do you feel a sense of dread with each day or often wish that you could have a more fulfilling life experience but don't know where to begin to create that for yourself? Have you experienced a vague sense of unfulfillment that you just can't shake? Do you look for things outside yourself to fill you up, such as excessive shopping, blanking out in front of the TV, overeating, or using alcohol in excess? Or do you keep yourself so busy you have no time for the things that make you happy, or even for quiet reflection? Do you often find yourself complaining about your work, relationships, health, finances, or goals?

If you answered yes to any of these questions, then you are operating within a scarcity mindset.

Scarcity consciousness is infectious and contributes to the insanity of humanity. Your life experiences are merely a mirror reflection of your own particular thought and feeling patterns. You may not even be aware of what patterns are not serving you if the ego has been running the show.

We covered defense mechanisms that create The Mask in Chapter 3, Self-Awareness. The ego desperately clings to The Mask for safety, and this fearful clinging perpetuates scarcity consciousness.

The authentic self is a divine representation of creation. There is no scarcity in creation.

COLLECTIVE SYSTEMS FAILURE

"Until you make the unconscious conscious, it will direct your life and you will call it fate." –Carl Jung

Operating unconsciously within the expectations of our social systems (family, school, work, government, religion, etc.) is limiting and does not encourage authentic living, which is the root cause of spiritual sickness. While collective cultural illness and elusive happiness may be the accepted norm in our society, you do not have to accept that existence for yourself. It is only when you become consciously aware of this fact that you can move differently in the world.

We are taught that we have to compete with others, be the best, play it safe, get a good job (that has nothing to do with our natural abilities), get the spouse, the house, the car, the kids, the money, and then, we will have made it.

What happens when you collect all of this and still feel miserable? You tend to blame external people, situations, and events for your unhappiness, like your spouse, your boss, your terrible job, your overbooked schedule—but the real issue is that you are denying your authentic truth because you are living the life you were told would make you happy.

The systems that are currently in place are not designed for you to realize your purpose—people end up slaves to these systems. They are designed to support the structure of their own life cycle, not the lives of the people who keep them operating. Most people are walking through life on auto-pilot, only vaguely aware of this fact and of their own unfulfillment.

You can choose something better—and when you do, you become the creator of your own life.

LIVE ON PURPOSE

"Find out who you are and do it on purpose." –Dolly Parton.

Becoming familiar with the intricacies of your core self helps to build the inner resilience necessary to become unbreakable in your authenticity. It is never too late and it doesn't matter what has happened in your life thus far, you can still experience the life you desire. We cannot know how the circumstances we have endured will help us get where we need to be; we cannot immediately see how these experiences are helping us move closer to accessing our authenticity and living through the lens of the core self.

First, you must give yourself permission to embrace your true, authentic self. It is up to you to be willing to unlock that door.

The confidence you receive from operating within your highest function of the core self allows you to access your vulnerabilities and learn to not be afraid of what you find. Practicing vulnerability is a practice in self-acceptance. In order to live an authentic existence, you must allow yourself to get vulnerable. On the other side of vulnerability is self-empowerment: the understanding that you are powerful beyond measure.

GETTING INTO THE FLOW

Do you know what it's like to be in the flow? In the flow, everything seems to unfold at precisely the right moment; serendipitous moments occur spontaneously, and interrelations between seemingly unrelated things (not coincidental but synchronous events) happen often. I call this experience the dance with the divine flow of collective universal energy, where it feels like your life is supporting you instead of pushing against you.

This state can be described as a feeling of profound peace, even in the midst of unknowing. It is peace beyond understanding. When you operate from this higher vibrational level, you will experience synchronous events that unfold as intuition takes over the consciousness, creating the life experiences you desire.

You begin by peeling back the layers of external conditioning and then learning how to understand and trust your core self. We will explore various ways to get into the flow in later chapters, but know that to remain in the flow state, you must get rid of everything that is not you.

"Knowledge of the self is the mother of all knowledge. So it is incumbent on me to know myself, to know it completely, to know its minutiae, its characteristics, its subtleties, and its very atoms." –Kahlil Gibran

REMEMBER YOUR DESIRES

Manifesting like a Goddess requires you to know your truest desires. If you have been placing your own wants and needs to the side for a long while, it can feel hard to remember or even to allow yourself to want anything beyond what you already have. Lack of desire creates stagnation. It's necessary to get very clear on what it is that you actually want for yourself. We will cover more on this concept in later chapters. For now, you can set the intention to uncover your deepest desires so you can manifest them. All the answers are within; you simply have to remember what they are.

Showing up in your full authenticity and acknowledging your deepest desires feels like freedom. It feels like peace. It feels like joyous anticipation. It feels like home.

The only way to determine who you are is to figure out who you are not. Maybe you have a job that requires you to show up in a way that feels unnatural. This is very different from finding yourself in a challenging situation that encourages you to grow. Inauthentic living feels like you are living within a shell of yourself.

This is also true within the context of personal relationships. Maybe your family dynamics are such that you feel a high sense of anxiety when you are around certain family members. You may find yourself pretending that everything is OK when it's not. Pretending to be someone else or faking emotions to gain the approval of others will lead you toward bending to the will of others. And every decision you make will ultimately be the wrong one for you.

Instead of blaming external factors, you must realize that everything happening in your reality is a projection of the beliefs you hold. Think of your mind as the movie projector and everything you see as the projection of your mind. This does not mean that you should tolerate being disrespected just because your own fears or hang-ups are being projected back to you by others. But it does mean that you will need to show up for yourself by acknowledging the moments when you shrink yourself to fit into a mold for others—and then choose something different. Tapping into this awareness without judging yourself is crucial to breaking the barriers that keep you playing small. If you insist on judging yourself for being responsible for creating a reality you don't want, you will not be able to change it.

You cannot be in alignment with universal consciousness when you are not being true to yourself. And when you don't show up for yourself, you can't show up for others either. It's a lose-lose proposition. Being inauthentic is a huge waste of energy. It actually takes a lot more energy to mask yourself than it does to step into your authenticity. However, being authentic takes courage.

VULNERABILITY IS THE SEAT OF AUTHENTICITY

Conscious manifesting requires you to know who you are, and BE that.

I'm referring to your authentic self.

The way to tap into your authenticity is through becoming vulnerable —which requires copious amounts of courage. Just think of the courage it takes to enter into a romantic relationship—even love cannot be known unless you are willing to risk a broken heart. You must be willing to be vulnerable to experience anything meaningful.

Allowing yourself to be vulnerable is the most courageous act you can practice as a human being. The reason it's so scary is because of the underlying fear of what could happen once you have revealed your true self. No one likes to be judged, or worse, rejected.

Our evolutionary make-up translates judgment and rejection as a death sentence because we inherently understand our need for connection. Thousands of years ago, being ostracized from your clan was indeed a death sentence. This is still a strong story perpetuated by the reptilian brain.

Vulnerability is a practice in self-love and self-acceptance, and it's the only way to create true emotional intimacy in the relationship you have with yourself and others. Without emotional intimacy, you cannot experience real connection with others, nor can you come into wholeness within.

AUTHENTICITY REVEALS YOUR PURPOSE

On some level, you must experience the death of your false self in order to be born again into your authentic self. Every human must go through this process. There is a grieving process associated with this loss—

it's perfectly natural. Shedding away layers of the false mask can feel like a loss of identity.

If you are not this label or that, then who are you? Yes, it's uncomfortable to ask these questions, but it is necessary. Shedding the mask clears your path to true inner fulfillment. For me, this process felt like I was literally burning away layers of my identity. It was incredibly uncomfortable. I grieved all the self-oppressive ways of being that I once welcomed into my life with open arms and had adopted as my identity. Once I let it all go, I began to feel lighter, and I began to rise like the Phoenix.

Before you can discern your reason for being here on Earth, you must develop the practice of being true to yourself. When you stop pretending to be something you're not, your self-knowledge and self-worth will begin to grow organically and exponentially.

Having a strong sense of your true self will support your life's purpose. And having a sense of purpose is the strongest indicator of happiness. When you know your purpose, you have the power to choose it, and with that comes a huge sense of relief because you begin to understand your own power.

There will never be another you on this planet. Incarnating into this dimension is not an easy undertaking—it is actually a miracle. The simple fact that you are here on Earth proves that you are a powerful being. And you're here for a reason.

7

EMOTIONAL MASTERY

"Where knowledge ends...feeling and imagination begin." –Neville Goddard

YOUR THOUGHTS CREATE YOUR EMOTIONS, YOUR EMOTIONS dictate your actions, and your actions drive outcomes.

E-motion is the precursor to action; it represents energy in motion. You cannot always turn off your thoughts, but you can choose to reframe them so you can experience emotions that feel good to you. Reframing thoughts does not mean that you must always think positive thoughts so you can feel better.

It's true that manifesting your desires requires you to line up your energy with the energy of your desired outcomes, but you will never bring in your manifestation while pretending to be happy when you really are not.

Contrary to popular belief, "rising above" your emotions by stuffing them down and relying on logic so you can "get on with life" does not represent emotional mastery. To achieve emotional mastery, you must be willing to feel your emotions—all of them. Only then will your energetic vibration be pure enough to match your desired manifestation. Once your own energy is aligned with the energy of your desires, the actions necessary to co-create your outcome will seem almost effortless.

This is why it's so important to learn to master your emotions.

Learning to master your emotions is possibly one of the most difficult undertakings of the human condition. Ruled by the realm of the feminine, emotions can be unpredictable and volatile. Your task is not to gain control over your emotional body and the flow of emotion, but to instead hold space for your emotions by becoming fully present to them while they are flowing. You do this by becoming curious about how you are feeling and then honoring each emotion with your undivided attention.

The act of feeling your emotions (the art of being) represents the feminine aspect of self. If you refuse to become intimate with your own emotions, you will become lost in either inaction or wrong action.

This is because emotions are the cause of action. Even if you think you are choosing logic over emotion, I assure you that you are not.

Every single decision we make is based on our emotions—how we want to feel and do not want to feel. While our thoughts dictate how we feel, it is emotion that inspires action.

In the world of marketing, this is well-known. Engaging with consumer's emotions is how companies sell products. Consider how Apple has marketed their products. Their marketing platform worked amazingly well because the focus was on creating a raised emotional experience for the consumer. Their product launches are designed to be seductive. In fact, their marketing techniques are so effective that their customers have literally camped out in front of Apple stores so they can be the first to receive their latest products. The late CEO Steve Jobs referred to Apple customers Apple addicts.

Authors Robin Lewis and Michael Dart explain Apple's marketing research in *The New Rules of Retail*, revealing how to evoke an emotional response in consumers so that it leads them to addictive behavior.

"We believe neurological connectivity is achieved when a retailer, brand or service creates a strong psychological and emotional response that operates on a subconscious level for the consumer in a way that is typically not readily understood nor necessarily recognized by the consumer. As various research studies in the field of neuroscience have found, when people encounter an elevated experience, their brains release many chemicals. One in particular that has attracted a lot of attention is dopamine, which leads to feelings of euphoria, self-satisfaction and well-being, and which can also actually lead to addiction."

Television in the 1950s became a useful political marketing tool: an ideal platform for spreading fear-based marketing campaigns that play on people's fear of crime. Fear-based political tactics have perpetuated the oppression of Native and African Americans in the United States and many others all over the world. This tactic is ultimately responsible for the creation of the United States' school-to-prison pipeline, which is now utilized to support modern-day slavery, feeding corporatized prisons through oppressive court systems, kidnapping children off the streets, and plopping them into prison cells where they provide free labor and are bought, sold, and traded throughout the prison system nationally. This travesty could only occur through emotional manipulation of the masses through fear-based messaging.

Considering it has been proven that emotions can be manipulated to build billion-dollar companies, elect presidents, normalize medication that fueled an opioid epidemic, and imprison 25 percent of the world's population in the United States alone, it would make sense for humans to learn to become the master of their emotions. It is safe to say that if you are not the master of your emotions, it's highly likely that someone else is.

FEELING YOUR EMOTIONS

Emotions are largely unconscious. It's possible you may be only vaguely aware of the depth of your emotions, or you may be completely unaware of how deeply they run. Gaining full awareness of your emotional depth is not exactly easy since societal conditioning has largely deemed emotional expression as irresponsible, useless, and weak. We experience our emotions by feeling them, but most people are not taught how to create space for this. Our collective conditioning has put such a high value on producing results in the external world that emotions have become secondary. There are so many negative connotations attached to being in our feels. There are myriad prescription medications prescribed every day that help prevent people from doing so! Regardless of how we weigh the value of emotions, humans still feel them, even if they go unacknowledged.

The most dangerous belief around emotional expression is that some emotions are bad and are not supposed to be felt. If human beings were not supposed to feel certain emotions, we simply would not be able to experience them. Some emotions vibrate at a higher frequency than others —put simply, some feel good, and some don't. But when the experience of lower vibrating emotions are blocked, even the higher vibrating emotions become inaccessible—internal growth becomes stunted and dysfunctional patterns continue to repeat in endless cycles. The refusal to acknowledge a negative emotion through stuffing or numbing will also block the experience of positive emotions. When you suppress your emotions, you oppress yourself.

Since we possess the capacity to experience the full range of human emotion (we're human, after all), there is no emotion that can be labeled as bad. The emotional body is actually quite intelligent, and all our emotions have important information for us. It is only when we allow ourselves to feel everything that we become free.

Holding space for emotions to surface will help you get into the habit of loving and accepting everything you feel—which supports the development of an intimate relationship with your authentic self. It's how you get to know yourself.

In my experience as a coach, anger seems to be the most regularly suppressed emotion. This suppression begins in childhood. Children are often not allowed to express anger and are typically punished if they do. This is unfortunate, considering that anger can support the decision-making process and serve as a guide toward more positive outcomes. The expression of anger has the capacity to lift you out of the vibration of sadness and depression and propel you into action. When anger is suppressed for long periods of time, it can create inaction or wrong action —and loads of regret.

EMOTIONS AND MANIFESTING

There is a serious collective misunderstanding around emotions as they relate to manifesting. In some spiritual communities, there is a tendency to believe that in order to manifest, you must remain in a high vibrating emotional state 24/7. As you well know, it is impossible to be in a good mood all the time. Yes, manifesting requires you to find your inner joy and become excited about receiving, but it also requires you to face your lower-vibrational emotions so they can be healed and cleared. Stuffing your emotions lodges them in the physical body and eventually manifests as dis-ease. One way or another, you will be forced to deal with them.

Facing certain emotions can feel terrifying, but it's better to create awareness and allow your wounds to surface so they can dissipate rather than stuff them down. When emotions are suppressed, the focus shifts from how you feel inside to external details that are beyond your control, such as the story your ego has created to keep you safe.

FREE YOURSELF FROM THE STORY TRAP

The stories we create around why we feel certain negative emotions usually include a person (or system) who we feel has acted against us in some way. The tendency is to focus on the event that caused the pain, and then we begin collecting evidence that proves we were wronged. The last step in the story trap is to determine how to punish the wrongdoer. This is indicative of the punitive system we exist in—the unending cycle of victimhood where someone is always to blame and needs to be punished.

You cannot possibly understand why people choose to act unless you inquire. With inquiry, you achieve a new understanding of why an event occurred. It usually has nothing to do with the story you created around it. That story you developed came from how you interpreted the event, and nothing more.

"Blame is simply the discharging of discomfort and pain." –Brené Brown

When you cast blame, you hand over the responsibility of your emotional state to others. You now have to wait for someone else to do something different so that you can feel better. This means you are giving your power away. When you give your power away, you lose dominion over the quality of your life and block your own healing. Blaming others makes it impossible to discover the inner wounds that perpetuate the negative experiences in your life. Blame is how we've all learned to discharge the pain we feel without having to internally process it.

Since the truth of humanity is that we are all connected, who is to blame is irrelevant. Blame perpetuates the most dangerous collective belief there is: that you are separate from the rest of humanity. If this were true, it would mean that you are also separate from what created you. This is why the belief in separation is dangerous, and it could not be further from the truth.

Every negative emotional reaction to an external event is a result of an inner wound that is rising to the surface because it is ready to be healed. If you can reframe your perspective by recognizing that external conflicts are merely clues about the wounds you carry, then you can step out of the victim cycle, heal your wounds and reclaim your power. To reclaim your power in any situation, you must release your negative emotional attachment to it.

You do this by turning your attention away from the storyline that is running in the mental body and focusing on what is happening in the emotional body. This deactivates thought details of the story that brought this emotion to the surface. From there, you can relax your need to control external outcomes (which are usually beyond your control).

Emotions are for feeling and thoughts are for thinking.

Rather than ruminating over the story of what someone did to you, shift your focus to how you feel. Doing this allows you to access and acknowledge your emotions and take full responsibility for them. This does not mean that you shift the blame toward yourself. Refrain from assigning blame. You are simply taking responsibility for how you are feeling in the moment because how you feel matters more than the story. When you create the space to be with your emotions, you deepen your awareness of self and your role in the event. Only then are you free to manifest a different experience.

HOW TO DIFFERENTIATE FEELINGS FROM FACTS

Feelings are not facts. The facts of a story become tainted once you attach emotion to them because you begin making assumptions. When you act upon those assumptions, problems compound.

The cleanest way to differentiate feelings from facts is to begin with the event that brought up the feeling. Objectively review the storyline of a particular experience. Just state what happened—what was said, what you or another did, and any pertinent events that occurred, without attaching blame or assuming intent. Once everyone agrees on the details of what actually occurred, you have yourself a factual story.

"There is no fault or blame without prior agreement." –James Daves

Then, you can take that story and use it to determine at which point your emotions got involved. This is how you identify your trigger point. I recommend writing a story timeline based on facts alone, then pinpointing the moment within the storyline where you felt your emotional energy shift. This will help you to identify the trigger. Usually, the trigger comes from an unconscious emotion tied to a wound we still carry from an older, painful experience.

Triggers occur in patterns. For example, if you felt anxious and embarrassed when your best friend gave you unsolicited advice about your food choices, or unappreciated because your boss never came through on that raise you were promised, you can bet you have felt those feelings before in another scenario. You can simply ask yourself, "When have I felt anxious and embarrassed before?" or, "When have I felt taken advantage of or unappreciated before?" More than likely, you have many examples of feeling the same emotion, maybe even around the same trigger point.

Taking it a step further, you can also ask yourself, "When was the first time I felt this way?" You may not reach the answer immediately. That's OK. Give yourself the space to explore the question. The answers surrounding what you're feeling will surface without much thought. Simply creating space for the answer to surface will help you receive it. Do not overthink the question. Let the answer come in its own time.

Once you have your answer, you have just uncovered an unconscious wound that you most likely didn't know you had. The wound will continue to play in a loop, showing up as various conflicts in your life until you stop associating with the storyline and acknowledge the emotion so your wound can heal.

When you care more about how you feel rather than the story your ego is focused on, the details of the story fade away, and the emotion takes center stage. By focusing on the emotion alone, you become inwardly focused rather than outwardly focused. What is going on inside of you is so much more important because it is your emotions that actually affect your choices and therefore create your external reality.

"BY-YOU" FEELINGS

I first learned about "by-you" feelings in a non-violent communication class as a grad student at American University. They are a powerful starting point for identifying underlying emotions. "By-you" feelings are words used to describe how someone else made you feel. Some examples of "by-you" feelings are: abandoned, betrayed, used, and cheated. What do these words have in common? Someone had to do these things to you.

In conflict, it becomes so easy to use "by-you" feelings to describe your emotions when you're focused on the story the ego has created. "By-you" feelings do not describe true emotions, but you can use them as a starting point to get closer to the truth of what you're feeling.

"By-you" feelings serve as a launching pad for you to locate your true, underlying emotion, but you must be willing to move beyond the "by-you" feeling toward what is beneath the surface, or else you will get stuck there. Trust me, you do not want to get trapped pointing the finger inside a story you cannot change. If you do, influences beyond your control will become your master, and you will remain at the mercy of what someone has done to you. In this space, the only way to feel better is for another person to do something different. If they do not, then you remain in perpetual suffering. Blame and punishment are the only tools available in this scenario, and no real resolution can come from that.

Here is how you can use "by-you" feelings to transcend the blame cycle. Especially in a fight, flight, or freeze state, it may be difficult to first create a factual story timeline so you can access your underlying emotions. In these moments, you can use "by-you feelings" in a simple three-step process.

1. Begin with the story you are telling yourself.
2. Acknowledge the "by-you" feeling that describes what someone did to you.
3. Locate the underlying emotion and allow yourself to feel it.

Here is an example of this process:

Lisa shares with her co-worker Cheryl the details about a project she's working on. Cheryl interrupts her and says, "Oh, you are doing that the wrong way. I can show you a better way." Lisa's feelings are hurt, and she becomes emotionally charged.

The Process:

1. Lisa asks herself, "What story am I telling myself?" Her story is: "Cheryl is insensitive and rude, and doesn't care about how I feel."
2. Lisa locates her "by-you" feelings. She decides she feels insulted and invalidated.
3. From there, Lisa can then locate her true, underlying emotion beneath the "by-you" feelings. She actually feels embarrassed, self-conscious, and worried that she's not good enough. She can then ask herself what information these emotions are trying to give her.

Now that Lisa has accessed her true emotions, she is empowered because she has claimed dominion over her own emotions by acknowledging them. She can now work on healing the wounds associated with how she feels. No one had to change their behavior for her to do this. Instead, she changed the narrative and took her power back.

Think of a time someone wronged you. Then, identify the story you told yourself about it, and then take a look at the "By-You Feelings List," located in the back of this book. Identify the "by-you" feeling that comes up for you. There may be more than one that resonates. Write them down.

Next, have a look at the "Feelings Inventory List," also located in the back of this book. Look for the underlying emotion beneath the "by-you" feeling. If you rarely consider your emotions beyond the limited words of "happy," "sad," "angry," and "bored," then this list will help you better capture the depth of what you're feeling.

You can use this list to take responsibility for how you feel and take your power back.

Taking responsibility for your emotions allows you to build emotional intimacy with yourself, self-soothe, develop resiliency, heal, and become the master of your life. You cannot heal the injured places within that you are unwilling to acknowledge.

It's up to you to take full responsibility for what you're feeling. When you care more about how you feel rather than the story your ego is focused on, you deactivate thought details and activate your emotional body where the important information lives. From this place, you can be gentle with yourself because your intention is focused on strengthening your relationship with yourself.

The only way out of emotional pain is through it. In choosing to identify and acknowledge how you feel, you have nothing to lose and everything to gain.

8

COMPASSION

My understanding of compassion came to me in a dream. I saw words floating in space, and it looked just like this: come, passion. I woke up immediately and wrote down what I saw. As days passed, the understanding behind the dream became clear to me. Our passion is born from compassion. Stay with me as I explain further.

First, let's explore compassion and what it really means. Here are two very different common definitions for compassion:

Definition 1: Sympathetic pity and concern for the sufferings or misfortunes of others.

Definition 2: Showing empathy, care, concern, and sensitivity to others. Other words to describe compassion include: understanding, tenderness, gentleness, mercy, love, consideration, humanity, and humaneness.

You can see that definition #1 describes sympathy, and definition #2 describes empathic caring.

The English language is tricky because there are often multiple conflicting definitions for one word, and in this case, the misunderstanding of compassion lies within the difference between sympathy and empathy.

Sympathy is feeling sorry for another without taking the time to understand the details of their pain. When you feel sorry for someone, you are not offering understanding—you are offering pity. You disempower others when you feel sorry for them. It's the same when you feel sorry for yourself; you disempower yourself with the same energy. No new possibilities can come from the energy of sympathy.

Empathy, on the other hand, is putting yourself in another's shoes so that you fully understand that person. In those moments, we recognize our shared humanity, and then we feel and extend compassion organically. Having empathy for yourself in moments of despair means that you focus on developing an understanding of what is happening within you, without judgment, so that you can uncover new possibilities for a more positive experience.

Compassion is an emotional response to empathy that inspires altruism. It supports three basic human needs: to be seen, heard, and understood. It helps us recognize our shared humanity, and that recognition drives us to act passionately in service to others. Compassion is empowering for the giver and the receiver.

Let's explore the definition of passion: intense, driving, or overmastering feeling or conviction; a strong liking or desire for or devotion to some activity, object, or concept, the emotions as distinguished from reason.

Passion does not operate through logic or reason; it is rooted in the emotional body. Passion is the fire in our bellies. We experience passion by feeling it, and it fuels our desire to take action. To explore passion in the context of desire always leads us to connection, whether it is through love for another or something we love doing—it is always about love. When you are in love, you share that love in connection with another. When you are doing something you love, you want to share that with others. This is because we are wired for connection. Creating the space for passion allows you to lead a passionate life in service to others from a purposeful place, which is the actualization of your highest self. From this place, you not only empower yourself but also create connection with others. This is what compassion is all about.

Compassion is a fundamental component in the process of manifesting. In order to consciously manifest, you must recognize your connection to everything. Practicing compassion helps you do this, and also fuels your passion to act in alignment with your authentic self, and ultimately, your purpose.

When you focus your energy on what you are passionate about, you begin to vibrate at the level of joy. And when you raise your vibration to the level of joy, you are in alignment with the energy of creation. This is your cue that you're on the path to manifesting consciously.

Serving from a place of purpose sparks passion. We are always serving others in some way, whether we're *passionately* serving from our purpose or *passionlessly* serving out of obligation. We cannot get out of service. Even if you are working at a gas station, you are serving other people by accepting their money so they can fill up their gas tanks and get back to serving others.

When you give through service in ways that feel really good inside, you begin to discover your greatest passions in life, which support your purpose—and that is why you are here.

Compassion and passion are interconnected and help align you to your purpose, which represents a higher actualization of self. Your higher self can be felt through your Goddess energy. When you are in your Goddess energy, you can create a life that you're passionate about, which is what conscious manifesting is all about.

Think about all the things that spark your passion. How can you use what you're passionate about to serve others?

PRACTICING COMPASSION FOR OTHERS

It's important to understand what it looks like to have compassion for others. First, I'll tell you what it's not. Practicing compassion does not mean allowing your boundaries to be crossed, nor does it mean feeling sorry for people. These two habits disempower us and everyone around us. Sympathy is a degradation to humanity. And because we are connected to every living thing, we hurt the soul of the planet when we degrade others. Listening to others complain and agreeing with them to make them feel better is also not a practice in compassion. It is an act of commiseration that perpetuates misery in your sphere of influence.

Compassion empowers everyone in your sphere of influence. Practicing compassion means practicing empathy (putting yourself in the shoes of others instead of separating yourself through judgment) and then offering loving service in some way. Compassion is not just reserved for people who are suffering or those who are obviously in need. You can extend compassion to anyone at any time in endless ways. You can give the gift of compassion by chipping in to help someone out when you are able and when it feels good to do so, listening to others when they are ready to share, making eye contact, or offering a smile. The compassionate energy you extend to others will be paid forward 100-fold. Compassion is such a powerful energy that even when people witness an act of compassion that is not directed toward them, they are still inspired to carry its energy forward.

Active listening is a beautiful way to show compassion for others. We all want to be seen, heard, and understood. To practice active listening means that you are really listening to what another has to say and taking all of it in without an agenda. It's so easy to stop listening, especially when you feel cornered or attacked. Preparing what you're going to say for when another is finished talking is a strategy rooted in self-defense. If someone is blaming you for something, it's easy to fall into the trap of defensiveness.

Sometimes, the energy of defensiveness is less obvious. Let's say your child or your younger sibling is having a problem they are working through, and they decide to share with you what's going on with them. If your immediate reaction is to give unsolicited advice, you are in self-defense mode. I know this sounds counterintuitive, but your perceived concern may actually be a fear of feeling anxious about what they are going through. And if we cannot bear it when our loved ones suffer, we cannot actually hear them. Usually, this happens when they need to be heard the most. Offering unsolicited advice is a defense strategy and can be emotionally invalidating to the receiver.

The 12-month conflict resolution facilitation certification program I teach in the Transcend Into Oneness Experience (that includes all I learned from Sylvia) is heavily focused on actively listening as a way to resolve conflict. Active listening is always about the other person. You repeat what you heard the other person say to make sure you heard what they wanted you to hear. If you are really listening, you can begin to identify the underlying message—often what is not being said.

How do you know if you've succeeded in active listening? Simply ask, "Is that what you wanted me to hear?" And you will get your answer. This form of communication can feel really awkward at first, but if you keep at it, your relationships will be better for it. Once you have heard what they wanted you to hear, you can ask certain questions to help them open up even further. You can ask, for example, "What would you like for me to know about that?" "Is there more?" It's important to continue reflecting back what you heard until they have no more to share.

Offering space for someone to be seen, heard, and understood is one of the most compassionate acts there are. Practicing compassion raises the vibrational frequency of every person, place, and thing in your environment. Conscious manifesting requires you to remain in a high vibration as often as possible, so you must create the environment for this to occur. Practicing compassion will help you do that.

PRACTICING SELF-COMPASSION

"We can't practice compassion with other people if we can't treat ourselves kindly." –Brené Brown

Self-compassion looks like showing up for yourself—allowing yourself time to rest, reflect, and practice filling your own cup. When your cup is empty, you have nothing to give anyone else. You end up feeling overwhelmed, exhausted, and passionless. Extending compassion to yourself means that you take the time to get to know yourself so you can give yourself what you need in any given moment. If you haven't extended compassion to yourself in a while, you may not truly understand what your needs are, much less realize that you have the power to give it to yourself.

As a single mom, I had an extremely hectic schedule with a full-time job, my son's school and sports schedules, and attending college classes. I was literally busy every waking moment. When I finally got some downtime, I didn't know what to do! So, I created more things to do when I really could have used the rest. I was so used to being in motion that I never gave myself a break until I became so exhausted that I got sick. Practicing self-compassion could have helped me avoid all that.

You can start right now by asking yourself: what do I need right now that I am not allowing myself to have?

Humanity's ability to understand their own needs has become increasingly rare, complicated, and difficult because so many people have become disconnected with their inner selves. Maybe you have no idea what you need right now. If you don't know what you need, you can't give it to yourself—not even the simplest things in life.

A very simple example I can give you is of a friend of mine who spent the first 20 years of her life dealing with painful stomach aches that reliably came after eating meals. She eventually removed certain foods from her diet, and immediately, her stomach aches disappeared. She was so used to living with stomach pain after meals that she thought it was just a natural outcome of becoming satiated. She had no idea that she could feel any differently until she became so tired of feeling bad that she decided to open herself up to the possibility that she could in fact feel better.

It's the same for emotional pain. When you acknowledge a particular negative emotional response that you experience on a regular basis, you can begin to do something about it. Emotional pain may surface around a particular person or memory or when you hide your authentic self. The discomfort you feel is trying to tell you something.

Paying attention to how you feel and what you need in any given moment by leaning into the discomfort so you can understand its message is the way through. Moving through the pain is the way out.

I know I keep preaching this point, and it is so important that this won't be the last time: self-awareness is everything. Creating awareness of your own needs helps you give yourself what you need and also communicate your needs to others. When you don't get what you need, not only are you miserable but so is everyone around you. If you want to manifest better relationships, you may only need to follow this one piece of advice!

Think about this: everything is an energy exchange—attention, money, love, etc. So pay yourself with your own energy. If you want more energy of any kind from another, you have to give it to yourself first.

The self-awareness journey can feel exhausting at times. It's important to be gentle with yourself while learning these concepts and putting them into practice. You are, in essence, rewiring years of conditioned programming, which requires lots of energy but is necessary if you want to create a different life experience. Self-compassion includes time for rest and recuperation while you are recalibrating.

Self-compassion actually shifts your energy toward the vibration of joy. This is important to remember because what you focus on expands.

I was not able to find my passion (that led me to my purpose) until I developed compassion for myself. I decided to go out on a limb and do something nice for myself every single day. Eventually, that one thing grew into three things and then into five things. I began to notice that I was spending more time happy, relaxed, and peaceful rather than tired, stressed, and pissed off. My overall existence became infinitely better. And I also got better at discerning my own needs. I learned how to meet many of my own needs by myself.

Your happiness is your responsibility. That doesn't mean that you have to do everything yourself. It simply means that you have to know what you want and make sure you get it, even if you have to give it to yourself.

HOW COMPASSION CONNECTS US

When you are feeling a negative emotion and having a hard time climbing out of that emotion, sometimes reaching out to another who is in need or is suffering can help. Why would you do that when you feel crappy? Because it helps you recognize your connection to something outside of your own misery.

Oneness (our connection with everyone and everything) is recognized through compassionate acts. The energy of compassion reflects the truth of our connection.

The act of serving helps you get back into connection with universal consciousness, which is the energy of co-creation. This is when you naturally begin working alongside Source consciousness and co-creating with the universe.

❦ 9 ❦

INNER CHILD HEALING

"Behind every independent woman, there is a broken little girl who had to learn to get back up and never depend on anyone." –Anonymous

WHILE I AM NOT A PROPONENT OF GOING IT ALONE AND refusing the help of others, the work of accessing your Inner Child for the purpose of your healing is a solo journey. Even if you have the help of a guide to meet your Inner Child, you still have to do the work. No one can do it for you or better than you.

My Inner Child healing journey began in 2017, and it will never end. I have dedicated my heart to my Inner Child, and I promised to give her what she needs when she needs it. Today, I have recaptured my child-like wonder by giving her a safe space to be. I listen to her when she speaks. I give her space to use her imagination. I shower her with all the love I have to give. The catalyst to my own Inner Child healing work was the excruciating pain of my marriage falling apart. I figured if the world was my reflection, I was attracting the people, places, and things that created my experiences. These experiences showed me the wounds I had carried into every important relationship. It even dictated the types of relationships I attracted into my life.

I delved into the work of reintegrating little Sara back into my life. It was equally beautiful and painful. And it was so worth it.

We all have Inner Child wounds to tend to. The areas where you did not receive the love and support that you needed as a child are the areas that you must heal. If you ignore these wounds, it will become extremely difficult to step into your own power and access the magnificent Goddess within you.

Leaving traumas unhealed will only leave you trapped in resentment, victimhood, and stagnation until you choose to take personal responsibility for your own healing.

The path to manifesting like a Goddess includes reparenting, which means taking full responsibility for your little self—and not judging, but instead loving all the aspects of you.

REPARENTING THE INNER CHILD

Very early in life, and possibly even before birth, every human being receives early wounding messages that control how we see ourselves and the world around us. These messages also create our concept of a higher power. If you learned that doing something your parents didn't like would get you punished, then it's quite possible that you did two things: you abandoned the part of you that wanted to express yourself in that particular way, and then, in adulthood, you transferred your experience into a belief—if you did that thing again you would be punished, but this time by a higher power. This is called parental transference.

A cognitive approach to changing this type of programming does not work because the rational or logical part of the brain is not responsible for emotional programming. As a child, you absorbed all kinds of information without analyzing it. Children take in the information they receive at face value, and that information creates the belief systems that they carry into adulthood. Because the logical brain is not responsible for this programming, using logic cannot change it. You must tap into your emotions by beginning with your earliest painful childhood memories and allow yourself to feel all of them.

Old emotional wounds are deeply buried in the emotional body; they are sometimes beyond conscious awareness. The suppressed anguish and torment lying beneath the surface can cause all types of physical and emotional illness if it goes unacknowledged. There is no way to get around feeling emotional pain. The only way out is through the pain.

There is also a common misconception that your Inner Child is the part of you that needs to grow up and manage their emotions better. This could not be further from the truth! Your Inner Child is a forever child that once existed on the physical plane, and now, her energy forever exists outside of the third dimension. In our 3-D reality, we perceive time as linear, but actually, time is fluid. If you were floating in empty space, you would not have any concept of time. If this concept seems a little far out, consider this truth according to quantum physics—there is only now. Everything that ever was and ever will be is happening right now. We will further explore the concept of time in Chapter 23, Bending Time, but for now, understand that every aspect of you, past, present, and future, exists right now. This means your childhood self is very relevant in your life today.

If your Inner Child has not received your attention and loving care, she will eventually make herself known to you through painful emotional experiences so you can address your wounds. It's better that you continually reach out to her and check-in rather than wait for her to come to you. The way to handle her is to honor her and let her be herself. In doing so, you'll find that your adult self can also relax as you begin to understand that you have the power to reparent yourself. When you regularly show up for your little self, you are essentially rewriting the story of the past.

HEALING THE WOUNDS OF THE INNER CHILD

Even thinking about healing Inner Child wounds can feel scary, especially if you experienced significant trauma as a child. A friend once said to me, "I can't do this because it was so bad; I'm afraid if I go back to that place, I'll get stuck there."

You do not have to go back and relive the past. What you are doing is connecting with your little self who experienced the trauma and developing a relationship with her. The only time you get stuck there is when you leave your Inner Child to fend for herself. You can see the proof of this in the negative patterns in your adult relationships and life circumstances.

Remember, e-motion is energy in motion. Think of your emotions as wires that lead to your internal subconscious programming. In order to release and heal the wounds associated with these early messages, you must shift out of the logical brain and open your heart so you can feel your way through. Opening your heart allows emotions to surface and be released. Then, you can use your imagination to create a different story, one where you are now the parent of your little self. You can do this better than anyone can because no one knows what you need better than you.

Many holistic healing modalities are based on the idea that every illness and injury is a physical representation of an emotional wound that is in need of healing. Your body is intelligent and will alert you to an emotional injury by giving you a physical representation of it.

You can also think about this as your Inner Child screaming her head off and acting out horrendously because you have gone missing. That is exactly what children do when we don't pay them loving attention. Once you turn inward and face her, you will discover a hurt and terrified child who just wants your attention and love.

I began to recapture the essence of my Inner Child by remembering all my favorite things I liked to do as a child: playing with my toys, dancing, spending time with friends, and staring at the indigo sky. Today, I give myself permission to play through imagination, dance, yoga, meditation, being in nature, creating art, and using tarot cards, runes, and rituals. While tarot, runes, and rituals are not practices to be taken lightly, they help me tap into my imagination and open the door to the unknown.

I also committed to a regular meditation practice with the intention to tap into my Inner Child's energy so we could become reacquainted and I could help her heal. My experiences using this healing technique inspired me to create the Inner Child guided meditation that is available in the *Manifest Like a Goddess Experience*.

However, you can simply bring this book with you to your meditation cushion and guide yourself through the process by reading the meditation yourself. This meditation will empower you to rewrite your programming and grow your self-love in ways that you never dreamed possible. It may feel scary to revisit the past, but as you know, the only way out is through. It's important that you do not rush through this process.

If you lead with your masculine essence, simply change the feminine references (she, her) in this meditation to he and him. Keep a journal nearby so you can record your experiences once you're finished.

INNER CHILD GUIDED MEDITATION

Find a quiet space where you will not be disturbed and bring your journal with you. Make sure you are in a comfortable seated position with your spine straight. You can use a meditation cushion or a pillow to align your spine.

Close your eyes, allow your body to begin to relax.

Breathe in through your nose, allow your belly to fill with air like a balloon, five counts in and release the breath, five counts out.

Take a deep breath in through your nose and fill your lungs with air. Exhale through your mouth, releasing all the stress in your body. Allow the rest of the world to be as it is for the time being while focusing on the presence of your body.

Become aware of the space that your body is occupying.

Let your breath drop down into your diaphragm, allowing it to flow more smoothly. Relax your forehead, your eyes, your cheeks, and your jaw. Allow a slight smile to surface around the corners of your eyes and mouth. Notice the breath in your nostrils. Feel the soft touch of the breath flowing in and out as you inhale and exhale.

Feel yourself entering into the present moment. Bring your attention to the room, noticing anywhere you're hearing noises, the temperature of the room and any smells you're noticing.

Allow your breath to flow uninterrupted, smoothly and continuously and similar in duration, so each breath in is the same length as each breath out.

Allow your shoulders to relax and drop into the awareness of your inner state. Allow your forehead to relax, now your jaw, eyes, and mouth. Now relax your neck, arms, chest, belly, spine, thighs, calves, feet, and toes.

Feel your heart expanding as you continue moving your attention within.

Scan your body, from head to toe. Ask yourself where the painful childhood trigger is located in your body. Do this without judgment. Where do you feel it? It may show up as a heaviness or pain in your heart, solar plexus, hips or shoulders, literally anywhere. It may be so big you feel it everywhere under your skin. Even if you don't feel its presence in this moment, you can imagine where the wound might be lodged in the body.

Trust any answers you receive.

Bring into focus what hurts the most right now, any slight or magnified emotional or physical pain that is present in your conscious awareness. Notice what is trying to get your attention.
Tune into this area without analyzing the details about the pain that is present. Simply feel your way through with love, openness, and acceptance.

Sit with the knowingness that you are about to experience profound comfort as you step into the energy of the loving ferocity of a mother bear protecting her cub, moving closer toward your Inner Child and any wounds that are present.

Ask yourself: how old is this part of me?

Bring your attention to the times when your emotional reactions to this pain may have played out in your life, revealing vulnerable and unhealed wounds.

Now, ask your Inner Child, "What is this about?" Be patient and allow your young self to reveal to you what created this wound.

Trust and allow what comes up without judgment.

The answer may come as a feeling, a voice or a flash of a vision in your mind, a sound, color, symbol, or a message from your gut—NOT a logical deduction. Trust whatever information you are given, no matter how it manifests. You cannot think your way out of this; you must feel your way through it. Trust your subconscious to connect with you, and welcome this connection with feelings of love and devotion so your Inner Child will know she can trust you.

Be fully and lovingly present with what you've found. Don't judge or turn away. Radiate love from your heart and hold the space for your little self to feel heard and supported.

Let her speak to you. Allow her to take all the time she needs.

Pledge that even though you don't know the healing answers right now, you will never abandon her again. Sit with your little self as long as she needs you.

Let her know she has been heard.

Declare with all the love that you can muster that you are going to help her heal and develop and that the greatest mission now is to create this essential, integrated relationship with your little self.

Allow your Inner Child to come to you and give her a big hug.

Thank her for being vulnerable and trusting you enough to share this space together. Let her know that you are here for her whenever she needs you.

Notice her smile. Feel the sincere love she feels from you. Now, she's ready to go off and play.

Notice all the strength you have just gathered from this time with your little self.

Know that she is feeling safe and secure. Know that your little self is safe and that you are safe.

Feel the gratitude in your heart that you could offer this gift to her.

When you're ready, slowly bring your presence back into the room. With your eyes closed, feel the weight of your seat. Wiggle your toes, your fingers, and adjust your position if that feels good.

Move your head from side to side. Raise your shoulders up, and let them fall. Give yourself a big hug for all the amazing inner work you just did, feeling a profound sense of gratitude for making the connection.

Slowly open your eyes and come back into the room.

Next, take some time to journal your experience. Write down how you felt and what you learned. This will help you release the residual emotional pain as well as give you a reference point for later.

❧ 10 ❧

UNCONDITIONAL SELF-LOVE

WE'VE COVERED A LOT ABOUT SELF-AWARENESS AND HOW developing an intimate understanding of who you are, including your wounds and your true desires will help you manifest like a Goddess. The practice of self-awareness without judgment leads to insight that not only has the power to grow your self-worth but also change the trajectory of your life path. As your inner knowledge expands, you will naturally feel more love for yourself just like when we get to know our partners and friends better, we love them more. Let's delve into some important truths, and then I will ask you to check in with yourself to see how they resonate with you.

FIVE FUNDAMENTAL TRUTHS

1. You are an expression of love.
2. You are a beautiful and magical divine being who is loved beyond measure.
3. You are a powerful manifestor who can create any life experience.
4. You are a gift to this world and possess unique gifts that can never be replicated.
5. You are a perfect expression of Source consciousness.

Pay attention to what happens inside of your physical and emotional bodies when you absorb these truths. How do you feel? Loved and acknowledged? Or are they uncomfortable and difficult for you to accept? Pay attention to your reaction, because your reactions are your clues to whether or not you truly believe it.

If these fundamental truths feel uncomfortable, that's OK. In this chapter, you will learn some practices that can help you settle into the awareness of them and accept them as the truth. It requires self-honesty, self-devotion, curiosity, and patience.

WHAT DOES IT MEAN TO LOVE YOURSELF UNCONDITIONALLY?

Unconditional self-love means that you love and accept yourself for exactly who you are in every single moment. This is easier said than done. The problem is that throughout childhood and early adulthood, your authentic self may have gotten lost in a sea of beliefs transferred to you by others who told you who you were supposed to be.

There are two main elements of unconditional self-love: honesty and devotion to self. When you learn how to get really honest with yourself, you can fall in love with all the beautiful parts of you and witness that love mirrored back to you in the external world.

Honesty: In order to cultivate self-love, you must become intimate with the inner workings of yourself so you can uncover those parts that were buried due to the fear of not being accepted. Once you uncover your inner workings, your job is to lovingly accept them.

Devotion: You entered this world with a unique set of badass natural talents, gifts, and abilities. If you have not devoted yourself to finding a way to use your innate gifts, then it's possible that you have abandoned those aspects of yourself and have felt unable to step into your purpose.

Being devoted to developing an intimate relationship with yourself is a crucial component to manifesting. When you are devoted to and honest with yourself, you will begin to develop an awareness of your deepest desires that reflect who you are truly meant to be and what you are meant to do in the world. Your desires also serve as a reflection of how you will serve others using your natural talents, gifts, and abilities. When you acknowledge your true desires, you are on the path to authenticity, and then you can allow yourself to dream bigger. If you want it, it is meant for you.

Your true desires will not feel like a longing. They will just be. Yes, you will feel the passionate energy associated with your truest desires. However, this feeling is very different from the uncomfortable longing for false, lower desires, which are merely illusions that your defense mechanism created because it felt too scary to own your power and let yourself have what you really wanted deep down.

There are many reasons why the belief "you can't have everything you want" exists. Maybe you feel that you don't deserve it, you haven't worked hard enough yet, or maybe you were taught that it is selfish to want too much.

When I was a kid, I was told repeatedly, "You can't have everything you want," so many times that it became firmly anchored in my reality. I believed it so much that I also taught this belief to my son at a very young age. I would sing him the Rolling Stones song, "You Can't Always Get What You Want," when he would beg for something he really desired that I thought I could not give him. What if I instead brainstormed with him ways to figure out how to achieve getting those desires met? If I had known better, I would have chosen to empower him to go after his desires rather than convincing him to settle.

ALLOW YOURSELF TO HAVE DESIRES

There is a very important reason we have desires. If all the people in the world stopped desiring, not one more creation could come into being. So, allow yourself to want. Your desires are the designer of your reality. We will never stop desiring because it is from our desires that we create.

We use our imagination to tap into a desire and then bring that desire into existence by imagining the details of what is possible. And we were born knowing how to use our imagination. No one had to show us how. It is a natural human gift that we possess because we are creators. We're taught to believe that our imagination is not valuable, yet this super-human tool is used to create everything in our existence.

However, if your desires cause you pain, then allow yourself to look deeper into that desire and ask yourself why you want this thing that causes you pain. This will help you get closer to understanding the difference between your true desires and ego-driven (fear-based) desires. You can feel loved-based desires in your heart. It feels like your heart is expanding. Fear-based desires feel more like contracting, which is associated with the feelings of longing or yearning, which feel awful.

My heart was completely crushed when my former husband left me. He actually left 13 times, and each time I felt like he reached into my chest and ripped out my heart. I longed for him to return, even after he entertained a months-long affair. I was willing to forgive him for literally anything as long as he would come home.

It wasn't until I was able to uncover the underlying wound associated with this longing that I realized he was only serving as a mirror that reflected back to me my own belief that I didn't matter. Once I healed that wound, I realized that this feeling of longing was attached to a false, fear-based desire that was merely a cover-up for my true desire: to matter.

If you're longing for a particular person to fulfill you in a romantic partnership, you can ask yourself, "Why do I want this so badly?" "Why does this desire cause me pain?" "What feeling am I chasing?"

When you are yearning or longing for something, you are using a false, fear-based desire as a cover-up for the true desire. In my situation with my marriage, I felt abandoned and betrayed ("by-you feelings"), and I longed for validation of my worthiness. Underneath the "by-you" feelings were my own actual feelings of unworthiness, insecurity, and loneliness.

Beneath the longing, my true desire was that I wanted to matter.

I began the process of Inner Child healing so I could rewrite the script and matter to myself. If I had felt I mattered, I would never have stayed so long in a toxic relationship.

If you uncover an old wound such as this, then do the work with your Inner Child so you can stop attracting people and situations that mirror your wounds back to you. Feelings of longing are not actually about anyone else; they represent the wounded aspect of self that is longing to heal so you can move into wholeness. No one can do this for you.

When I uncovered my underlying emotion and my true desire (of wanting to matter), I stepped into my power and gave that gift to myself. I stopped repeating painful patterns and began creating life situations and experiences that bring me joy.

FOCUS ON WHAT YOU DO WANT

Another collective issue that must be overcome is the habit of focusing on what you do not want. The ego likes to take control by focusing your attention on all the things you do not want. This is where you must flip the script and begin to explore what you actually do want.

This is not to discount the importance of learning what it is that you don't want. Duality is the driving force in our 3-D reality, and it's how we learn our most important lessons and get to know ourselves. Having uncomfortable experiences can be your greatest teacher in figuring out what it is you actually want, as long as you don't get hung up on the trauma of those experiences. Remember, there is a tendency to apply stories around perceived failures or difficult moments. Those stories will keep you trapped in the trauma drama of the past and create more fear, which is debilitating. Then, it can feel impossible to try something again, or to do something you've never done before. The fear-based question becomes: "What if [insert bad thing] happens?"

Becoming stuck in the painful emotions of what you have lived through becomes a mind trap full of "what-ifs." Instead, thank your experiences and find the lessons in them. You have gained valuable knowledge from every experience you've ever had. There is always a way to achieve your desires, and it is never too late.

SELF-PARTNERING

Self-partnering means that you devote time to yourself to honor your own needs by giving yourself what you want and need when you want and need it.

Self-partnering is a bit different than Inner Child healing. Just because you are feeling a lower emotion doesn't necessarily mean that your Inner Child is screaming for attention. Usually, the pain of the Inner Child feels unbearable, and the emotion cannot be accessed without concentrated effort. When you are feeling a lower vibrational emotion like irritability, it could simply mean that you are hungry or tired. If you feel anxious, it could mean that you just need a break.

Ask yourself what you need in these moments, and then give it to yourself. Consider self-partnering the tool you use to give yourself exactly what you need, exactly when you need it.

When I first began the practice of self-partnering, I had to think hard about what I needed in a given moment. I hadn't given much thought to my own needs for so long that I didn't have any ideas about what I could give myself. I thought that maybe I didn't need anything—which was far from the truth. I had not allowed myself to indulge in desiring anything because I thought it was selfish. This faulty belief kept me from designing my own reality and experiencing joy, which is my divine right. It is also your divine right to experience joy.

There is something incredibly magical about taking time to focus on what brings you joy. If you create the space to really think about what you can do each day to show yourself love, you will come up with many ways to do it. It doesn't have to be extravagant or take up a lot of time.

When you begin to show up for yourself, you will notice people, places, and things will also show up for you in your external reality. And when you begin to meet your own needs, you will develop self-trust. As you begin to trust yourself, you will notice that you have the ability to notice your wants and needs more easily. The most amazing outcome of trusting yourself is becoming aware of your intuitive nudges. Self-trust expands intuition.

In Chapter 8, Compassion, I explained to you that I began doing one nice thing for myself each day. My practice grew to three nice things, and today, I've graduated to five nice things. The beauty of this practice is that it brings multiple gifts. Not only will you begin to expand your intuition, but you will also begin to notice that you have even more time to do even more nice things for yourself that uplift you. After a few weeks of doing nice things for myself every day, I noticed that I ended up with more time to devote to myself, and my quality of life rose significantly. I stopped spinning my wheels and began to think more clearly. I was able to carry out my responsibilities more efficiently, have more fun, and receive more help. My hope is that you will take this idea seriously and show yourself some delicious unconditional love every day so you can watch the quality of your life rise to new heights.

USING THE "LOVE LANGUAGES" TO LOVE YOURSELF

To get started on figuring out what in the world I actually wanted, I began with the book *The Five Love Languages* by Gary Chapman. If you haven't yet read this book, I highly recommend doing so. It not only taught me how to love others in the way they wanted to be loved, but it reminded me of my own needs and how to communicate them and express love to myself.

This book describes five main ways we give and receive love. These are: acts of service, gift-giving, quality time, words of affirmation, and physical touch. Get creative with these love languages, and imagine the many ways you can show yourself some love! If it feels strange to think about showing yourself love, then remember that the quality of your life depends on figuring this out. You can choose to give yourself no love and live an unfulfilling life, or you can choose to love yourself at every opportunity and spend your days feeling happy and fulfilled. What you focus on expands. The choice is yours.

Here are a few examples from my self-love list:

Acts of Service: Yoga (only if I really WANT to do it), getting a pedicure, massage, or facial, having breakfast in bed or cooking myself a delicious, healthy meal.
Quality time: Lighting candles, journaling, taking a nap, reading, meditating, spending time with loved ones, dancing with others or by myself.
Words of Affirmation: Speaking aloud all the wonderful attributes I possess and saying "I love you" in the mirror. Writing down all the things I like about myself.
Physical touch: Snuggling with my partner or my cat, giving myself a hug, wearing silky or soft clothing, and taking a bubble bath.
Gift-giving: Buying myself flowers, taking myself shopping or to a nice restaurant by myself (or with others), and being open to receiving help from others.

I encourage you to use the love languages to figure out ways to show some love to yourself on a regular basis.

There will be times when you are unable to give yourself the exact thing you need in a given moment. When you are unable to experience the thing you're wanting to give yourself, allow yourself to want it anyway without feeling bad about not getting it. Do give yourself what you're able to give, and open yourself up to the feeling of gratitude for being able to give yourself anything in that moment. This expands the energy of allowing and receiving, essentially opening the door to getting even more of what you want. It is incredibly empowering to be able to trust yourself to meet your own needs.

11

RADICAL GRATITUDE

WE CAN SPEND SO MUCH TIME AND ENERGY ANALYZING WAYS to overcome pain in the quest for happiness when the solution is actually very simple; yet the simple solutions are the ones we ignore because our analytical brain believes that the solution is somehow supposed to be complicated.

Before I understood the importance of gratitude, I never stopped long enough to be grateful for anything. Once I achieved one goal, I immediately moved on to the next. I thought being grateful for achievements was weak and that I was willing to settle for what I had accomplished so far. I believed that if I allowed myself to be happy with what I had, I wouldn't accomplish anything else.

I had trained myself to move through the world in this way because I was afraid to stop. My underlying belief was that I was running out of time, and I felt like I was behind in every way. I started college as an adult, so in my mind, I was already seriously behind in my career, and I had to catch up fast.

Being a single mom, I was constantly on the go. There is not much any single parent can do about their busy schedules except to schedule time out for themselves. I never considered scheduling time for myself as an option. I was too attached to being the hero. I loved hearing from my son how much he looked up to me and believed I could do anything—this fulfilled the hidden need that I had: to matter.

If I had given myself permission to stop and look around, I would have seen that I had so much to be grateful for. Instead, I expended all the energy I could muster at all times because I was determined to succeed as the perfect mom, employee, student, neighbor, friend, sister, daughter, and granddaughter. I believed that stopping to smell the roses was how people became complacent, and that was not going to be my fate. There were too many people relying on me—most importantly, my son. I believed I had to show him that it was possible to succeed in the world so he would believe that he could also. The problem was that I didn't believe in myself, and I felt like I was on the edge of failing all the time.

I also thought that if I was grateful for things like my car that broke down on me all the time, it meant I was settling for what I had and I would not try to improve my circumstances. This created a world where nothing was ever good enough. I cringe when I look back on those days.

There was no joy in moving through the world that way. I began to have the same expectations of everyone around me that I had of myself. I was trapped in my defense mechanism and making fear-based decisions at every turn. As you can probably imagine, I wasn't very much fun to be around. Yet, I was doing the very best I knew how at the time, as we all do.

All that effort I expended was nothing more than a waste of energy. If I had allowed myself to slow down and appreciate what was around me, I would have been able to experience more joy on a regular basis, and it's possible that I would have made some very different choices about the direction of my life. I didn't allow myself to even want joy. What I decided was that I was supposed to work hard so I could catch up with everybody else. Little did I know, the people I was trying to catch up with were living their own special versions of hell. I finally got to the place I thought I wanted to be, and it was a barren wasteland.

Gratitude is the creator of joy, and being in joy is how we human beings create. Being grateful decreases stress and increases peace and joyous anticipation, which attracts abundance in all areas of your life.

When my son transitioned, this realization hit me like a ton of bricks. While I was in the grief pit, I felt like all the work I had put into creating a good life for him meant nothing, and I had failed as a mother.

Today, existing on the other side of grief, I know better than that. I no longer beat myself up that way, because I was simply doing the best I could with what I knew. Today, what I know for sure is that the memories that are like precious jewels to me are the ones where my son and I were together, laughing and having fun—the times where we were in full appreciation of each other and in the moment, experiencing joy. We weren't setting goals and working to achieve them. We were not doing anything, really. We were just being. This realization snapped me out of my faulty belief system. Experiencing the greatest loss imaginable changed the way I thought about everything. I now spend the majority of my time in the energy of radical gratitude. I allow myself to be grateful for everything, even if it is a traumatic experience that I've learned from.

My radical gratitude practice has transformed my life in ways I could not have imagined. Radical gratitude means to move through your days looking for things to be grateful for. Expressing gratitude is the fastest way to uplift your vibration, and this is important because you attract what is a match to you.

When you practice radical gratitude every day, you not only manifest more things to be grateful for in your life, but you also speed up your manifestation timeline in ways you never dreamed possible. Being grateful requires a lot less energy than fear-based thinking. Gratitude actually eliminates fear-based thinking because you cannot think both love-based and fear-based thoughts at the same time.

There is a seemingly magical element that exists in the energy of gratitude. When you are grateful for what you have, more things to be grateful for appear. We get what we focus on.

I used to think that having an actual gratitude practice was just another thing I would have to add to my already never-ending to-do list. I didn't realize that it was the most important thing I could do every day. And it isn't time-consuming. There are 86,400 seconds in a day. It only takes sixty seconds to write your daily gratitude list. And it only takes two seconds to say, "Thank you."

GRATITUDE REWIRES YOUR BRAIN

There is another important reason to adopt a gratitude practice. It sparks the most highly evolved areas of your brain.

Practicing gratitude with repetition helps you tap into neuroplasticity, which is the ability of neural networks in the brain to change through growth and reorganization, so neurons are able to make new connections. Practicing gratitude also produces positive emotions that fire up the hippocampus, the brain's center of learning and memory. Strong feelings get stored in the long-term memory, and it is long-term memory that creates the human belief system—on a basic level, this is how we become socialized.

Practicing daily gratitude actually frees you from emotional suffering and will make you happier and physically healthier. When you are happy and healthy, you have the inspiration and self-discipline to achieve your goals.

CREATE YOUR RADICAL GRATITUDE PRACTICE

If you hold the energy of gratitude in your conscious awareness, you will rapidly change your life and begin to create a more satisfying reality. You can look for things to be grateful for throughout the day and also extend gratitude toward others. Simply shift your focus from potential problems and what you don't have to potential wins and what you do have. Before you know it, you will have created a new habit that feels amazing, and the problems you need to solve become transformed into goals you want to achieve.

It pays dividends to grow the joy in your heart. And it also uplifts everyone around you and makes the world a more joyful place to be because you're not only elevating your vibration but also the vibration of everyone and everything you come into contact with.

Have you ever made eye contact and smiled at someone in passing for no other reason than because you could? This is an expression of gratitude for goodness. When you express gratitude in this way, straight from your heart, it will be noticed by the person receiving it and felt in their heart. Sharing gratitude is a win-win because it allows us to lift the collective vibration and anchor the consciousness of Oneness through our connection with each other.

Every single chance you get, remember to say "thank you" for every little thing, even if you're quietly thanking yourself. Gratitude is ultimately your gift because it feels really good to be thankful.

DEVELOP A RADICAL GRATITUDE PRACTICE

To make this a daily practice, you can begin by choosing to write down what you are grateful for at the end of each day. There are literally millions of things to be grateful for. Today, I'm grateful for the ability to write this book, for the roses that have bloomed in my front yard, for my sweet cat snuggling next to me, for waking up in my comfortable bed, and the new sofa I'm getting tomorrow. There was a time that I was writing down things like, "I'm grateful to have gotten through another day," "I'm grateful I have all my limbs," and "I'm grateful for my eyesight because without it I wouldn't be able to witness the sunset." Even if you have no limbs or sight, if you only have the capacity to think about what you are grateful for, you can be grateful for your conscious thoughts. You always have something to be grateful for.

I highly encourage you to start a gratitude journal so you can begin your practice. My gratitude practice began with writing ten things I'm grateful for in my gratitude journal every night before bed. This practice put me in the best mood before I went to sleep and that carried over into the next morning. Over time, I began noticing all sorts of things throughout the day to be grateful for, and I would make a mental note to add it to my list that evening.

Today, my Radical Gratitude practice consists of writing in my gratitude journal at night and quietly giving thanks in the morning for the beauty of every new day and anything else I'm feeling grateful for in that moment before my feet hit the ground. I say thank you for the sunshine, the birds chirping, and my comfy pillow. You get the point. With practice, you naturally begin to live in the energy of gratitude. I write my list just about every day. And I keep my gratitude journals, so when I'm feeling down, I can go back to them and see all things I have to be grateful for—there are many. Every single time I do this, my spirit is lifted within seconds.

USING GRATITUDE TO MANIFEST

Another important element of my Radical Gratitude practice is to show gratitude for all the things that are on the way to me. After you write down your ten things that you are grateful for having or experiencing now, you can flip the page over and write ten things that you're grateful for that are on the way to you. I call this my Manifesting Wish List. Write them down using present-tense language as if they have already happened. For example, if you want a new car, you will write, "I am so grateful for my brand-new car! I love driving it!" And that's it.

My favorite part is revisiting those pages months later so I can see what I've manifested. It's a great reminder of my own inner Goddess power.

BEWARE OF TOXIC GRATITUDE

I will warn you, there is a way to take the practice of gratitude too far. Beware of using gratitude to avoid negative feelings or to judge yourself for having negative feelings. This is a toxic space that blocks self-awareness and self-love, and therefore blocks your manifestations.

I've found this to be a pervasive issue in working with clients who have tried a gratitude practice to feel better and to manifest but to no avail. A woman I coached struggled with toxic gratitude. She judged herself for feeling negative emotions and beat herself up for not instead looking on the bright side of life and feeling grateful for what she had. And she had a lot to be grateful for. She had a wonderful husband, a healthy child, and a successful business, but she struggled with severe negative self-talk and worried constantly that she was failing in her relationships and not meeting her potential. So she decided to begin a gratitude practice. This is where it went sideways; when she felt bad, she would say to herself that she had no right to feel bad because she had so much. She used her gratitude practice to beat herself up for feeling bad. She judged herself for feeling negative emotions and then guilted herself with her gratitude practice, believing that she "should" be grateful. This did nothing but support the stuffing of her own emotions through this emotionally-invalidating attack against herself.

The time to practice gratitude is not when you are in a low vibrational state unless you can truly see beyond your current emotion and enter into a place of sincere gratitude. If you're having trouble doing this, save your gratitude practice for when you are in a neutral state or higher. Do not use your gratitude practice as a weapon against your negative emotions. Your negative emotions are not your enemy. They have important information for you, so allow the space to feel whatever you feel and know that you can go back to feeling grateful later on.

❧ 12 ❧

INNER RESISTANCE

"What you resist persists." –Carl Jung

IF YOU ARE STRUGGLING WITH MANIFESTING, AND NO MATTER what you do, you can't seem to manifest what you want, there may be an unconscious part of you that is not on board with your conscious desire and is therefore creating resistance. In order to manifest like a Goddess, you must deal with your inner resistance.

Inner resistance is caused by two aspects of self that are at odds with one another. These two opposing forces reflect the fragmentation of self, which is the splitting apart of two or more aspects of you that want different things for different reasons. You cannot come into wholeness if you suppress one aspect of you that wants something different than what the other aspect is trying to achieve.

Being in the energy of resistance manifests as procrastination, confusion, inability to make decisions, fence sitting, not living up to your own expectations, acting in ways that are out of integrity, inability to complete projects or tasks, and being unable to manifest specific outcomes no matter how hard you try.

When you're setting your intentions to manifest, if all the parts of you are not on board with what you say you want, then you will subconsciously sabotage your manifestations. Usually, there is a fear present of what it means to actually have what you want, and these fears are not always obvious. This creates a split in self, and if it goes unchecked, it can wage an inner war.

When you resist the part of yourself that wants something different than or opposite to your conscious intention, you must acknowledge that resistance. Suppressing any desire, whether consciously or subconsciously, will block your gifts because your conflicting desires are working at cross-purposes with each other. Everyone experiences resistance. When you can face it and resolve it, you can manifest what you want much easier.

We are all fragmented on some level at certain points in our life, so if you notice this happening within yourself, it's time to honor all the parts of you that want different things by giving each one a voice.

The refusal to acknowledge every one of your needs, even if they are at odds, is an act of resistance. When opposing desires go unacknowledged, it creates stagnation. Just like when you refuse to honor your emotions, when refusing to acknowledge all of your needs, you will either become debilitated by inaction or take the wrong action. It can feel like working hard to achieve your desires yet feeling as if you're making very little progress or achieving no results at all as if you are running on a hamster wheel.

This is because there are two parts of yourself that are trying to go in different directions. The result is: you go nowhere. This is what I call being stuck in a loop. To break the stagnation, you must find the resistance, acknowledge it, and address it so you can get all the parts of you on board with the conscious decision-making process.

When you discover and acknowledge the deeper truth, you may decide you want something different. But you will never know if you don't try.

Here are some case studies of client hurdles that serve as perfect examples of inner resistance. The names have been changed to maintain confidentiality.

Case study #1: Jessica is struggling in her marriage. She loves her husband deep down, but her marriage has lost its spark, and she feels unappreciated. One day, Jessica believes the right thing to do is to end her marriage and find another man who is right for her. The next day, she cannot bear the thought of leaving her husband. They have so many wonderful memories together, and her vows mean everything to her. She thinks maybe they can work it out. She decides to stay but gives only a part of herself to the relationship.

Jessica is on the fence. She hasn't decided with full certainty to stay or go and therefore cannot give 100 percent to the relationship. If she decides to stay and not deal with the aspect of her that wants to end her marriage, she will remain in resistance. She has essentially hopped on the fence, and there will be no movement in either direction. She will eventually exhaust herself, which will create further stagnation in the relationship, and the aspect of her that wants to end her marriage will still be in opposition to the aspect of her that wants to save it. The fragmentation she feels could create enough issues that the marriage will end without her having to be the one to end it.

Usually, there is a subconscious fear hiding in the background. She eventually discovered that her marriage was struggling because she had a fear of intimacy, and it felt safer to end her marriage rather than show up vulnerable and state her innermost needs, which felt like putting herself at risk for heartbreak. It became up to her to figure out what her subconscious fear was, so she could return to wholeness and make a fully conscious decision.

Sitting on the fence only makes your butt hurt and disempowers you because you have decided not to take action in either direction, so decisions will eventually be made for you.

Case study #2: Mandy wants to have a baby. She's a healthy and fertile woman and has been trying for years to get pregnant. Her heart hurts from all the trying and failing. Her doctor says there is no medical reason why she cannot get pregnant. Mandy is refusing to acknowledge her fears around whether she will be a good mother. The aspect of her that is in resistance to starting a family is excited about her plans to grow her career. She also didn't have good role models growing up to show her how to have both a happy family and a successful career.

She is frightened by the idea of having a family and a successful career, and that she might have to choose between losing her autonomy or failing as a parent and ruining her child's life. These opposing aspects of herself could be blocking her from getting pregnant. It's up to her to get honest with herself regarding her conflicting desires: the desire for a successful career and the desire to start a family. Then, she must deal with her fear of losing her autonomy and also failing as a parent.

Suppressing any of your desires pulls you out of joy and therefore out of the energy of receiving. All desires must be acknowledged, especially if they are in opposition to each other because opposition only strengthens the fragmented parts within you. It's like two people digging in their heels and stubbornly refusing to budge on their stance, except they are both you.

Case study #3: Janet hates her job but thinks that if she uses the affirmation "I love my job," she will begin to find ways to love it, or maybe another job will magically appear. She decides to stay where she is until something else better comes along.

Telling yourself lies is a practice in inauthenticity and deepens the divide of the self. Using manifestation tools like affirmations before you have cleared resistance will actually deepen the resistance.

A truthful acknowledgment will bring you back into wholeness. "I don't like my job, so it's up to me to figure out what I love to do so I can manifest work I love into existence." Another is: "It's up to me to figure out why I keep playing out this same painful career experience that creates disruption, chaos, and stagnancy in my life."

These statements pull you out of victimhood and shame and give you your power back.

THE RESISTANCE PAYOFF

If you haven't yet created the life situation that you consciously want for yourself, then there may be an aspect of you that wants to hold on to whatever is keeping you from achieving what you want. Simply put, there is a payoff somewhere.

Logically, we think that we want to be rid of resistance, but what if there is a part of you that is not on board with releasing the resistance? The truth of this can be so painful to see that we would rather deny it than face it. But, if you are in resistance to a painful truth, you are also in resistance to your awareness of it.

You may believe that you desperately want something, and yet there is a part of you that might not want it at all. Becoming curious about the fragmented aspects involved in your inner conflict can help you reveal a greater inner truth, which allows you to determine what it will take to get every aspect of you on board with your conscious desire. Or you may actually end up deciding that you want something completely different for yourself. The goal is to stay curious and open as the objective observer so you can get to the truth of what you really want.

Maybe part of you wants to succeed as an entrepreneur, but there is a suppressed aspect of you that does not want to have success in this area because your parents always played it safe. The suppressed aspect of you may believe that you would lose connection with your family because they would not be able to relate to you if you went on to achieve the things they were never willing to try. The part of you that does not want success is the part of you that is terrified of the disconnection between you and your family.

Understand that resistance is present because all the aspects of self are begging to be recognized, validated, and understood. Ignoring any aspect of you is the same energy as discounting someone else's feelings instead of trying to figure out why those feelings exist.

There is nothing wrong with being in resistance in the short term. We are all in resistance from time to time, and we will continue to experience it in different ways as we grow and discover more about ourselves. It's when the resistance is not recognized and dealt with that we find ourselves stuck and unable to manifest our desires.

ACHIEVING WHOLENESS

A fragmented self is a lost self. You cannot abandon any aspect of yourself if you want to be able to manifest your desires. All the parts of you deserve to be seen, heard, and understood. When you acknowledge all the parts of yourself, you move out of fragmentation and into wholeness.

It's also easy to fall into the trap of denial when it comes to self-abandonment. Trey's friend once said something I will never forget: "Denial means, 'don't even know I am lying.'" I never forgot that. It's amazing what children can teach you if you're open. When you deny certain aspects of yourself, you end up spinning your wheels into the land of excuses for why you can't have what you want, and you will keep trying to no avail, all the while believing that you are making the right decisions for you and those around you. You essentially become a victim to the fragmented parts of yourself that you are ignoring. If you are not making decisions from a place of wholeness, you are not only hurting yourself but also everyone around you. It leaves you feeling trapped in a world full of expectations, including the ones you place upon yourself.

The path to wholeness is through practicing non-attachment, which requires curiosity and objectivity. When you lead with curiosity, you can move into the role of the objective observer.

This is when you can lean in and get to know these various aspects of yourself. As the observer, you set aside fear and judgment and stop the identification with either stance. You are neither extreme because you are both, and you take on the role of the observer who is holding the space for the two extremes so you can reconnect the fragmented parts of you.

In this space, you have become the multi-partial representation of self that holds a safe space for all aspects of you to be seen, heard, and understood. The definition of multi-partial is: trusting and validating each of the realities and truths of all parties, and not favoring one over the other.

Your goal is to find a way that all the parts of you can REALLY have what they want. When you hold space for understanding, all aspects of you can be heard.

When you love and accept each part of you as you would your own children, sibling or your best friend, that part of you is no longer hiding behind the veil of judgment. This aspect of you becomes free to express her desires and finally feels understood. Then, you are ready to make room for both aspects to join together to devise a new plan so all your needs are met.

When you are whole, there are no more decisions to make, only actions to take.

You can practice by bringing both parts of you together for a conversation. This may sound like a strange thing to do, but it is simple, and it works. Taking on the role of the multi-partial observer allows you to hold the space for the conversation to happen.

I created an Inner Conflict guided meditation to support this conversation. The audio version is included in the *Manifest Like a Goddess Experience*, or you can simply set the stage for this conversation yourself using this written meditation.

INNER CONFLICT MEDITATION

Find a quiet, comfortable space where you will not be disturbed. Keep a journal nearby to capture your experience.

Tap into the energy of the inner conflict that you are experiencing. Allow the conflict to surface in your mind's eye. Usually, internal conflicts show up as indecisiveness. What are you having a hard time deciding? Who are these aspects of you in conflict? Choose one aspect to focus on for now.

Lovingly allow this aspect of yourself to show up exactly how it wants to. You are holding a safe space for it to emerge. Ask this part of yourself, "What do you want me to know about how you're feeling right now?"

Allow the answer to come. It may come to you in words you hear, in a vision, or a symbol. Allow the answers to come in whatever way this aspect of you is able to communicate this information.

Feel into this information and recognize the validity in what you've discovered. Tell this part of yourself that it has every right to feel this way. Recognize that this aspect of you is trying to keep the totality of you safe. Thank this aspect for protecting you, and send her loving energy.

Watch how this aspect of you responds to the love you have offered. Tell this aspect that you are safe. Let it be known that you are working with universal energy for the highest good of all aspects, and she can relax in the knowing that all is well and she is protected.

Ask this part of you to help bring in the opposing aspect of you with loving energy so she can also be heard.

Now, with all the love you showed the first aspect, lovingly allow the next aspect of yourself to show up exactly how she wants to.

Continue holding a safe space for this aspect to emerge. Ask this part of yourself, "What do you want me to know about how you're feeling right now?"

Allow the answer to arrive however it does; in the words you hear, in a vision, a symbol, or however the information needs to be communicated.

Feel into the information you receive, and recognize the validity in what you've discovered. Let this part of yourself know that it has every right to feel this way. Recognize that this aspect of you is trying to keep the totality of you safe. Thank this aspect for protecting you and send her loving energy. Watch how this aspect of you responds to the love you have offered. Tell this aspect that you are safe. Let it be known that you are working with universal energy for the highest good of all aspects of yourself, and that she can relax in the knowing that all is well, and she is protected.

Allow the conversation between these two aspects of yourself to unfold for as long as it takes to achieve understanding.

Ask all the opposing aspects of yourself to face each other and see one another through the eyes of love.

Feel the love emanating from you as the observer, to all the parts of you. And feel the love emanating from all the parts of you to the wholeness of your being. Thank them all for their incredible gifts and for working so hard to keep you safe. Let them know they no longer have to hide in judgment. They are free to express their needs and desires and finally be acknowledged and understood. Let them come together and devise a new plan, one that allows for new possibilities.

If an answer doesn't reveal itself right away, let them know the answers to the dilemma are coming from universal consciousness—the answer is on its way to all the parts of you that need closure in this matter. Ask them all to be patient, and rest in the knowing that they don't have to figure it out alone. The answers will come in divine timing. There is nothing else they need to do but wait for the soul's input—they will know it when it arrives.

❧ 13 ❧

RAISE YOUR FREQUENCY

"The whole existence is vibration and so are thoughts. If you generate a powerful thought, it shall become a reality." –Sadhguru

EVERYTHING IN EXISTENCE IS ENERGY THAT IS VIBRATING AT A particular frequency—including you. Your thoughts are responsible for creating your emotions, which vibrate at certain frequencies. The level of your vibration determines what you are able to manifest.

You can think about different frequencies as radio stations. As you tune into a particular station, the radio transmits the frequency of that station and you hear a particular type of music. Just as with all frequencies, music has the ability to make you feel, bringing to the surface all sorts of emotions—including joy, courage, longing, and sadness. It can also grind your nerves and produce anxiety. Music can ignite literally any emotion, depending on who is listening to what.

You can easily change the radio station, and an entirely different emotion can surface as the music changes. You have the ability to choose from a variety of radio stations to tune into, but you can only tune into one at a time. If you are tuned into a station that plays music you don't like, then you have to be willing to change the station, or else it will continue to play over and over the same types of songs that drive you mad. Energetic levels of consciousness operate in a similar way. The energetic frequency you are tuned into determines how you feel. This chapter explores the energetic spectrum of consciousness and will help you identify and change your frequency as needed so you can raise your vibe.

THE SIGNATURE ENERGETIC FREQUENCY

The Signature Energetic Frequency (SEF) represents the general energetic state that a person vibrates at the majority of the time. Your SEF is formed from your unique life experiences, perspectives, and the beliefs you have picked up along your journey.

It is the energy of your beliefs that form your SEF. This energy enters your being and then vibrates out into the universe, creating everything in your reality. If you don't like your current reality, then you must change its energetic frequency by first changing your own. Only making external changes in your physical reality may suffice for a while, but eventually, the same energy will boomerang back into your reality again if you haven't changed your internal station. You will keep attracting more of the same experiences. If you are noticing uncomfortable patterns repeating in your life, then it's time to focus on what is going on within you and make necessary shifts.

THE MAP OF CONSCIOUSNESS®

The late scientist, author, director of The Institute of Spiritual Research, and founder of the Path of Devotional Nonduality, Dr. David Hawkins, created the Map of Consciousness® to show the various levels of consciousness that we can experience as humans.

Dr. Hawkins performed more than 250,000 muscle testing calibrations over 30 years with multiple research studies that were conducted by The Institute for Spiritual Research, Inc. He defined a range of values that correspond to levels of consciousness which include certain attitudes and emotions. With a logarithmic scale of 1 to 1,000 and the Map of Consciousness® he developed, Dr. Hawkins defined the classification and characteristics of these energy fields. The calibration figures do not represent arithmetic but a logarithmic progression. For instance, level 300 is not twice the amplitude of 150; it is 300 to the tenth power. An increase of even a few points represents a major advance up the scale.

Dr. Hawkins' research has transformed the way many perceive consciousness. His Map of Consciousness® is a guide to determine how high or low one is on the scale at any given time. In his book, *The Map of Consciousness Explained*, he describes that people rarely rise more than five points up the scale in a lifetime. If you have not studied Hawkins' work, I highly recommend you do.

I was able to significantly raise my SEF after sitting in a pit of grief (level 75) for more than a decade. I'm not saying it was easy, but it was doable because I so strongly desired a better life experience. As human beings, we experience the full range of human emotion; we do not necessarily vibrate at one particular level for an entire lifetime. It is possible to get stuck in one part of the spectrum for quite a long time, though. However, if I can change my SEF, you can change yours too.

THE BLOOM OF CONSCIOUSNESS

The Bloom of Consciousness is my interpretation of Hawkins' Map of Consciousness®.

The full color illustration of the Bloom of Consciousness is located inside the cover of the front of this book. Please refer to it as you read this chapter.

After spending some years studying Hawkins' map, I made two important changes to the language. I made these changes because I realized there was a fundamental issue with the way some words in the English language are understood and misunderstood. Throughout this book, definitions of certain words in the English language are explored; ones that seem extremely contradictory and therefore cause confusion. The critical changes I made to create the Bloom of Consciousness are in the language to serve as clarification of certain labels that I define a bit differently. For instance, Hawkins' placed "Desire" at level 125 because he equates desire with suffering and explains it as denying, disappointing, craving, and enslavement.

In this book, we explore the meaning of pure, authentic, love-based desire, which is not in alignment with the energy of suffering. When you desire something and it feels good to want it, that energy vibrates at a much higher level. The energy of a love-based desire is a higher-vibrating frequency than that of Hawkins' definition of desire, which equates to suffering.

The absence of desire is dangerous. Without desire, there is no joyous anticipation, and that is when stagnation occurs. It is the energy of loved-based desires that moves us higher up the Bloom of Consciousness toward the vibration of "Joy."

In the Bloom of Consciousness, "Yearning" replaces "Desire" at level 125. Yearning is defined as a feeling of intense longing for something, and therefore vibrates much lower, closer to the range of suffering. "Desire" is situated higher up the spectrum at 325, between "Willingness" and "Acceptance."

When you develop the willingness to acknowledge your loved-based desires, you become able to accept them into your reality while simultaneously accepting your circumstances as they are and also accepting yourself as you are, which is divine creation. The embodiment of the energy of "Acceptance" does not mean you stop desiring or moving in the direction of your desires.

You begin the manifestation process by being willing to imagine and feel the energy of your love-based desires and practice acceptance for what is as you continue rising higher toward the vibration of "Love." Then you can rest in the knowledge that the universe will deliver your manifestations to you in such a way that supports the highest good of all, so there is no reason to choose suffering.

You can use the Bloom of Consciousness to determine where you sit on the spectrum and identify your SEF. Your SEF is important to understand because it determines what you are a vibrational match to. The more often you experience "Joy," the higher your vibration rises, and the more it can stabilize it over time.

The energy you embody runs the show—always (consciously or unconsciously) co-creating with the universe and then dictating your response to external stimuli. It determines how high or low on the vibrational scale you are able to move in a given moment. For instance, if you are generally vibrating at a lower frequency, such as at "Fear," it will take a lot of energy to get you vibrating at the level of "Acceptance." If you generally vibrate at the level of "Neutrality" or "Willingness," you can more easily reach the level of "Love."

Sometimes, the SEF expresses itself through more complicated patterns. For instance, I used to know someone who regularly vibrated at such a low energetic frequency that he could not handle high vibrating frequencies for long periods of time. His SEF often repelled the high vibrating energy of external stimuli. This person once had to leave a concert before it was over because he felt the music was so amazing that he just could not stand it any longer. His low SEF also caused serious problems in other areas of his life. When people reached out to offer him love, he would run away because he could not accept the energy of unconditional love. Experiencing feelings of love and security felt especially dangerous to him because it was so far outside of "the known." Higher vibrating energy contributed to an internal system overload because it took so much of his energy to move higher up the vibrational spectrum. As a result, his SEF was repelling all the goodness in his life.

"Never give anyone more than they are emotionally capable of receiving, or they will have no choice but to hate you for it." –Elizabeth Gilbert

I call this hitting your Joy Ceiling. When you hit the peak of the high vibrating energy that your SEF can tolerate, you tend to quickly head back down the spectrum. The goal is to break through your Joy Ceiling so you can more readily access the frequency of "Joy" and with more regularity. It may feel uncomfortable to practice raising your SEF at first, but the only way up is through.

It is the norm in Western culture to unconsciously choose to be a victim of the roller coaster of life instead of consciously choosing to become the observer of it. The good news is that you can change this pattern, and therefore raise your SEF at any time. When you become the conscious observer of your reality, you are able to tune into a higher frequency and enjoy a brand-new, high-vibrating life experience.

Like a fish in water, it is difficult to recognize that you are vibrating at lower levels when it is a lower vibration that you are used to existing in. Allowing yourself thirty days to work on raising your vibration is enough time to begin to notice a shift in your usual notch on the vibrational spectrum. There are ways to raise your SEF so that you can begin operating at a higher vibrational level and continue doing so even when you are not paying close attention, so you can enjoy all the high vibrating experiences that will begin to boomerang into your life.

The information in this chapter will help you determine where you are on the spectrum of the Bloom of Consciousness and raise your frequency with more ease, no matter what circumstance you find yourself in.

If you're unsure of where you normally exist on the vibrational scale, you can figure it out. Simply carry a little notebook around for about a week—or use your phone's recorder to keep a journal of when your emotions change throughout the day. Record your emotional shifts for one week and keep track of how long you stayed in any particular emotion. Unless you are dealing with some pretty unusual circumstances, you should be able to look at your notes after seven days and have a pretty good idea of your SEF.

You magnetize to yourself every experience in your life. Your energy is always vibrating out into the universe, attracting like energy and thus creating your reality. Raising your frequency is the path to changing your reality and manifesting your heart's desires.

To manifest like a Goddess, you must plant your seeds of intention while in a high frequency, and you do this by first clearing your energetic field—that means cleaning up all inner gunk that is clogging up your manifestation pathway and preventing you from reaching the vibration of "Joy." Setting intentions without first getting yourself into alignment to match what you are asking for will not help you create your desired outcome. You must be a vibrational match to what you're asking for.

The clearest indicator of your energetic frequency is your emotional state. As we have covered in earlier chapters, e-motion is energy in motion —it doesn't matter which emotion you embody, you are always manifesting your reality based on what you are feeling—as your external reality is created from your emotional body.

You can raise your SEF by changing your daily routines and habits and choosing new experiences that increase your happiness.

THE MAGIC OF SOUND

"The first manifestation of the infinite Spirit was through the cosmic sound vibration, and the closest utterable human approximation to this sound is Om. The Om sound is a symbol of Anahata, the uncreated word vibration not produced on account of any friction while all other sounds are produced on account of friction. It is a self-created, total field of energy akin to what modern scientists contemplate as the quantum event, infinitely interconnected, self-organizing, and profoundly intelligent to be the central idea, the blueprint, and the element of the universe." –Hindustan Times

The vibration of sound exists between the world of form (the seen) and the formless (the unseen). Harmonic sounds, such as what we hear in nature or when an instrument is played, form intricately beautiful patterns. Have you ever seen how sand moves with the vibration of beautiful music? It actually moves into shapes, forming geometric patterns that we see in nature. Unpleasant sounds, like banging or screaming, form patterns that are jagged and rough.

Sound is just above solids in terms of frequency and therefore serves as the bridge between the abstract and the concrete. This means that sound is the tool of creation in the material world, and we have direct access to this tool to create anything we want. You can give yourself the opportunity to play around with different sounds by playing music (even if you are just creating a beat) or listening to beautiful music or the sounds of nature.

WATCH YOUR WORDS

"In the beginning was the Word, and the Word was with God, and the Word was God..." –John 1:1

Words are one of the most powerful tools available to us. In manifesting, we use both the written word and the spoken word to create. We tend to pay much more attention to the words we write than the words we speak. The spoken word carries even more power, however, because it is sound, and it was sound that sculpted the structure of the universe. There is great power in the spoken word, and we can create anything we want by using it.

When you speak words into existence, you are creating your reality and your future experiences. Speaking your truth aloud and allowing others to bear witness to that truth is intentional spell casting, a form of conscious manifesting. Uttering things you don't mean is a form of unconscious manifesting. Either way, you're manifesting.

Because you speak things into existence with words, consider all words spoken as spells. The reason this is true is because they have their own vibrational frequency which has the power to create your reality. Using your words wisely empowers you to create change in your external experience. While thoughts carry their own energetic vibration, they do not contain the same power as words. You can always choose to change a thought. Once words are spoken, they are out in the ether.

The words you speak can either raise or lower your vibration and have a powerful ability to guide your subconscious. Both positive and negative words spoken aloud have a major impact on what you create, and they also have the power to shift emotions. Just think about what happens when you speak to a person and your words negatively impact them. You can't take them back if you try. If your words carry a high vibrating energy, and therefore have a positive impact, then you have the power to change someone's life for the better with just one sentence, and the listener will never forget it.

Words have an incredibly powerful impact on those who hear them, and they vibrate out into the universe into infinity.

Also, beware of the words of others. People in your energetic field who are looking for validation by spreading their negativity around is not only toxic for them, but also for the person listening. Since words are energy, negative words serve as an attack on the listener and everything else in existence. When you allow others to complain incessantly in your presence, you are essentially supporting that person in lowering their own SEF as well as your own. I had the fortunate pleasure of meeting three Jain nuns from India during a Unitive Justice workshop taught by Sylvia in Richmond, Virginia. The nuns shared with the group how negative thoughts, even about the self, is energy that goes out into the universe and melds with the collective energy of All That Is, which causes emotional violence in our world.

I do not want you to give yourself a hard time every time you think a negative thought. Our current collective nature does not support the total absence of negative thought. However, we can become open to this awareness and choose something different when we recognize that our thoughts have become negative.

You can watch your words with even more care. You will manifest better outcomes for yourself when you focus on what you want instead of what you don't want. For example, saying, "I don't want to lose [fill in the blank]," represents an imagined fear-based outcome that you don't want. And what you resist persists.

Practice choosing loved-based, direct speech over passive, fear-based speech. Shifting your focus to what you do want will also shift your language and speed up your manifesting timeline. You will actually feel the difference in your body when you change your language. It is not necessary to become perfect in your language and thoughts—it's instead something to strive for. You will never have full control over your thoughts. But with practice, you can increase your loved-based thoughts, emotions, and words, and you will experience an organic shift in the direction toward your desires.

MEDITATION

"Ego says, 'Once everything falls into place, I will find peace.' Spirit says, 'Find peace and everything will fall into place.'" –Unknown

Did you know that having a regular meditation practice can permanently strengthen the most evolved area of your brain? It enhances cognition, creativity, and positivity. It encourages the release of dopamine, oxytocin, and endorphins, which evoke sensations of happiness and calm. It is the fastest and most efficient way to raise your SEF.

Meditation allows you to go within and access the depths of your divinity, which is as expansive as the universe. As you go within, the smallness of the world disappears and the unlimited expansiveness of all that exists enters your awareness.

Sitting still for even a few minutes each day can help you connect to the divine nature that transcends thought. It doesn't matter what kind of meditation practice you choose—do whatever feels good. You can meditate in silence or with music, with eyes open or closed, and use guided meditations or practice walking meditation. The point is to be in the present moment for as long as possible.

If you're saying to yourself, "I'm not good at meditation," I want you to know that you actually are. We've been so conditioned to pay attention to what is happening in the external world and check off our to-do lists that stopping feels impossible. This nonstop doing has created the chattering mind of the ego, which wants to run the show. If you've tried meditating but your mind would not shut off, and then you became frustrated and quit, here is your chance to try again—this time with a different perspective.

Consider your chattering mind. It begins to go wild when you become still. What do you do when that happens? Do you argue with it? What happens when you tell it to stop? My guess is that it keeps on chattering until you find something to do that diverts your attention—maybe watching TV or running errands, and it still may continue chattering in the background.

Diverting your attention away from yourself is the ego's goal. The ego is essential to our being because we cannot get out of doing. While doing is an essential aspect of the human experience that represents masculine energy, it is not the same as the ego's intention to divert your attention away from yourself. The ego is expressed as an over-functioning of the brain, and the brain is a tool we use to analyze the past, or what we already know to be true. Having an over-functioning brain is like giving a super-computer full control over your life. The computer only knows what you've programmed, and then it experiences that past programming in the present.

Tapping into the heart space, which is the place of knowing, lessens the ego's grip and helps you enter into the present moment.

The state of nothing from which all things came represents the universal feminine essence. It is the expansive, magical, mystical darkness where nothing and everything exists. In this space, you are both nothing and everything. The feminine essence does not fight the ego; she surrenders to it. She is open to receiving, so she listens. Have you ever just listened to your mind chatter to see what it is really saying? What if you were not attached to the messages at all? What happens to that chattering voice when you turn to that voice with love? I'll tell you—it stops. It stops because the ego is an empty shell with little substance. It is a tool that we use to get by in the material world. When we begin to see it as more than that, it can trick us into believing it represents who we are, when it does not and never will.

Your substance is beneath the messages of the ego. It is found within the silence of the present moment. When the ego begins its chattering, just listen. When it stops, stay present. When you're sitting in meditation and you become conscious of a thought, just notice it and allow it to float by without having to do anything about it. You will never turn off the mind completely. Let it do whatever it wants to do and turn your focus toward your inner substance, which is more grand and powerful than you can imagine. Its power is accessible through presence.

Another way to have an amazing meditation experience that I've discovered is through the practice of floating. Many cities have float tank options where you can float for an hour or so in 1,000 pounds of Epsom salt water, which is heated to the same temperature as your body. It is meant to be a total sensory deprivation experience. I recommend floating without sound or light and without touching the edges of the tank. It will not take long for you to recognize your connection to All That Is.

My first float tank experience was some years ago in Venice Beach, California, where I floated for about two hours inside of what looked like an old restaurant walk-in freezer. I put in my earplugs, hopped in, and shut the door. Time disappeared and so did I. I could not feel the edges of the tank with my fingers or toes. The water was the same temperature as my body, and I could see nothing and I could hear nothing except the sound of my breath, which was surprisingly loud with earplugs in. It was the first time I had ever given that much attention and respect to my breath. I listened in awe and felt its power. I don't think it was long before it hit me that I was a part of the universal consciousness. It wasn't a logical thought. It was a knowing. Other times in the float tank, I experienced spiritual breakthroughs and received messages that also came through as a knowing.

GRATITUDE

We covered gratitude in Chapter 11 and the importance of keeping a gratitude journal. Periodically revisiting your gratitude journal entries can be a powerful practice. What are the recurring things or experiences you feel grateful for? Find those recurring entries and reflect on them. Speaking them aloud will add power to them and fuel your frequency, raising you to an even higher vibration.

Adding a couple of minutes in the morning before you get out of bed to reflect on your list can help you raise your vibration and positively impact your entire day. Remember, anything that shifts your emotional state from positive to negative raises your vibration and helps you create the outcomes you desire.

When I wake up in the morning, I ask myself how I want to feel that day. I wait patiently for the answer to come. I do not get out of bed until I feel the emotions I chose flowing through my body.

SUSTENANCE

Consuming foods that are alive is the fastest way to clean up your energy and raise your vibration. I always encourage clients who want to manifest quickly to rid their diet of all animal products and replace them with fruits and vegetables—foods that are alive with the energy of the sun. The sun is the Earth's life force; we cannot survive without the energy of the sun. These foods naturally vibrate at high frequencies. Eating food that is alive provides energy that is very different than eating food that contains the energy of trauma, which can be lodged in the bodies of slaughtered animals. Pay attention to how certain foods make your body feel. When you eat foods that are low in vibration, you are more at risk for disease, anxiety, and depression.

If your doctor agrees, you might consider just experimenting with a vegan diet for thirty days and see how you feel. If a change in diet is not for you, I highly recommend shifting your diet to vegan on the days surrounding the dates of your manifesting rituals. The three-day dark moon phase is a good time to do this.

Visit the Tools for Manifesting Like a Goddess in the back of this book to learn how to use the moon phases to manifest.

When I decide to set intentions, I begin the day before the new moon by consuming food that is grown from the sun's energy. I keep this diet for three full days—the day before I set intentions, the day of, and the day after. I've noticed that I feel lighter and clearer when my diet is clean. Your energy needs to be as clean as possible when you're sowing your seeds of intention. You will notice your intuition heighten and you will more easily be able to open up to the energy of creation.

GROUNDING

Being out in nature is another rapid way to clean your energetic field and raise your vibration. Standing barefoot on the Earth has purifying effects for the body.

Humans used to walk barefoot and sleep on the earth. Our collective lifestyle does not allow us to make direct contact with nature as much as we used to, so it's important to intentionally make time to connect with Mother Nature every chance you get. Walking or standing barefoot on the earth is incredibly cleansing.

There is a vast supply of electrons on the earth's surface and research has shown that connecting your bare skin (especially your feet) to the earth has amazing health benefits, including better sleep and reduced pain.

The earth's surface, whether grass, dirt, mud, or sand, has a limitless supply of free electrons that support the body's biological rhythm and can actually reset your biological clock and cortisol secretion. It also neutralizes free radicals in the body, which can reduce inflammation.

The beach is my favorite place in nature. It brings me so much joy to be near the magnificent, mysterious ocean. While being in nature is always grounding, visiting your favorite place in nature has the power to uplift your vibration in ways that nothing else can.

FINDING FLOW THROUGH PLAY AND MOVEMENT

We are human beings, not human doings.

We are here to explore our surroundings and imagine what we want to create. We can do this through play. We tend to devalue play just as we devalue the imagination. Your imagination is divine creation at work. You co-create with the universe through your imagination. This requires you to be in the present moment, where energy can just flow.

Play requires imagination and often some sort of large muscle movement. It is through movement that energy becomes unblocked. If you're feeling stagnant, take a few minutes to stretch or take a walk, or do anything that requires moving your body. If you are noticing that your body feels tight or sore, this could be a perfect time to move it. Of course, listen to your doctor and follow their advice. I have noticed that when my body feels tired, the more I move, the better I feel, especially during my Ashtanga yoga practice. Once upon a time, my yoga teacher used to say to me, "If you're sore, come to class; if you're sick, come to class; if you have cramps, come to class; if you're hungover, come to class." There was literally no reason to not come to class unless you had a fever. Every time I went to yoga class when I felt bad, I left feeling much better.

Another way to shake out stagnant energy and raise your vibration is to dance. What better way to move with the divine flow of energy than to dance with it? You don't need a dance partner. You can dance by yourself! I suggest getting creative; for instance, I love jumping on my bed. A few years ago, I decided to play my favorite music and dance on my bed, and it was such a freeing experience. After teaching certain workshops, I send people home with a list of things to try, and dancing naked on your bed is one of them. I can't think of anything else that can pull you out of lower vibrational energy faster than dancing naked on your bed to your favorite song. It may seem silly, but it's empowering and freeing. Be willing to try new ways of aligning yourself with the divine flow—do whatever it takes.

It is when you're in the divine flow that your manifestations begin to unfold, and at precisely the right moment. Serendipitous moments occur spontaneously, and interrelations between seemingly unrelated things (not coincidental, but synchronous events) begin to occur. This represents the dance with the divine flow of universal energy, where you can feel the universe supporting you, because you have recognized your connection to All That Is.

A sense of profound peace is realized in the flow, even in the midst of unknowing. When you exist in this space, you can experience what is referred to as peace beyond understanding.

❧ 14 ❧

INTUITION

"The intuitive mind is a sacred gift and the rational mind is a faithful servant. We have created a society that honors the servant and has forgotten the gift." –Albert Einstein

I BELIEVE THE REASON WHY INTUITION REMAINS A MYSTERY TO so many is because people are largely accustomed to relying on the analytical mind to solve problems and make decisions that are solely based in logic. If you have a habit of relying on the analytical mind to understand everything in your reality, you may experience difficulty receiving and accepting the messages brought to you by your intuition. Just as you cannot think your way out of feelings, you also cannot analyze your way into understanding intuitive messages. Accessing intuitive messages requires you to listen to the wisdom of your soul.

Francis P. Cholle, founder of the Human Company and lecturer on the subject of intuitive intelligence, defines intuition as sensation (a gut feeling or a hunch) that appears quickly in consciousness without us being fully aware of the underlying reasons for its occurrence. It is a process that gives us the ability to know something directly without analytical reasoning, bridging the gap between the conscious and unconscious parts of our mind.

Deepak Chopra also defines intuition as a form of intelligence that is beyond the rational mind. He describes it as contextual, relational, and holistic, with no win/lose orientation. In spiritual traditions, it is believed that intuition eavesdrops on the mind of the universe.

To develop your intuition is to learn to still your mind, ask your question, and feel the answer in your body. The ability to receive these messages lies in being able to decipher the sensations moving through your body. Feelings of fear, anxiety, or any other lower vibrational emotion will block intuitive messages and instead offer you a different type of information that you'll want to pay attention to.

I think of these different types of messages as the two distinct aspects of your inner voice.

We all have an inner voice. One aspect of the inner voice is attached to emotion. It brings messages forth to shine light on lodged emotions that reside within the hidden recesses of the emotional body, which are essentially stuck energy. I refer to this part of the inner voice as the shadow. This is not a negative connotation. The shadow has an important role—its messages bring to light any stuck emotional energy that is ready to be released.

We also have a non-dualistic inner voice that represents the seat of universal wisdom, which offers truth. This aspect of the inner voice is what is known as intuition. Intuitive messages come straight from the soul, which represent our inner knowing and are not attached to any emotional component.

The soul aspect of the inner voice is not as attached to outcomes as the shadow aspect is because the soul knows that it is experiencing life as a human being for the purpose of learning. This learning will happen either with ease or with suffering, but it happens nonetheless. However, the soul does not expect the human aspect of self to suffer unnecessarily, so it offers wisdom through intuitive messages that can be used as a guide toward the path of least resistance in the name of harmony. That is what the universe is always doing—creating harmony—and since the soul is a divine aspect of universal consciousness, it has a role in this as well.

My dear friend and teacher, Albert Moore, author of *Eyes In The Mirror: Everything Changed When He Met His Soul*, says that on Earth, we are in the "Forgetting Place." We have forgotten our innate knowledge and power. But we have something called Free Will, so if we have the desire to remember and tap into universal consciousness, we can. If you have been consistently ignoring your soul's messages for a long while, it may feel impossible to access them. But I assure you that the messages are there, and you can learn how to open yourself to them.

It's important to understand that both aspects of the inner voice are equally valuable because they both have information you need. Think of the shadow's messages (emotional information) as coming from the more human part of you, and the soul's messages (intuitive information) as connected to the all-knowing universal consciousness which is also part of you.

SHADOW MESSAGES

Shadow messages are based in the emotional body and released through the physical body. In earlier chapters, we addressed how your emotions serve as your internal radar system, alerting you to go within so you can see what information they are trying to give you. Because your feelings are not facts, shadow messages can sometimes feel almost cryptic. Analyzing your emotions does not help, it only creates more confusion.

If you feel you are getting an intuitive hunch but it is attached to an emotion such as sadness, grief, jealousy, anxiety, or anything that feels bad, consider this information as coming from the shadow aspect of your inner voice and trying to alert you that something within needs attention. Interestingly, the same goes for positive feelings. If you feel you are getting an intuitive nudge based on feelings of excitement or elation, that is *also* the shadow aspect of your inner voice, possibly attempting to latch onto something outside of you in hopes that the external thing will bring peace, which is a false promise. The peace you're seeking is within and cannot be found "out there." I am not saying do not trust your emotions. What I am saying is that messages tied to emotions come from the shadow aspect of the inner voice, not the intuitive aspect.

Shadow messages can bring up all sorts of emotions, which is not an indicator to take action in the external world. It's instead your cue to practice inner reflection. The shadow ignites strong emotions so that you will pay attention and begin to understand what is happening within your emotional body so you can move into harmony.

When you feel a negative emotion, you can thank your shadow

messenger for alerting you that there is a wound within you that is ready to be healed. If you ignore the message, it will continue to resurface as conflict, often becoming stronger until you pay attention. Shadows cannot exist in the light, so honor this aspect of yourself by leaning into the shadow messages you receive and bring them into the light.

INTUITIVE MESSAGES

Have you ever just known something without having proof? What did that feel like? If it was an intuitive message, the information came to you maybe in a whisper or a flash of insight with no emotional component. It just came as a knowing.

Intuition, which I refer to as messages from the soul, represents pure knowing that is not attached to any emotion. Intuitive messages come from your soul, the part of you that is directly connected to universal consciousness. They can help guide you in your decision-making if you're able to listen to them.

Intuitive messages have no emotional charge—even if you consider yourself to be an empath who can feel what others are feeling. Being an empath is not the same as being intuitive. Picking up on other people's emotions is different than tapping into intuitive knowledge.

The intuition's delivery will feel as unassuming as knowing your car is parked outside of your house. There will be no emotion tied to it. This is when you know your soul is talking to you. Even if the message you receive is unnerving, the delivery of the message itself will not be. It will just be.

If you have not been listening to your intuition for some time, these messages may be less apparent to you, so you will want to pay special attention to your hunches and give them the space to come through. They may arrive as a whisper or a vision, as an inspiration, through a song that pops into your head, and also in dreams. Accessing the message requires stillness and the ability to know when to be still, or you will lose the message. Don't discount any messages you receive. When you feel you've received an intuitive message, write it down as soon as possible. Your soul will begin speaking to you loud and clear when you set the intention to pay attention.

IGNORING YOUR INNER VOICE

Your intuition will often offer you information that you need to make big decisions, but you must be open to receive the message. When you ignore your soul's messages, you are blocking access to the divine insight designed to help you choose the highest path.

Sometimes intuitive nudges seemingly come out of nowhere. Maybe while you're driving your car or while you're in the shower. It's easy to ignore your intuition at these times, because usually you are getting ready to focus your attention elsewhere. In these times, intuitive messages can be so fleeting that you may not feel the need to pay attention. When you ignore your intuitive messages, what comes next is regret. How many times have you gone against your intuition only to say later, "I knew it!" "If I had only listened to my (heart/gut/intuition)!" I know how frustrating that is.

I have ignored my soul's messages more times than I can count and instead just went along with the ideas or desires of others, often to keep the peace, even when I knew I needed to go in a different direction. Every time, I was sorry. I haven't ignored my intuition in some time. Even when it tells me things I do not want to hear, I listen anyway. I consider my intuition my guardian angel. It's never steered me wrong. I promise, the more work you do to grow your self-awareness and self-love, your ability to hear and trust your intuition will strengthen.

When you ignore your shadow messages, you are essentially running from yourself. Your body will eventually communicate this fact to you through illness or injury to get your attention. And the universe, which is always co-creating with you, will show you through signs—often repeating negative patterns which will become more and more painful until you listen.

The system programming we've all experienced is responsible for silencing the inner voice. If you're struggling to hear either aspect, it means that at some point in childhood, your inner voice was most likely disregarded by others when you shared these messages. You learned to listen to others' perspectives instead—and the inner voice was eventually replaced by other people's voices.

STRENGTHENING YOUR INTUITION

You can practice strengthening your intuition with the use of divination tools such as runes or tarot cards. There are literally hundreds of divination tools that you can use (I also use a pendulum when I am looking for a yes or no answer). Be sure that you do not overuse them by asking the same question over and over again until you get the answer you want. If you try to manipulate the answer, you will not uncover the truth.

When I began to focus on strengthening my intuition, I began using the tarot to help me still my mind and be present with the information that the cards provided. This helped me learn to trust myself. Today, I have several tarot and oracle card decks that I use almost daily. I allow myself to choose whichever deck I feel an energetic pull toward, and I pull one or two cards and feel into the images and descriptions. Tarot cards date back to the 18th century, and there are seventy-eight cards made up of major and minor arcanas. It takes some time to study this deck in order to learn how to reveal their messages. Oracle decks, on the other hand, usually have message descriptions right on the cards, so there is less of a need to interpret what they mean. There are no rules regarding how many cards should be in a deck or what symbology they include. You can begin pulling oracle cards to read for yourself by either reading the message or simply gazing at them to see what images stand out. I have found it to be a powerful practice for strengthening intuition.

I allow my mind to rest and focus on what I am feeling when I hold the card in my hand. Then, I look at the image to see what stands out. There are times when I see something brand-new in a particular card that I've never seen before, which alerts me to pay closer attention to what I'm noticing without overthinking. I allow whatever messages to come to me that need to come. I have learned to trust them. If I recognize that I am feeling frustrated as I'm reading cards, I stop. I will also stop if I recognize that the message I received came with an emotional reaction. I know at that time the soul's messages are not coming through. This means it's time for me to switch gears and let go of what information I'm asking for and bring my focus to the emotion that came up within me. It's my cue that the shadow aspect of my inner voice has a different message for me that I must pay attention to before I can receive the soul's messages.

I also pull runes on most days to give me some insight regarding the path my soul wants me to take for the highest good of all. Pulling runes is a practice I began a couple of years ago, back when my dear friend Delanea Davis was writing her book, *Rune Reading Your Life*. I devoured her book and immediately created my own runes with some small flat rocks that I found by the river. In her book, Delanea explains that runes are a means of divine communication. The runes I pull provide me with a roadmap and help me decide what to focus on. Again, I allow my intuition to guide me based on the runes I pull, paying attention to the meaning behind each rune and what information comes up when I pull it.

By far, the most powerful way to strengthen your intuition is through meditation. If you want to develop your intuitive muscle, then commit to a meditation practice. Strengthening your intuition will help you begin to trust yourself more, and self-trust grows self-love and the awareness of who you are—a divine aspect of All That Is. The key to unlocking your intuition rests in your ability to become aware of the fleeting messages that come without emotion and can even seem somewhat unassuming, and then acknowledge them.

❦ 15 ❦

ONENESS

"In the stillness of your presence, you can feel your own formless and timeless reality as the unmanifested life that animates your physical form. You can then feel the same life deep within every other human and every other creature. You look beyond the veil of form and separation. This is the realization of Oneness. This is love." –Eckhart Tolle

Oneness: the fact or state of being unified or whole, though composed of two or more parts.
Separation: a point, line or means of division; an intervening space or gap.

WE LIVE IN A WORLD WHERE OPPRESSION, HUNGER, POVERTY, violence, illness, war, and destruction reign. This is due to the collective belief that we are separate—and this creates a lack mentality based in fear, and the belief that our success and safety can only be secured by competition, punishment, or greed. We are destroying precious resources, creating massive suffering for living beings, and harming Mother Earth.

While separation on some level represents the experience of our current existence, it does not represent the whole truth of what is happening here. There exists an overarching absolute truth, and that is

Oneness. This truth is so simple, yet its simplicity boggles the analytical mind.

All sacred texts speak of Oneness, yet it remains elusive. We see that our physical bodies are not attached to other physical bodies. We see that we are not the chair we sit in or the car we drive. The concept of Oneness seems to go against everything we experience in physical form. And for a long time, science backed up the notion of separateness.

Newtonian physics explains one aspect of our reality, that we are made up of atoms that are composed of separate particles: protons, electrons, and neutrons that exist as subatomic particles that are floating around in empty space.

While Newtonian physics represents part of the truth, it does not tell the whole story of who or what we are. This limited view supports the idea that we are simply matter which has no connection to other physical objects or beings that are made up of separate particles.

It wasn't until quantum physics was discovered that we began to see things differently. We now know that while the Newtonian laws of matter apply at the gross physical level, a more fundamental reality exists beyond matter—an all-encompassing field of energy where separation does not exist. It is actually the space between the particles that make up who we are. When you look at these subatomic particles under a microscope, you can see even more of what is referred to as empty space. We now know the space is not empty—it is energy. This "gap" between matter is what actually connects us. In this gap exists the mystery of creation. It is the energy of the mysterious feminine essence that created everything from nothing.

Quantum physics teaches us that we are all constituted from the same energy. Every living thing is created from the same material. We are connected to everything; in essence, we are pure consciousness expressing itself in different forms. We are life, trying to know itself. Quantum physics affirms our interconnectedness.

I remember a time when I was sitting in a coffee shop with a woman I had just met. We talked about Oneness and how everything is made up of energy. Then she said something that I will never forget: "Matter is 99.9999999 percent empty space. If you took out all of the space inside of our atoms, the entire human race would fit into the volume of a sugar cube."

We are made up of the same energy and we are always impacting one another through the ripples of energy that emanate from our being. This is because we are individual aspects of one whole. Another dear friend of mine once suggested I think about the entire human race as a big pie that is cut up into 7.5 billion slices. Each slice has its place within the pie. Because we are at different places within the pie, we see things from a different angle and therefore have different perspectives. This is true even for the slices that are situated right next to each other.

Not one person is having the same experience, and that is because life is trying to know itself. And for life to know itself, we incarnate as individuals with our own unique perspectives, talents, gifts, and abilities; yet we remain connected to the whole of consciousness. We are inextricably connected to the whole and yet here, as human beings, we are having this individual human experience for the good of the whole.

The truth of this did not arrive into my conscious awareness as a sudden flash of insight. It is a knowingness that occurred over time. I once moved through the world experiencing my own perceptions that created my subjective reality, which affirmed my separateness from everything. I believed it was me against the world. And in order for me to survive, I always had to have a strategy of attack. This attacking I was doing was also an attack on myself, as everything I tried to control served as a boomerang of energy that was giving back to me everything I put out into the universe. The universe is forever working to create harmony through the balancing of energies, and this is our karma. Through the lens of separateness, karma is understood as revenge. But through the lens of connectedness or Oneness, karma means learning—this is what we are doing here.

Along my spiritual journey, the concept of Oneness became clear to me as I sought to understand my own pain and the pain of those around me. This understanding came to me over time through meditation, practicing vulnerability, and finding the courage to love. I was able to understand what I inherently knew deep down through the teachings of unity consciousness with Sylvia and many other teachers that opened me up to a new perspective. Even though I knew this information in my heart and had gained the tools to embody the concept of Oneness, I could not yet put it into practice. I had some healing to do first.

When my son transitioned, I felt completely separate from everything and everyone. I was angry. I cursed the universe. I cursed God. I cursed the people who were with him that fateful night. I cursed myself.

My logical understanding of the concept of Oneness fueled my desire to believe that the universe was always working for me, my son, and everyone because we are an integral part of All That Is. But another part of me felt like my son was cheated out of life. And there were so many others who had been cheated out of life. How could the universe (or God, Creator, or Source consciousness) love him or me, or anyone, if this was allowed to happen? Hate began to grow in my heart like a cancer. Even though I wasn't openly displaying these emotions, my energetic vibration was being reflected back to me in my external reality in the most peculiar ways.

When I looked back on that time, I realized that I was stuffing all the anger and confusion I was feeling. The more I stuffed those feelings that were tied to the grief of losing my son, the more anger and confusion began to show up in my reality. I had never really had enemies before, yet I was feeling attacked at every turn as one conflict after another began to manifest in my life. The confusion I felt continued to build, and I found myself buried in so many conflicts that I became paralyzed.

Every one of those experiences served as my mirror, trying to show me what I was carrying around inside of my emotional body. But I was so focused on trying to figure out who was to blame that I couldn't see that I was creating this reality for myself merely by refusing to deal with my own pain. I had no true understanding of the pain that lived inside of me. This lack of self-awareness threw me into victimhood, and I stayed there for a time.

I couldn't see how the lower vibrational energy I carried was creating all this conflict. The conflict was offering me many perfect opportunities to bring that pain to the surface and deal with it. Still, I refused, and continued to unconsciously manifest a painful life situation for myself. It wasn't until I went within and faced the pain of this significant loss that I could step out of the experience of separateness and into the experience of Oneness.

The perception of separateness supports the belief that we must rely on ourselves to get by, so we do whatever it takes to get our needs and desires met, regardless of the impact on others. This way of moving through the world is pretty common because most of us know no other way of being.

When our actions cause direct or indirect harm to others, we will eventually see that harm come back to us. It is a simple yet profound truth that our thoughts and actions create an impact that affects the whole, directly or indirectly. In order to make Oneness known collectively, we must begin with ourselves. As we elevate our own consciousness, we lift everyone else. This is how we embody the concept of Oneness, together as one.

When we recognize the truth of Oneness, that we are one small piece of the divine whole that can never be destroyed, then we can relax into the knowing that the universe would never want to hurt itself, and therefore would never hurt us. This shift in perspective allows all unnecessary suffering to end. The universe is not acting against us; it is working for us all the time.

Albert asked me to consider the possibility that I chose every single painful experience I've had. He asked me to consider that before I incarnated into human form, I went shopping at the cosmic grocery store, walked down the aisles, and placed into my basket all that I wanted to experience in my next life. I chose my place in the pie—my place of birth, the culture I would grow up in, my parents, my sex, the perspectives I would adopt. And as I formed the plan, there were other souls also picking out their experiences and collaborating with me to help life unfold in the perfect way so everyone would be supported in their personal learning experience.

The conversation between souls sounded something like:

My soul: "I would like to experience immense loss in these particular ways so that I can more deeply understand the concepts of compassion and Oneness. Would you be willing to participate in helping me to learn this through bringing these experiences to me in these specific ways?"

Soul family member: "Since you are me, and I love you so much, I would be honored to provide you with what you need to grow during your next lifetime. In order to do this for you, I must endure certain experiences that will allow me to show up for you in this particular way, and some of those experiences will be extremely painful, but I will also be able to develop an awareness of what I need to better understand. For you, I will do it."

My soul: "Thank you for supporting me along my journey. I love you."

Soul family member: "It is my absolute pleasure to do so. I love you too."

The truth of Oneness is embedded in the idea that the universe is working for you—because you ARE it. You cannot manifest consciously without recognizing that you are working with the divine and *as the divine* to bring your desires into your reality.

REMEMBERING YOUR RELATIONSHIP WITH SOURCE

"You are not a drop in the ocean. You are the entire ocean in a drop."
–Rumi

All of us naturally have a relationship with Source consciousness. There is nothing you need to do to create this relationship. You only need to remember and acknowledge it.

Our understanding of Source consciousness becomes skewed as we become socialized within our first established system in early childhood— the family dynamic. As children, we see our parents or caregivers as all-knowing and larger than life. We believe everything they say is true. In essence, to us, they're gods.

Even if we don't believe everything they tell us, this scenario establishes our beliefs about our Creator and the universe. Essentially, we replace our earliest authority figures with what we would consider to be a spiritual or religious version of our Creator. This is called parental transference—we transfer the beliefs from experiences we have of our caregivers to create our belief systems surrounding the omnipotent consciousness, which becomes our new authority figure. Our experiential definition of the concept of "authority figure" dictates how we experience Source consciousness.

There are three beliefs that are created from this experiential definition:

1. The universe is working with you and for you.
2. The universe is working against you.
3. The universe is neutral and is neither helping nor hurting you.

If the universe is out to get you, there is no way to win, and you live in perpetual victimhood.

If you had punitive authority figures, then your God is a punishing God. If your first authority figures felt like adversaries, God will feel like an adversary, and you will view God through the lens of separation and will most likely see the universe as working against you instead of for you. You will feel punished for doing things that God deems wrong.

The belief that the universe is conspiring against you feels like the odds are stacked against you and there is no way to win. Good things that enter into your life may be viewed as a cruel trick that will eventually lead to suffering. This is when you might begin trying to outmaneuver, placate, and barter with the universe.

If you believe that the universe is neutral and is neither helping nor hurting you, then you are operating under the belief that you are separate from it, and from this space, you are unable to co-create and, therefore, unable to consciously manifest. This belief comes from a subconscious resistance to the parental/God transference. However, what you resists, persists. Those who disconnect from their relationship with Source will often find another way to transfer the parental authority—often through political affiliations and fighting against the wrongdoings of certain leaders throughout the world. This supports separation through fear-based thinking.

A prime example is the belief that if your candidate wins, life will be good again. The outcome might be as relevant as a football game but still creates a sense of relief for a short time until you get pulled into the game again. This supports the idea that you are never safe for long, which only perpetuates the illusion of separation and, therefore, continued, prolonged suffering. If you believe the universe is neither helping nor hurting you, consider how you may have transferred the authority your parents had over you onto seemingly larger authority figures that you believe somehow dictate your life. This idea may trigger a defensive response in you, but I ask you to remain open to the possibility that this may be true.

It might on the surface seem that it is a better alternative to believe in a neutral universe rather than to believe in a punishing God. However, believing in a neutral universe can also trap you in the dream of the human experience, and often, nothing anyone says or does will be able to pull you out of the dream. That is, unless you have a supernatural experience that is so profound that it wakes you up and reminds you of who you really are—All That Is. Supernatural experiences are often associated with some level of pain in order to get your attention. That is precisely what happened to me.

Even though I always felt there was a higher power, I spent most of my life believing the universe was neutral. I was raised by responsible and loving grandparents who I could credit with giving me an amazing childhood. I saw how their actions created their experiences, and I came to believe it was up to me alone to create the life experience I wanted to have. In early adulthood, my manifesting practice only included me, myself, and I. And I had to work around the clock to get what I my wants and needs met! It was my subjective truth, until it wasn't.

After my son crossed over, I began having experiences I could not explain. Then, slowly, I began to remember all the supernatural experiences I had as a child—everything that happened during meditation and playing around with energy with my brother and my dad, even astral projecting and being visited by unknown beings. I began to remember and wake up to the truth of who I am, which is part of everything.

You are also a part of the whole. Therefore, you can allow Source to show up in any way that feels good to you. But in order to consciously co-create with Source, you will have to choose to believe that you are part of the whole. If you open up to this idea, you will begin to find proof that the universe is on your side and does indeed have your back. We are always co-creating with the universe because we are it—we are an extension of the truth of Oneness. We cannot create alone, as nothing is created alone. Becoming conscious of this truth is why many of us are here.

The experience of Oneness happens through purity of consciousness, which occurs in presence, or in the now. This can be achieved through meditation, conscious living, inviting in harmony, showing up vulnerable and authentic, and recognizing our shared humanity.

Sylvia explains Oneness this way:

"In the unity worldview, separation does not exist. What happens in any part affects the whole; thus, we demonstrate our 'specialness' as individuals, not by excluding others, but rather by [equality]—inclusion without exception, doing unto others as we would have them do unto us. As the beliefs that bind us to duality are shed, our awakening mind realizes our individual self has a non-dual relationship with creation as a whole; the self and creation are both manifestations of one undivided unity. We need not seek for unity—it is our inherent nature. Our task is to seek and find all of the barriers we have made against it, the false beliefs and illusions we project on our world to maintain the illusion of separation. When we recognize that the world is not dualistic, we wake up in the worldview of unity. This worldview promotes the understanding that everything is interconnected and balance is perpetually maintained."

I would like to challenge you to explore your own beliefs around how you experience Source consciousness. Ultimately, you are supported no matter what you believe, but when you can reframe your relationship with the universe by seeing your forever connection, you are able to consciously co-create with it, and you can move through life with more ease. Embodying the concept of Oneness is a beautiful way to live your life because it will set you free.

❧ 16 ❧

NON-ATTACHMENT

Manifesting like a Goddess requires you to recognize our interconnectedness and practice non-attachment regarding specific outcomes. This chapter explains the dualistic nature around attachment by exploring four terms: Healthy Attachment, Unhealthy Attachment, Detachment, and Non-Attachment.

Here are some simple definitions of these terms for the purpose of this chapter:

Healthy Attachment: Recognizing our connection with All That Is and taking love-based action based on that belief.
Unhealthy Attachment: Relying on specific people, places, things or outcomes to feel complete or whole.
Detachment: Taking fear-based action based on the belief of separation. The outcome is separation, resentment, or indifference.
Non-Attachment: The ability to be the objective observer while recognizing your connection to everything. The outcome is peace.

Our inherent connectedness means that we will form attachments, and what we believe about those attachments will determine how we feel about them. We are relational beings and therefore cannot get out of forming attachments. How you relate to and handle your attachments dictate whether they are a source of freedom or needless suffering.

REFRAMING DESIRE

Before we dive into non-attachment, it's important to understand how desire impacts attachment.

The biggest block to manifesting that I have witnessed, first within myself and later with clients is the attachment to specific outcomes. We humans have a tendency to become so attached to our desires that we yearn for them. Yearning is painful. In order to relieve the pain, there is a tendency to force, push, and coerce situations to our liking. When the outcome is not what is expected, we suffer. This is why Hawkin's positioned the energy of "Desire" so low on his Map of Consciousness® explained in Chapter 13, Raise Your Frequency.

While desire in itself is natural and necessary, yearning vibrates on a much lower frequency. Yearning forms an unhealthy attachment to desired outcomes, which causes suffering.

Desire is a pure, conscious acceptance of destiny. Our true desires are what is meant for us. When you practice non-attachment, desire doesn't feel like yearning. Desire in its purest form is a higher vibrating energy that comes with the conscious understanding of what you want and what you don't want. You can desire something and still practice non-attachment to that desire. Yearning represents unhealthy attachment and causes intense feelings of longing for something that you've lost, been separated from or have not yet achieved. The energy of yearning will actually repel your desires.

HEALTHY AND UNHEALTHY ATTACHMENT

Healthy attachment is rooted in love. We are innately wired for connection. This is the reason why babies become immediately attached to their mothers. Attachment is rooted in survival. A sense of belonging is felt and love is shared. But inevitably, the child grows up and begins to develop autonomy. Their innate preferences begin to blossom. They begin to discover themselves.

Children are constantly absorbing information about the world around them and learn at a very young age that some of their desires conflict with what their caregivers want, and they learn what they need to do and who they need to be in order to keep their caregivers happy and maintain connection. When the need for survival is at odds with a child's authentic expression, the child suppresses their authentic self in order to maintain attachment. In adulthood, the behaviors that were adopted in childhood to maintain attachment can continue on the subconscious level and may become adult patterns of unhealthy attachment.

Unhealthy attachment is a fear-based construct of the mind that comes from the fear of loss of connection. This fear creates a need to control outcomes by forcing, pushing, running, hiding, or shrinking because we do not trust life to naturally unfold in ways that support the highest good for all. It can create the belief that we must attempt to control situations that are beyond our control. The result is suffering. Unhealthy attachments encourage the suppression of authenticity.

Psychologist, researcher, and addiction specialist Gabor Mate researched the top three risk factors for chronic illness:

#1 Automatic and compulsive regard for the emotional needs of others while ignoring one's own.
#2 The automatic and rigid identification with duty, role and responsibility, rather than the needs of the self.
#3 The automatic suppression of negative emotions (feeling responsible for the way others feel and the fear of disappointing anyone).

These three risk factors are adaptations that are usually formed in childhood and are automatically suppressed. It is not a conscious act. While the need for attachment is important in childhood, when we reach adulthood, authenticity becomes more important because it is crucial for self-actualization.

When you are not showing up authentically, you are not in tune with your own needs and will eventually disconnect from your spiritual, emotional, and physical bodies, which are all intertwined. For instance, you can feel emotion in your heart and also your gut, and you can sense their intelligence. Ignoring the messages from your authentic self requires you to stuff emotions and neglect your own needs, thus creating illness in the physical body.

Suppressing your authentic self will block your blessings.

DETACHMENT

Detachment is also a fear-based construct of the mind and creates a need to control outcomes through avoidance and numbing emotions because of the inability to trust life to naturally unfold in ways that support the highest good for all. It is used as a tool to disconnect from others and from our emotional bodies when connection is threatened. Detachment is a byproduct of the belief in separation.

When the ancient collectivistic practice of non-attachment was adopted by Western spirituality, the concept was processed and understood through the lens of an individualistic culture, which is responsible for the idea that we are independent of others and our actions do not affect the whole. This misunderstanding became anchored into our spiritual practices, creating confusion about attachment. This has created massive suffering.

In Western spirituality, there is a pervasive idea that we should release our attachments and practice detachment in order to alleviate suffering. However, detachment is simply a different form of control that creates a different kind of suffering. Stuffing emotions, pushing people away, and forcing ourselves to be OK with whatever happens creates a feeling of numbness and disconnection from life. When you attempt to disconnect from yourself and others, you cut off your ability to connect to life itself—and you can no longer feel your divine connection to Source consciousness because the stories of separation have taken a front seat.

In his book, *An Uncommon Bond,* Jeff Brown explains that detachment is a prison of avoidance—the New Cage movement that is practiced by the walking wounded—those who attempt to control outcomes by running from pain, abandoning their own feelings and emotions, and closing off to the feelings and emotions of others in order to achieve peace. The idea that detachment is the path to peace is one of the greatest lies ever told. There is no peace in separation.

Unhealthy attachment keeps you hyper-focused on the stories of the mind, while detachment keeps you perpetually running from those stories. Either way, you become chained to a story and lose your freedom.

Both unhealthy attachment and detachment are extreme fear-based reactions to our perceived separateness. They are choices which are rooted in the belief that you are separate from everything. Clinging too tightly or pushing away your desires are both fear-based reactions that block the blessings that are waiting to manifest into your reality.

Practicing detachment is the act of separating yourself from whatever is causing you emotional pain because the connection poses a perceived danger to the autonomous self. Separation may offer a sense of freedom and peace in the short-term, but it is limited and therefore an illusion. When you recognize that you are connected to everyone and everything, you break the chains of your own self-imprisonment and experience true freedom.

NON-ATTACHMENT

The collectivistic mindset of ancient cultures supports the truth of our connection. The individualistic mindset of the West supports the truth of our uniqueness. You do not have to choose to believe one or the other as both are true. Non-attachment supports both the truth of our connection and individual autonomy. The blending of connection and autonomy is the path to self-actualization.

The individualistic mindset supports the idea that connection and autonomy oppose each other and relying on others is weak. You can see the problem with this limited way of thinking, considering that nothing is created alone.

We can be both autonomous and connected at the same time. We can be uniquely authentic and recognize our sameness. The truth is, we cannot self-actualize outside of connection. We must be both autonomous and connected if we want to live in harmony with ourselves and the rest of humanity.

Non-attachment is rooted in connection and the understanding that we are part of everything. In the practice of non-attachment, we can relax into the knowing that events that cause pain are actually opportunities to learn more about ourselves and become more connected. Non-attachment does not require you to abandon yourself in order to belong. You can put yourself first, celebrate your uniqueness, and still belong. And if others do not accept you for who you are, you are free to love them from afar, while still recognizing your connection with them.

It is only through the lens of connection that we realize that all is well —that all our desires are always met exactly on our terms because we are not separate from the divine universal consciousness. In that realization, we can let go of the clinging anxiety that comes with unhealthy attachment and the emotional numbness that comes with detachment. When we practice non-attachment, we are free from both extremes and are able to coexist with everything inside a new paradigm where both individuality and the collective are celebrated.

WHY YOU SUFFER

Spiritual teacher Deepak Chopra has a profound outlook on why people suffer: "You suffer because: you don't know who you are and [you] identify with your ego and cling to transitory experiences [and are] afraid of anything that is unpleasant, [...] including death."

The practice of non-attachment provides the opportunity to practice self-awareness and trust in the universe and your forever connection to it. Chopra explains how you can move into non-attachment by asking yourself these simple questions:

Who am I?
What am I?
What do I want?
What am I grateful for?
What is my purpose?

Simple questions require simple answers, but it can feel like the answers to these questions are not so simple! The answers do require a certain level of self-inquiry in order to reach a place where you become not only self-aware but aware of your awareness. In that moment, you have become the observer of your surroundings and of yourself. This is when you enter the unknown, where new possibilities exist.

As you begin answering these questions, you will see that everything you are has to do with connection. When you truly understand this, you will not want to create further separation. You will want to lean in and create deeper connections regardless of what pain is present.

We are relational beings. And if we are being honest, there is nothing more important than our connection with the people we care about the most. Relationships mean more to us than money or any material possession. The reason material possessions mean anything to us is that we mostly think they dictate the types of relationships we can have. Think about what it would be like to have all of your needs met and the ability to do anything you wanted as long as you lived. Sounds pretty good, doesn't it? Now think about trading connection for security. What if you had to live out the rest of your life completely alone? Would security matter so much to you then?

The biggest gift our relationships give us is the opportunity to achieve self-awareness. Every relationship you have in your life will offer you this opportunity and will usually present itself as conflict. The only time you miss this opportunity is when you race for the victim's seat. When conflict arises, the collective conditioned pattern is to move out of your natural, peaceful state and into a state of unhealthy attachment or detachment, which presents as fight, flight, or freeze. Much of human suffering comes from how we react to conflict. When you are faced with conflict, practicing non-attachment will not only help to bring resolution faster, but will also alleviate suffering.

PRACTICING NON-ATTACHMENT IN CONFLICT

Practicing non-attachment during conflict will help you move into the role of the objective observer so you can move toward resolution. When conflicts go unresolved, the energy of the conflict lives within you, and you suffer. This stuck energy blocks your manifestations from entering into your reality.

Practicing non-attachment means that you can let go of the stories created by the mind and go within to locate the emotion that is tied to the story. As we covered in earlier chapters, attaching stories to your pain gives the ego full control and throws you into perpetual victimhood. To move out of victimhood, it's necessary to release your attachment to the story in order to get straight to the heart of what is truly happening within you.

This means that you refrain from detaching from people who have triggered your wounds. Detachment is never the solution. The solution lies in the recognition that you have a role in your own suffering. When you can show up for yourself and sit with your own pain and appreciate the message it has for you, then you can also sit with other people's pain and not take it personally. Non-attachment supports the practice of empathy for the wounds others are dealing with, along with the understanding that all the suffering we've witnessed is something we can take responsibility for on some level because what impacts the people in your reality is also impacting you, and vice versa.

Detaching from what we perceive to be the cause of our own pain creates a disconnect within self, and detaching from the cause of other people's pain creates a disconnect between you and others. Either way, you are running away from yourself.

"When self is known, all is known." –James Daves

What if you release your attachment to the story around who is right and wrong? What if you adopted the idea that you were looking at an external reflection of yourself instead of some separate being that you are in conflict with?

All relationships serve as a mirror. Connection is necessary to develop a profound understanding of self. They reveal to us everything about ourselves that we have suppressed.

The practice of non-attachment in conflict supports the understanding that we are all connected, and that your pain is my pain, and my pain is your pain. Yet, we do not wallow in suffering. We lean into and address the pain so we can reach resolution. Practicing non-attachment when you are experiencing pain around a situation (that includes another person) is to recognize the concept of Oneness—to see others as you and love them as yourself.

This is what the Buddha meant—to be able to hold the awareness of non-attachment to any extreme.

When we move into conflict with another, we have an amazing opportunity to learn something new about that person and also about ourselves; we grow our self-awareness and strengthen our bonds with others simultaneously as we seek to understand. Regardless of who you are in conflict with, both of you have an opportunity to recognize each other's shared humanity and open up to possibilities that were once hidden beneath the surface of the storyline that you both helped to create.

Everyone at some point has had the experience of feeling closer to a person after a conflict was resolved. That's because conflict is the bridge between separation and connection. It is a gift that serves to expand our understanding of our interconnectedness. We see proof of this through synchronicities that arise through recognizing our shared humanity, and we witness this by leaning into conflict and allowing new information to be revealed. In this space, we not only recognize our sameness, but also appreciate how our differences add value to our lives by offering a new awareness.

Synchronicities are always present, but we do not see them unless we are open to them.

❦ 17 ❧

SYNCHRONICITY

Synchronicity: the simultaneous occurrence of events which appear significantly related but have no discernible causal connection.

SYNCHRONICITY IS A CONCEPT THAT WAS COINED BY analytical psychologist Carl Jung, who defined the term as an acausal connecting togetherness principle—a meaningful coincidence. We are all part of Source consciousness and therefore we are all connected with everything that is. Synchronicities are validation of this fact.

You can think of synchronicities as signs or clues from the universe that arrive in your conscious awareness to let you know that you have been heard and action is being taken on your behalf. We are always receiving signs from Source consciousness, but are you recognizing them?

My experience with synchronicities began after my son crossed over. They came in the form of floating feathers that landed in my lap, hummingbirds flying right up to me and staring me in my face (sometimes for 20 seconds or longer!), phone calls from my son's phone number precisely at his birthtime, finding dimes in the strangest places, his favorite song playing when I am feeling down or during important moments, and many more unexplainable happenings.

After other family members crossed over, I experienced even more strange events, such as lights flickering, seeing license plates with the names of my loved ones on them (for example, LOL TREY), and hearing random conversations in public where a stranger would say something exactly in the way my loved one would have said it, exactly when I needed to hear it. One morning, a glass of water that I placed on my bedside table fell over seemingly by itself. I woke up to the sound of glass crashing to the floor. Once I calmed down, I checked my phone, and I had just received a text that my son's father had just passed away.

Signs can arrive in any form—through nature, animals, coins, numbers, electrical glitches—anything that feels meaningful to you. They are sometimes the random songs you hear or sightings out in nature, such as a rainbow or a butterfly, or a feather floating by. Signs can also show up through numbers in repeating sequences such as 11:11, 222, 333, 444, 555, or any series of numbers that are significant to your life in some way, such as your birthday, birth time, or anniversary date.

Author and medium Laura Lynn Jackson, who wrote the book, *Signs, The Secret Language of the Universe*, explains this phenomena. She wrote, "The other side will use strange and unlikely occurrences—cellphones acting weirdly or receiving inexplicable texts and calls, lightbulbs flickering or burning out," to get your attention.

Laura goes on to say:

"The conductive force behind any sign is energy. The universe is made of matter and all matter is essentially condensed energy. The Other Side comprises the light and energy of all our souls put together. Energy, therefore, is a currency that binds us all—the connective tissue of the entire universe. Albert Einstein cited the connection between matter and energy, stating, 'Mass and energy are both but different manifestations of the same thing—a somewhat unfamiliar conception for the average mind.' Our Teams of Light on the Other Side can manipulate energy fields in a way that makes them ideal for sending signs."

Since we are all made up of the same energy, we also have the ability to manipulate energy fields. And we can ask for these fields to be manipulated on our behalf to experience synchronous moments. This is how we co-create with the universe. All living beings generate electromagnetic energy. Animals can sense electromagnetic fields and can use the Earth's magnetic field to orient themselves and navigate their environment. The

Journal of Experimental Biology calls it "nature's GPS." Put simply, we are all working with the same stuff. It's a similar concept to how the ancient Polynesians (mentioned earlier in this book) navigated the ocean without maps.

Two years after Trey passed, I had already received hundreds of signs from him. So many that I could not deny they were happening, but I still sometimes doubted what it all meant. Then, I was introduced to an incredible woman named Denise Dolan, who is a thought leader, medium, and inner wisdom development coach. Within minutes of meeting her, I learned that she was great friends with many of my friends! We even ended up at the same friend's gathering shortly after we met. My son would have known that it was important for me to have a connection like this with the person he would choose to come through. And she was the perfect person.

I decided to have a session with her, and it changed my life forever. I was able to release my grief and understand why things happened the way they did, and that everything was happening exactly as we planned it. On my way to the session, my phone began playing a meditation app all by itself. It repeated the words over and over, "I am not the body, I am not even the mind." When I arrived at her office, I could not turn it off. I tried turning off my phone, but that didn't even work! I had to remove the battery for it to finally stop.

At the beginning of our session, Denise tapped into Trey's energy and verified certain things about his physical life experience that she would not have otherwise known. This was Trey's way of letting me know that he was there. What I learned about myself, Trey, the human experience, and what we are all doing here is a story for another time, but I knew that my life would never be the same. He told me to find a mantra to use during meditation and chant it often. He said, "Don't overthink it, just let it come to you." During this session, a wave of peace rushed over me, and it has never left.

After our session, I drove straight to my mom's house. The radio came on by itself and began playing a Christmas song I used to sing to him, "All I Want For Christmas Is You" by Mariah Carey. I would sing it and he would laugh and beg me to stop—it's a wonderful memory I have of us just being silly and having fun.

When I got home, I opened my email and saw a message that came through while I was on the way to my session with Denise. It was an email from YouTube with only a link to a video of a mantra for protection that was uploaded that very morning. I had never received an email from YouTube before. The mantra was a beautiful phrase that was put to music and sang in Farsi. Farsi is the most beautiful language I've ever heard, and Trey knew that. The video was one hour, eleven minutes and eleven seconds long: (1:11:11). It sounded angelic to me, as it repeated, "You are my Advisor, You are always with me. You preserve, protect and care for me." The email came through at Trey's birth time, 11:44 a.m.

Synchronicities have become a part of my daily life. They are often recognizable to those who have lost a loved one. Passed on loved ones are not the only ones who can send messages to us and you do not have to experience this type of loss in order to receive them. I believe the reason why so many of us who have lost loved ones see these signs is that they become easier to recognize, because our loved ones know precisely what to send our way and when to do it so that it is meaningful to us. Those who have crossed over have full recognition of their inherent connection to the one life force, and since we are conscious of our connection to their energy, we more easily witness the signs they initiate. My experiences with the signs Trey sends me is how I learned that I could ask the universe, that same one life force, for signs. When you open yourself up to this possibility, you will begin seeing them.

Becoming a conscious manifestor requires you to pay attention to the synchronicities that your connection with the divine is always offering you. Practicing what you learn in this book will help you recognize these signs. As you open yourself up to this possibility, you will become astonished by all the amazing ways universal consciousness interacts with you. Eventually, these occurrences will become so commonplace that you will consider synchronicities as a natural part of daily life. This is when life becomes magical.

SYNCHRONICITY OR COINCIDENCE?

The logical mind cannot make sense of synchronicities because it attempts to understand them through the lens of separation. Often, synchronicities are misunderstood as random coincidences. Coincidence is considered to be a remarkable concurrence of events or circumstances without apparent causal connection that happens by chance.

However, synchronicities are validation of our connectedness, and in order to recognize them, we must strive to understand them through the lens of connection. This does not require analytical thought. Think of synchronicities as your direct line to divine universal consciousness that is communicating with you through the energy of the feminine essence, which of course, defies logical explanation.

It is not the job of the masculine essence within to analyze synchronicities through logical deduction, because these messages are beyond our capacity to understand with the logical mind. Our patriarchal system has conditioned us to dismiss what we cannot logically explain. The logical brain cannot make sense of synchronicities. They are understood by the heart.

Feminine energy flows through the heart space, and the heart has a consciousness of its own. It doesn't work as the brain does—you will not be able to logically deduce the wisdom you receive from the heart. As you practice receiving synchronicities, listen to the wisdom of your heart instead of analyzing whether or not the synchronicities are real or what they mean.

> "I beg you to have patience with everything unresolved in your heart and to try to love the questions themselves as if they were locked rooms or books written in a very foreign language. Don't search for the answers, which could not be given to you now, because you would not be able to live them. And the point is to live everything. Live the questions now. Perhaps then, someday far in the future, you will gradually, without even noticing it, live your way into the answer." –Rainer Maria Rilke

USING SYNCHRONICITIES TO MANIFEST

You can use synchronicities to help you manifest. Synchronicities can sometimes serve as signs or clues from your external environment that arrive at the perfect time—they offer insight on whether to take action or be patient. They can also serve as validation for your thoughts and feelings and even serve as a reminder that you are not alone.

The synchronicities you experience will be unique to what is meaningful to you. Signs arrive in myriad ways and are only limited by what you are willing to accept. These signs can arrive without any effort on your part. Your job is to notice them and pay attention to what you were just doing, feeling, or thinking, and you will begin to understand their meaning.

You can also ask the universe to give you signs, but you must be patient and realize that our concept of linear time is an earthly concept and irrelevant to divine Source consciousness. Patience is required when divine timing is at work.

Asking for a sign requires a higher level of trust than merely being open to receiving signs. You make your request and then practice non-attachment to the outcome. If you find yourself in constant pursuit of a sign or wondering whether you may have received one or maybe missed it altogether, you are overthinking; your sign cannot materialize nor be recognized. Knowing that it's on the way to you is a practice in non-attachment. You must trust that it will arrive when you least expect it. Simply ask for a sign and then let go. Just as with intuition, it will arrive as a knowing; you will know it in your heart.

When you receive your sign, you become a witness to a magical synchronous moment.

SYNCHRONICITIES IN THE FORM OF TESTS

The universe will test you. This idea is often misunderstood as the universe punishing you. The universe would never do that—you must instead think in terms of *what is* rather than applying labels such as good or bad. These tests aren't to serve as any type of punishment but to simply help you get clear on what it is that you want and to make sure that you are actually ready to receive what you've asked for. The universe will test whether what you've asked for is a true desire based in love or a lower desire based in fear. It will also test your self-worth to make sure you can openly receive it.

If you have put an intention out into the universe, your sign may unfold as an opportunity to take action in order to set your manifestation in motion. Taking action is the masculine component to manifesting. You can redirect your actions and make changes as needed when it *feels* right to do so, which is how you incorporate the feminine aspect.

Sometimes, it isn't until we get what we thought we wanted that we understand that the details surrounding the initial desire are not exactly conducive to our happiness. I call these signs the beta test. Beta tests will help you get crystal clear on what you want by bringing you options so you can decide which path to choose. Let's consider the commonplace explanation of beta testing in the physical world with software products, and then apply this idea to the beta testing concept in manifesting:

"Beta Testing is performed by real users of the software application in [a] real environment and can be considered a form of external User Acceptance Testing. It is the final test before shipping a product to customers. Direct feedback from customers is a major advantage of Beta Testing. This testing helps to test products in the customer's environment." [1]

For software, beta testing means your software is close to performing as designed. In terms of manifesting, you can think of beta testing as your intention being very close to manifestation. Beta tests often arrive as a physical manifestation to help you have an experience to make sure that you actually want what you've asked for. You become a "real user" testing in a "real environment" for the purpose of external User Acceptance Testing—the final test before the universe ships the customer (you) the product (your manifestation). It is to your advantage to test it to see if it works for you, and then provide direct feedback so the universe can support you by making adjustments when needed.

Think of beta testing as the universe's way of testing your willingness to play along with it. You may receive a manifestation that is only part of what you asked for, but not the whole enchilada, to let you know that Source has heard you and is working alongside you to help you manifest your desire. Your patience is being requested.

Sometimes, the universe will test your willingness to settle. For example, let's say you have set an intention to land a particular type of job in a particular location with a certain salary. The universe may bring you the type of job you asked for with a bigger salary than you asked for, but the location is less than desirable. This is the time you must remember to trust, and know that the test is occurring to ensure that your self-worth is in check and you feel that you deserve to receive what you asked for. Or, it's testing your readiness and making sure you really want what you've asked for.

You will not be able to manifest something that you believe you don't deserve. If you have low self-worth, you will take the beta bait (the unfinished product) every time. Consider this a blessing. If the universe gave you what you wanted when you weren't ready for it, you would quickly learn that you weren't ready, through overwhelm, self-sabotage, or lack of appreciation, which can create massive regret later.

Your beta test is not the final product. A beta test is only part of what you asked for and may offer other options for you to consider. The final product is a manifestation that includes everything you wanted, or something better, and you take it because it feels right to do so.

Utilizing synchronicities to manifest requires the self-awareness to recognize internal blocks that come from self-worth issues. It also requires faith that the universe is working on your behalf. The more you grow your self-awareness, the higher your self-worth becomes. These key components will help you practice the patience and the self-worth required to not settle—and wait for what is actually right for you. This requires radical trust and believing that you deserve exactly what you want. What you want exists. Do not settle until you get it.

The trial and error that beta testing offers through synchronicities create opportunities to experience unknown elements that you may have overlooked but are somehow attached to what you're trying to manifest. In manifesting, the details are what matter because it's in the details that you begin to become clear on what your truest desires are.

If you have set your intentions to manifest love in your life, and you have been less than clear about what you want, the universe may bring multiple opportunities to experience love so that you can learn what you really want. If you have set clear intentions, and you take the beta bait, you will have missed your opportunity to receive exactly what you asked for.

Let's say you asked for a partner who is loyal, honest, emotionally available, good-looking, passionate, and loving. Before you know it, you've manifested a potential partner. They seem to have all the qualities you asked for, so you jump into a relationship without first making sure you're not dealing with beta bait. After a couple of months, you realize that your once seemingly perfect partner is emotionally unavailable. You have allowed yourself to become attached to this person, so you begin to overlook this aspect of them or make excuses for them. You might even have a talk with them about this need of yours to emotionally connect. It's possible that your person will seek to understand your needs and work on providing what you asked for. It is also possible that they will not or cannot give this to you. Do not waste your time waiting for the dynamic to change or trying to teach them what it means to be emotionally available. The longer you spend doing this, the longer you will block what is meant for you.

I remember trying to teach a former partner by example what it meant to live in integrity. I did this for years and to no avail. Do not waste your time trying to make other people become who you want them to be. Allow them to be who they are, and if who they are doesn't support your desire for the type of relationship you are trying to manifest, then move on in love. The universe cannot do it all for you, nor can it make other people change or manipulate their free will. You must be willing to make the right decision for yourself, even if it hurts initially.

✤ 18 ✤

UNDERSTANDING YOUR PURPOSE

"Be who you were created to be, and you will set the world on fire." –St. Catherine of Siena

EVERYONE HAS A PURPOSE TO FULFILL. IF YOU DID NOT HAVE purpose, you wouldn't exist. Manifesting is a lot easier when you understand your purpose and choose to live into it.

To manifest your desires, you not only need to be clear about what you want and why you want it, but it's also important to understand why you're here, wanting anything. You've chosen to read this book for a reason, and there is no better reason than to open yourself to the possibility of considering your purpose on the planet. In this chapter, we will delve deeper into an aspect of self-awareness that will help you to understand why you're here so you can begin to make your purpose clear.

Without purpose, it's difficult to make decisions, and making solid, clear decisions is required in the manifesting process. When you don't know your purpose, it's easy to get stuck on the fence, which feels painful because it will tear you into fragmented pieces. Getting clear on your purpose will provide you with the inspiration you need to take inspired action and co-create with the universe with more ease.

I will explain the concept of purpose in terms of an idea you may already be familiar with. I can thank my former corporate life for this lesson and for providing the structure for how to get clear on my own purpose.

You may be familiar with the organizational concept of mission, vision, and values or MVV (of course there's an acronym for that). The MVV makes up the whole of an organization and is designed to give employees and leadership a clear understanding of where they are going as a company, what it will take to get there and the reason why they are doing it in the first place. In the corporate world, the vision is considered the far-reaching aspiration that can never be fully realized as long as the company is in business. If the vision is ever completed, there would be no need for the organization to exist.

An organization's mission represents a multitude of smaller goals that support the never-ending journey toward the vision. You can think of the vision as where you're going and the mission as what you'll do to get there. Values serve as the moral compass that guide decision making about the way the mission will be done. Together, mission, vision, and values provide a clear direction for an organization.

The following is a case study by Levi Strauss & Co. It is a great example of values implementation and why completing missions that are in alignment with a set of predetermined values is crucial.

"The Case Study: Child Labor in Bangladesh" in 2017 provides a prime example of a company making values-based decisions. Levi Strauss & Co. based this decision on their company values, which helped them solve a serious issue.

> "When Levi Strauss began to source its manufacturing overseas, the company developed a set of principles called the Global Sourcing and Operating Guidelines for overseas operations and suppliers. One of the principles covered the use of child labor: Use of child labor is not permissible. Workers can be no less than fifteen years of age and not younger than the compulsory age to be in school. We will not utilize partners who use child labor in any of their facilities. We support the development of legitimate workplace apprenticeship programs for the educational benefit of younger people.
>
> Levi Strauss found that one of its contractors was employing children under fifteen in a factory in Bangladesh. The easy solution would be to replace those workers, but in Bangladesh, the children's wages may

have supported an entire family. And if they lost their jobs, they may have had to resort to begging on the streets. Levi Strauss came up with a different solution, one that supported its values of empathy, originality, integrity and courage: it paid the children to go to school. Levi Strauss continued to pay salaries and benefits to the children and paid for tuition, books, and supplies. Even though it would have been easier to just fire the child laborers and consider the problem settled, Levi Strauss was driven by its values to find a better solution."

Being clear on your values allows you to remain in your integrity. Your values keep you honest about why you're doing what you're doing.

Vision represents your purpose, mission represents what actions are necessary to live into your purpose, and values represent why your purpose matters.

CLARIFYING YOUR PURPOSE

When you know your purpose, you'll have no more decisions to make, only actions to take. You can ask yourself the questions listed below to help you begin to imagine what it would look like to live into your purpose.

Here are some questions you can ask yourself to help you formulate your own personal MVV:

Vision: What do you want?
Values: Why do you want it?
Mission: What will you do to get there?

You don't always need to know the details of the "how" or "when." Those details unfold in divine timing, and they always happen perfectly, even if it doesn't seem that way in the moment. Remember, in conscious manifesting, the "how" and "when" are none of your business (and the "who" is your badass divine self).

When you have clarity on your personal MVV, you'll be able to determine your purpose and the direction of your life.

Think of your personal mission like a video game. As you play the game, you have a mission to complete. Your successfully completed mission propels you toward your vision, but there is no end-game to your vision. Even if you beat the video game, there is a part two or another video game out there that you'll play at some point. Your missions throughout life represent the masculine essence and what actions you take to move closer to your vision.

However, you are not a human doing, you are a human being, which is why your vision dictates what types of missions you will accept. You can think of your vision as a journey with no final destination. It's all-encompassing, like dark matter. Even though your vision can change as you evolve, ideally, your vision is your foundational path, and you're in it for the long haul.

Your vision represents the feminine essence. In order to stay in alignment with your vision, you will need to take an active role, representing the masculine aspect of self. The blending of the masculine and feminine allow you to accomplish the goals (your missions) that are in alignment with your vision (your purpose). We tend to think about purpose as masculine, but it is very much defined by both polarities. Think about it like this: your purpose is extraordinary and unending. The actions you take with each mission helps you do your part to live into your purpose each day.

Missions are fruitless without vision—completing missions without understanding the reason behind them leads to a life without meaning. Having a vision without choosing a mission is also fruitless—it creates stagnation, feelings of hopelessness and a lack of focus. The masculine (doing) and feminine (being) aspects of self must work together in order for you to live into your purpose.

Values connect to both mission and vision, forming a trinity. Your personal values system determines the reasons why you take action. You use your values as a guide for how you want to show up and make an impact on the world. Consider your values to be the reason why you are doing anything in the first place.

Knowing your purpose will offer you clarity about what you really want, what you're willing to do to get there, and why you want to do it. When you begin living into your purpose, you will be able to make decisions with ease and feel good about them.

Conscious manifesting requires you to be decisive and clear about what you want to bring into your reality. Your whole self must be in alignment with your desires, or else the fragmented aspects of self—the other part of you that isn't on board with your conscious desire—will sabotage you every time. As a conscious manifestor, the intentions you set need to both be clear *and* feel good to you. When you set clear intentions from a place of wholeness, the universe can begin creating on your behalf.

My purpose is to anchor the consciousness of Oneness on the planet. This vision will be realized when every human being recognizes the truth of Oneness. I clearly cannot reach the realization of this vision in my lifetime, but I can certainly help in small ways through the missions I choose to accept. The missions I have chosen are guiding clients toward discovering their true purpose (so they can share their gifts with the world) and helping them learn how to manifest (so they can recognize their divine power) through my coaching program and this book—and teaching conflict resolution (to spread the awareness of our shared humanity). I've fulfilled many other missions that help me stay in alignment with my purpose, and I will no doubt choose many more in the future.

When it's time for me to choose a mission, I ask myself if that mission aligns with my personal vision. If the answer is no, I do not take it on. If the answer is yes, I then ask myself if it resonates with my highest personal values that include empowerment, truth, courage, lovingkindness, empathy, and connection. Since I am clear on my personal vision and values, my action-oriented decisions about what missions I choose are easy to make.

STEPS TO DISCOVERING YOUR PURPOSE

Here are some simple steps you can take right now to begin to gain clarity on your purpose:

1. **Personal values:** Give some thought to what issues you really care about. Why do you care about these things? Make a list of all the reasons why. You can use your list to determine your personal values that will, in turn, support your decision-making process.
2. **Mission:** Make a list of what you're most passionate about. How can you use your passions to support your values? What actions can you take that feel good to you? Write down ways you can take inspired action based on your passions.

3. **Vision:** What is the impact that you feel inspired to make in the world? Is there an overarching theme that supports both your passions and values? How can you use both to compassionately serve others?

PURPOSE AS THE PATH TO WHOLENESS

"Don't be afraid that your life will end, be afraid that it will never begin." –Grace Hansen

Living into your purpose is what brings you into wholeness. When you find yourself being pulled in many different directions, this is usually a sign that you are out of alignment with your purpose. Aligning with your purpose can help you harmonize all the areas of your life.

The simplest way you can begin to gain clarity on your purpose is by taking your passions seriously. Your passions will give you clues about how to formulate your missions so you can begin to take inspired action.

Your passions will ultimately lead you to take action on purpose. Understanding what your passions are will help you uncover the many creative ways you can take passionate action.

I want you to imagine that anything is possible and nothing is off-limits. You don't have to make any major decisions or moves right now—instead, consider the possibilities of how you can embody a passionate life in service to others.

When you begin to consider possibilities without worrying about how it will happen, you will immediately begin to feel relief. Giving yourself permission to become joyful and excited about what is possible will raise your frequency and allow you to dream even bigger.

If you aren't exactly sure what your life's purpose is, play around with ideas you are passionate about and allow for trial and error. As with any aspect of self-study, the knowledge you gain through trial and error will get you closer to clarity.

The more familiar you become with yourself, the more you understand what you want and why you want it, and the easier it will be for your purpose to find you.

19

BOUNDARIES

YOUR ABILITY TO MANIFEST IS DIRECTLY IMPACTED BY THE health of your relationships, which are an indicator of your internal state and how you feel about yourself. Placating others or placing unspoken expectations on others is not truthful, nor is it authentic. If you do not express your true desires and move in the direction of them, you will quickly find yourself settling for something that can never offer you total fulfillment. If you place expectations onto others, you will find yourself repeatedly let down. The most loving act you can do for yourself and the people around you is to speak your truth and ask for what you need. Anything else is insanity.

Creating and maintaining boundaries in your relationships sets the stage for speaking your truth. Boundary-setting creates a safe space for you and everyone around you to relax into their authentic selves and fully show up.

Living without boundaries is dangerous in the context of relationship. A lack of boundaries creates inauthenticity and inner fragmentation, which means that you end up living in a false reality and also creating a false reality for those around you. Not having and communicating clear boundaries can also cause enmeshment. Those in enmeshed relationships are at risk of mistaking the other person's feelings for their own, which can lead to loss of autonomous development. This pattern usually begins in childhood and carries on throughout adulthood unless checked. A typical outcome of enmeshment is that one person in the relationship takes responsibility for the other's emotions, and the other becomes unable to take responsibility for their own emotions. A lack of boundaries also causes resentment as the people you care about continue to disappoint you by not living up to your unspoken expectations. This is how contempt grows and relationships die.

Boundaries are a critical component in every relationship. If you don't have them and communicate them clearly, your relationships are destined for failure. If you have not created and enforced boundaries before, the idea alone can feel threatening or even like a selfish act, but boundary-setting is actually one of the most loving acts toward another that you can make. It might feel counterintuitive to set boundaries because it can feel like you are breaking connection. But what you're really doing is breaking unhealthy relationship patterns that serve no one in the long run.

Every living being is wired for connection. We spend so much time hiding our truest selves out of fear of disconnection that we miss out on opportunities to give and receive love. When healthy boundaries are in place, giving and receiving love becomes a natural part of the relationship. Boundary setting offers a clear path to experiencing the joy and peace that comes with union.

I once was so afraid to speak my truth that I ended up spending years in bad relationships. I tolerated toxic work environments, romantic partners that were not right for me, and many one-sided friendships. Life became unbearable for me when I began experiencing a series of life crises. I had very few people to go to for support.

When my son went to prison, I felt like I could not share the details of my life with anyone in my large professional/friend group, which made most of my friendships surface-level at best. I suffered the trauma of the loss of five years without him and being constantly afraid of what he would go through. I kept my personal life to myself. I didn't want my son to be judged because he was in prison, and I didn't want to be judged either. I was living a lie. It was difficult to hold conversations with people. I was having silent panic attacks in the boardroom. I became sick, over-weight, and depressed.

I held back my truth to the point it actually began to create physical pain in my body. I began experiencing a painful ache in my throat. It manifested as a sore lump, like what happens when you feel overwhelming sadness that is begging to be released through a good cry—except I didn't feel like crying. I felt this pain all the time as I went about my day—on the train, at work, at the grocery store, when I was trying to go to sleep. I tried acupuncture, which took the pain away for only a few hours at a time. I took singing lessons to strengthen my throat chakra, which helped some, as the pain would subside when I sang. However, I was applying Band-Aid solutions to a deeper emotional issue. As always, the only way out was through. I had to speak my truth.

It wasn't until I began setting boundaries in all areas of my life, honoring my desires, and telling the truth about my life circumstances that this horrible throat pain went away for good. I began sharing with my friends what happened to my son, regardless of the outcome. They didn't judge me. Instead, they showed compassion and supported me in ways I didn't expect. It wasn't long before those connections transformed into meaningful and fulfilling relationships.

SPEAK YOUR TRUTH

"Be who you are and say what you feel, because those who mind don't matter, and those who matter don't mind." –Dr. Seuss

When you state your true feelings and desires, you are showing up fully in your authenticity and helping other people determine whether they can align with you. This is so important in the manifesting process because you will not align with the right people unless you own your truth.

There is a cultural standard in place that encourages holding back when it comes to sharing your authentic self and what you truly believe, want, and need. It can feel unsafe to be honest about your beliefs, feelings, and desires because it means you must become vulnerable. In not allowing your true desires to be known to others, you also hide them from yourself.

It can feel dangerous to speak your truth because of fear that it may create conflict with the people in your life or require you to become more exposed than you are comfortable with. If conflict with others feels like rejection to you, and authentic exposure feels dangerous, then it's highly likely that you have abandonment or betrayal wounds to tend to. When these wounds are in control, it can feel impossible to speak your truth.

Revealing your vulnerable self becomes most challenging when you have become emotionally triggered. In fact, it is much easier to cast blame in those moments and move into a fight, flight, or freeze response. In conflict, it is a challenge to not allow your automatic fear-based response system to take over in the form of lashing out, running away, or shutting down. Unchecked, this auto response can cause relationship death by a thousand tiny cuts.

Not only is this cycle a disservice to yourself because it blocks you from relaxing into your authentic self, but it is also unfair to those you care about. If you don't speak your truth, you will essentially create a false reality for the people around you. They will make decisions based on the false reality you have created by not being honest about how you feel, and those decisions will never be good for them or for you.

Another way a false reality can be created is through lack of communication because the people around you are forced to fill in the blanks through making assumptions. There is no way to put it lightly—I call this a mind fuck.

Saying what you mean is a practice in integrity and will help you to find peace within and eliminate the possibility of mind fucks. It may initially feel uncomfortable to acknowledge and communicate your truth, but I assure you, the sense of peace that comes with it is absolutely worth it.

The reason it is so difficult for many to show up vulnerable is because of the misunderstanding surrounding conflict. The purpose of conflict is to bring wounds to the surface that are ready to be healed, so it makes sense that conflict would trigger your wounds. Conflict is the bridge between separation and connection. The only way out is through.

However, communicating boundaries can help you avoid unnecessary conflict. I learned from relationship coach Bryan Reeves how to understand boundaries, create them, and enforce them. Bryan is one of many coaches I've worked with over the years and one of the most impactful coaches I had the pleasure of working with during my spiritual journey toward wholeness.

Here's a brief overview of what I learned from Bryan. If you want more from him, check out the References section in the back of this book for the link to Bryan's Boundaries Program.

EXPECTATIONS VS. AGREEMENTS

Expectations are unspoken desires that include the expected action of another person to meet certain needs, without communicating those needs. Consider every un-communicated need, whether met or unmet, an expectation.

You can expect to be let down by your expectations because no one can predict your needs 100 percent of the time. You must communicate them.

An agreement is a need that is communicated and agreed upon. Forming agreements is how you set boundaries.

SETTING BOUNDARIES

Bryan talks about the different types of boundaries that fall within two categories: requests and requirements. A request is a nice-to-have, while a requirement is a must-have.

Requirements are deal-breakers, and if these types of needs consistently go unmet over long periods of time, especially after clarification, the relationship needs to be evaluated to determine whether it should continue.

To get you thinking about how to begin your list, here is a list of some of the requirements I've expressed within the context of a romantic relationship:

- Call if you're going to be late.
- Do what you say you're going to do.
- Create and maintain a monogamous sexual and emotional connection.
- Instead of shaming, try to understand.
- Be present to my feelings instead of telling me how I should or should not feel.

- Have a desire and willingness to maintain open lines of communication in the name of honesty and growing together.

Requests work a bit differently. If you would like for your partner to help with household chores when you work late, but it wouldn't end the relationship if that didn't happen, you can consider it a request. A request is something that you would like to have but do not necessarily need to stay in the relationship. And if your loved one is not willing to meet this request, then you must be willing to accept that.

Here is a short example list of some of my requests that I have used within the context of a romantic relationship:

- I would like at least one evening of alone time per week.
- I would like to have dinner together on most nights.
- I would like us to schedule a date night out once a week and a date night in once a week.
- I would like you to wash the dishes when I cook.

It's important to give some thought to the difference between the two types of boundaries and what boundaries you would like to set before having a boundaries conversation. If your requirements have not been set, then petty arguments tend to happen when your partner does not live up to your requests. Not living up to requests are rarely the true problem; usually the underlying issue comes from not communicating your requirements.

Creating and enforcing boundaries does not have to result in an argument, nor should it. It is an act of love and can be done in a loving way. Have these conversations when everyone involved can be present and the energy between you and another is relatively neutral. Do not try to have a boundaries conversation in the middle of an argument. I have actually set a time in the future for myself and another to have the conversation. This creates space for us both to give some thought to what we want and need out of the relationship and how we want to communicate that.

When someone breaks a requirement, it is crucial to make it known as soon as possible and communicate how you're feeling about it. If it happens repeatedly, then a serious conversation needs to be had about whether everyone understands the boundary.

Unclear, low-vibrating relationships that lack boundaries can really screw up the manifesting process. Enforcing boundaries helps you stay true to yourself and maintain a clear understanding of what truly is happening within the context of the relationship, so you can make decisions that support the highest good for yourself and others.

❧ 20 ❧

EFFORTING

I LOOKED FORWARD TO SITTING DOWN TO WRITE THIS chapter because this concept represents one of my greatest lessons: learning how to surrender. For so long, I felt a constant, heavy load of responsibility on my shoulders. I was spinning plates all the time, hoping I didn't drop one and have them all come crashing down. I lacked faith in the universe to show up for me. The story I told myself was that the universe was neither working for me or against me, and if I wanted something, it was up to me to make it happen.

The defense mechanism I took on as a child supported the belief that I was good as long as I was successful and others thought well of me. This developed a fear of being worthless or without value apart from my achievements. When I was a kid, I would write extra book reports and not even for extra credit. I didn't know it then, but I was living out the pattern of my defense mechanism: "the achiever." I carried this into adulthood, and my defense mechanism often tried to work me to death. Defense mechanisms are the construct of the ego, with the end-game being self-destruction. Societal expectations confirmed my belief that I was supposed to work hard for what I wanted because that was the only path to success and the only way I would be worthy, accepted, and desirable in the eyes of others.

This is actually a pretty common wound. Just think about all self-help gurus out there with thousands of ideas about how to be more productive and successful. Many of these experts who share strategies about how to achieve success tend to focus on how to manage linear time to get the most done. There are schools of thought regarding the importance of waking up at 5:00 a.m. to churn out your best work or spending the first waking hours exercising before you do anything else. Following strategies on how to best manage linear time can sometimes be extremely helpful to achieve goals, but they can also be extremely limiting. For those who want to relax into the co-creation process and experience the journey toward achieving in the state of flow, flexibility is required.

The systems we've all been operating within were designed to keep us so busy doing that we rarely have time to question anything, much less use our divinely-given imagination to co-create with the universe.

I'm not saying that in order to co-create with the universe you have to throw out your planner or let go of the schedule that is working for you. What I am saying is that when you feel blocked or uninspired, sometimes the right thing to do is something else than what you planned, whether it means going for a run or taking a nap. You'll know if you need to redirect your energy based on how you feel. I have repeatedly found that pushing myself to do tasks or create when every fiber of my being does not want to do it (except my chattering mind telling me that I must) is a complete waste of time. Either nothing gets done or what I create has to be redone.

If I'm being completely candid, relaxing into surrender does not always come easy for me. I'm constantly learning how to further relax into the flow. However, I recognize that if I do not slow down and invite the universe to play, I will lose sight of why I'm working toward achieving a particular goal in the first place. If I lose sight of why, it's possible that the energy of my creation will not fully align to my purpose. This is the very reason I did not rush to finish this book.

While waiting for the right time to write this particular chapter, I wasn't as patient as I wanted to be. I wrestled with what I "should" be doing, even though I had just simultaneously wrapped up "Anchoring the Consciousness of Oneness World Summit," and experienced major life changes that required my full attention. I still find it curious how the universe stops me in my tracks so that I can more fully understand the concepts I'm writing about when it's time to write them.

I decided to trust and shelve the book instead of forcing myself to write when I wasn't yet ready. I waited patiently, as I had already learned that completing goals for the sake of completing goals equals an empty existence.

After six months, I was ready to begin writing again. I'll have you know that I am super lucky to have such a patient and supportive editor! If I had moved forward despite my intuition telling me to wait, I wouldn't have been happy with the end result. There was no logical explanation for the reason why I felt the need to wait. It was simply a knowing that came from within, gently nudging me to pay attention to my soul's messages. Shortly thereafter, life became stressful. My entire immediate family began struggling with illness, injury, or major life hurdles and massive changes, which tested my faith yet again. I believe that, on some level, I needed confirmation that I had embodied my own message and was able to walk my talk before this book was published.

During that time, I also recognized that some of the details in this book were no longer feeling like a complete match to my intended message, yet I had no idea how to reconcile that. Then, I made some incredible friends who helped me explore my ideas around how to articulate those nuances. I was able to surrender and allow the universe to provide what I needed to receive for the book to become complete. The result was a better book with less effort on my part to get it to where it needed to be. If I had plowed through, I would have had to rewrite many parts of it later anyway.

SURRENDERING IS NOT A BAD WORD

To many, the word "surrender" sounds like losing a war. That is a very masculine way of perceiving the idea of surrender. From the perspective of the divine feminine essence, surrender means to let go of control and allow the universe to co-create with you, and then be open to receiving your gifts. Allowing and receiving are both acts of surrender that ignite the magic of manifesting.

Surrendering can feel scary if you believe the universe is not working on your behalf. Once you have shifted your beliefs around your relationship with universal consciousness, you can relax and begin to trust that your desires will come without you having to fight for them, because the universe is always working for you. Efforting less is a practice in the art of surrender, which is your divine feminine right. It means you get out of your own way so you can create space for the best outcome to be realized, and sometimes, that means that you must be patient and allow the steps ahead to unfold before you.

THE NONACTION PHASE IN MANIFESTING

Doing the initial work of setting clear intentions is the first step in the art of manifesting. The second step is a nonaction phase; it requires you to trust and remain open to opportunities that you would otherwise miss if you're spending time trying to control outcomes. The third step is taking inspired action based on the opportunities that are presented to you. Like the second step, the fourth step also relies on nonaction—to receive what you asked for, even if it arrives in ways you don't expect.

I've said this many times in this book and it is so worth repeating: The "what" and "why" are what you want to focus on—not the "how" or "when." Once you relax into surrendering the "how" and "when," you will see that Source knows better than you how to get there and will help you arrive at your destination in a way that is often surprisingly easier than you could have imagined on your own.

Unexpected opportunities the universe presents to you can often help you manifest your desires faster and in ways that you never considered or even thought possible. This is the most magical and joyful part of manifesting. And vibrating at the level of joy puts you on the fast track toward manifesting your desires. The universe can show up in many ways to help you through people, opportunities, and personal breakthroughs that offer incredible "aha" moments. Creating the space for these opportunities requires trust.

Existing in the space between effort and surrender can be challenging, but if you pay attention to how you feel, you'll be guided in the right direction. If you are putting in effort and resenting it, that is a clear indicator that you must begin efforting less.

THE UNIVERSE WANTS YOU TO HAVE FUN

In childhood, duality begins to take hold of the consciousness, and the recognition of Oneness begins to fade into the background. However, at some point in adulthood, we begin to experience the tug to reconnect with the pure essence of the soul.

You are an infinite, spiritual being inhabiting a human body. Your soul does not care about controlling outcomes; it wants to experience the joy of Oneness. When you are feeling overwhelmed or stuck, this is your clue to stop what you are doing and have some fun. It is in the moments that we allow ourselves to experience joy and reconnect to infinite peace that we have our most inspiring breakthroughs. We gain insight into exactly what next steps we can take. This is working smarter, not harder. You cannot strategize your way to inspiration. It is a state of being that is dependent upon your awareness, meaning what you pay attention to dictates your view. If you only pay attention to a strategic plan and logic-based thinking, you might say, "I have to get from A to B by a certain time." That puts you into a worldview that is bound by space and time, which limits what you are able to achieve.

HOW EFFORTING LESS REVEALS YOUR CONNECTION TO UNIVERSAL FLOW

Many spiritual traditions and sacred texts explore an unexplainable force that we are working with to create our realities. What is this force and what is it like to be connected to it?

When it was finally time to write this chapter, I decided to share a portion of an interview about consciousness that I did with my friends Marti Spiegelman and Todd Hoskins for the Oneness Summit; this was another mission that took a lot longer than expected but came together with a lot less effort than you would expect.

Marti Spiegelman, executive mentor, professional development adviser, speaker, and founder of Precision Consciousness: Expert Training and Mentoring for Today's Emerging Leaders defined this force as consciousness.

"All of the cultures that I've been initiated into and work in around the world, basically every human culture comes to the same understanding of consciousness. It's got a different word, it may be held in a different image or different icons, but underneath it, it's the same idea, and it's a force. I love to go to the cosmometrist, those who study space. They are really looking at how the universe operates. They say that there is a constant stream of energy and information that's flowing in this space that we call the universe. And that's what they say consciousness is. And I have yet to find a culture that says anything else.

If you think about how a seed germinates in the ground and grows into some sort of plant, there are larger forces that are igniting that growth, and there are larger forces igniting human existence. And where does our life force come from? We don't make that up from our personal identity—it's a bigger force. Humans have always looked to the universe, to the stars and the sun and the moon to get a read on the bigger scheme of things. In so many of our traditions and our scientific lineages, we have statements from visionaries and scientists who all say that humans, in order to thrive, one of the things we need is a relationship with a larger force. That's how we get our blood flowing, that's how we get our energy. It moves through us, it informs us. If we just for a moment think about that big flow of energy and information that is the universe, that creates galaxies and planets and redwood trees; it creates us too.

Everything inside of us biologically and neurologically has come from outside of us, and something has to be moving it into us and through us. So if we say for a moment that this is consciousness, this big force, it seems that [...] we have a relationship with it, and it seems that in the modern world, we need to be in awareness to that relationship so that we can be in the best relationship with the forces that give us our presence here in the world." –Marti Spiegelman, Anchoring the Consciousness of Oneness Summit

Since we are always working with unseen forces, we can choose to do so with more ease and exist in a state of well-being rather than a stress state. This idea brings me back to an example I heard Marti explain about the ancient Polynesians, which I briefly mentioned earlier in this book.

According to Marti, the Polynesians navigated and mapped the Pacific Ocean a thousand years before the birth of Christ, without scientific inventions that were created centuries later. They were tapped into the awareness of their relationship with a larger force and therefore able to allow the world to move through them. In their experience of the world, the ocean moved through their consciousness and told them where they were. The ocean brought them information about where landforms were located and how deep the ocean was and which direction the currents were flowing.

To the Western consciousness, this sounds a bit woo-woo. But this is how consciousness works. The human capacity to collect accurate sensory data from the world requires a shift in awareness. It requires us to focus on this larger force that runs through us and everything else. If we were able to do this, we would begin to understand the world differently and what is possible. This way of being is counter-intuitive to the way we've been conditioned to perceive the world—as something separate from us.

"The world needs you to tap into this force that we call consciousness."
– Todd Hoskins

My dear friend Todd Hoskins, facilitator, coach, consultant, and adviser who speaks about consciousness said, "Energy is the capacity to do stuff." Todd went on to explain our misunderstanding of energy:

"The problem with our state of being and state of mind is that we take it all on ourselves. When we think we want or need more energy, we think that we have to collect the energy and figure out what to do with it all by ourselves. This is an overwhelming and unnecessary burden to carry. You do not have to carry the world on your shoulders. We've all been working way too hard.

This energy is always available to us, to flow in and through us, so we don't have to work at it so hard. What if the 'capacity to do stuff' is not contingent solely upon what you are willing and able to do? When you allow yourself to be in a state of being, you are receptive, so you can take in all of this awareness-based data so that action comes from your state of being. It is a relaxed state of unplanned effectiveness that you wonder how it even happened. That is consciousness.

By inflating the importance of our own existence in relationship to everything else, we developed instruments to measure the world, because we forgot how to be aware of the information that we naturally have access to—even though it continues to move through us. When we shift our understanding of our connectedness with everything around us, we can see that our outer world reflects our inner world. With this understanding, we can begin to open up to the idea that we are never alone."

–Todd Hoskins, Anchoring the Consciousness of Oneness World Summit

❧ 21 ❧

INTEGRATION

"To be yourself in a world that is constantly trying to make you something else is the greatest accomplishment." –Ralph Waldo Emerson

THE DEFINITION OF INTEGRATION IS TO COMBINE ONE THING with another so that they become a whole. If you are to come into wholeness, you must integrate all aspects of self, which means you integrate all aspects of life. Integration supports wholeness, and wholeness supports harmony.

We are always seeking ways to move closer to harmony—in our relationships with self and others, and by following through with responsibilities and meeting goals. Every pure desire to manifest anything is an energy that supports moving toward harmony. Our constant striving toward harmony is a mirror reflection of what the universe is always doing. The universal principles of harmony represent the expansive flow of life. We see this everywhere in nature. Everything, including us, is designed to be in universal flow. You know when you are in the flow because you feel harmonious—you feel joy.

It is a mistake to believe that achieving harmony means creating a constant balance in all areas of life. The quest for balance is actually pretty stressful simply because of the way we have come to understand balance.

We have been conditioned to perceive all the various areas of our lives through the lens of separation. When we separate different aspects of our lives, we end up separating the different aspects of ourselves, which causes inner fragmentation. This chapter explains why seeking harmony through balance as we know it does not work and why integration is the path to harmony.

These well-known definitions used to describe balance are based in separation:

1. A condition in which different elements are equal or in the correct proportions.
2. To offset or compare the value of (one thing) with another.

Our understanding of balance comes from the idea of having things in the correct value proportions, which is measured by how much time you give to certain areas of your life. We try to create equilibrium. Yet, the very definition of the word equilibrium even poses a problem: *a state in which opposing forces or influences are balanced; denotes two or more forces in opposition to each other.* The current collective concept of balance also seems to rely upon linear time, which actually perpetuates imbalance because all these seemingly separate aspects of life actually compete for your time and energy. This causes competition between different needs, which will eventually lead to suffering. Anything that creates separation leads to suffering.

Attempting to achieve balance in this way represents one of the biggest struggles of humanity simply because of the collective understanding that we are separate from everything. The tendency is to look at all the parts of your life (family, partner, friends, love, work, play, health, rest, vacation, etc.) as existing in separate boxes as if they do not interact with or influence each other, but actually, they all influence each other greatly.

When you experience stress in your career, it can impact your relationships and also your health. And when you experience a health problem, it impacts your ability to work and interact with your loved ones. The belief in separation can really get you into trouble because it requires you to attempt to evenly distribute your time between many areas. Attempting to achieve balance in all areas of life when one aspect is requiring more of your attention is impossible. The type of balance achieved through the lens of separation creates an experience that feels like walking on a tightrope while spinning plates in the air and hoping you don't drop one because the rest of them will fall—and you might too.

When you really think about it, weighing the value of your career versus your loved ones seems absurd considering that your loved ones are most likely the reason you want to succeed financially—so you can provide for them. But when you are working toward achieving balance through the lens of separation, weighing value is exactly what you are doing. Distributing your time according to value proportions that seem to oppose one another cannot create harmony because forces that oppose each other cannot harmonize.

You cannot use linear time to achieve balance because the only possibilities are what you can add or subtract. Considering each aspect of life as separate means you must also separate the various aspects of self by splitting yourself into various fragments. Seeking balance through separation causes you to step out of wholeness. And since wholeness is essential for well-being, the question becomes: how do you get around this?

The answer is integration.

Definitions of integration:

1. The act of uniting people, places, and things.
2. Any bringing together and uniting of things.
3. Combining or coordinating seemingly separate elements so as to provide a harmonious, interrelated whole.

Harmony is achieved through integration, which occurs when all aspects of life are in alignment with each other; this includes everything that is meaningful to your life experience. When you choose integration, you stop competing and begin working with the natural laws of the universe and are better able to co-create with natural forces. When you integrate all the parts of your life, you bring them together into wholeness.

When even just one area of your life is out of alignment, it becomes impossible to achieve full integration—just like a car may not run properly even if the smallest part breaks. When you integrate all the areas of your life, the various areas are able to nourish each other.

Integration happens when you deliberately combine two or more seemingly separate aspects into one. Discovering and stepping into your purpose is integrating your authentic self with how you serve and move through the world. Living your purpose will naturally create harmony that will positively impact the other aspects of life. Since society tends to place the highest importance on what one does for work above everything else, it's good news that we are now witnessing a collective shift toward integration in the workplace, as companies are beginning to recognize the need to operate in cooperation with the personal needs and aspirations of their employees, which include the whole person. There is still a long way to go in this area, but at least the idea is getting some traction.

According to UC Berkeley's Haas School of Business, work-life integration is "an approach that creates more synergies between all areas that define life: work, home/family, community, personal well-being, and health." Bringing together all areas of life supports harmony.

You can begin integrating in small ways, which will support further integration in larger ways, and that is when you will see your life begin to transform. You cannot predict how the unfolding will happen. Just begin where you are and start simple.

Maybe start with integrating quality time with your loved ones with a nature excursion and explore creatively together while getting exercise. This example integrates seemingly separate aspects of life (family, nature, health) into one so they can nourish one another. It can look like integrating work with play, which is relatively easy to do when you actually love doing what makes you income. You can integrate service to your community with making friends so you can expand your network while doing good in the world. Take on clients who are a joy to work with and whom you can see being friends with later. You get the idea. These are small examples that represent taking deliberate action for the purpose of creating wholeness. You can find ways to do this in any part of your life. Begin where you can, and you will continue to experience forward movement toward integrating even more aspects of your life. It may seem like a small step toward wholeness, but you will be surprised where it leads.

Integration does not include scattering your energy to the point where you are trying to complete multiple separate tasks at once. Multitasking essentially splinters your energy in various directions all at once (i.e., eating and working at the same time, looking at your phone when you're spending time with someone, rushing through one task so you can get to the next one). Scattering your energy pulls you out of the present moment because you cannot give anything your complete focus.

Conscious manifesting requires your full presence. The more you can blend all the parts of your life together, the better you will be able to stay connected to the present moment, achieve harmony, and manifest consciously.

HOW NATURE INTEGRATES

The universe is always seeking harmony through integration. Living organisms interact with their inorganic surroundings on Earth to form a synergistic and self-regulating, complex system that helps maintain and perpetuate the conditions for the expansion of life on the planet. We see this happening constantly in nature as Earth corrects for even the smallest separation. Organisms continue to evolve and integrate with their ever-changing environments for the purpose of creating harmony for the whole. If something in nature is not in harmony with its environment, then nature will create change in the environment so it can correct it.

You have also experienced this in your life. You've experienced change because change is the only constant. Either you created change so you could maintain or regain harmony, or the universe stepped in and did it for you in the name of something better. When you are truly ready for something better, you cannot stop change. If your life remains out of harmony for too long and you don't do anything to change it, you can count on the universe to eventually step in and create necessary changes in your environment to restore harmony, even if you resist. The more you resist change, the harder life becomes.

This is the difference between conscious and unconscious manifesting. Achieving wholeness means that you have created a life that feels good to you. The universe will not have to step in on your behalf and flip your life upside down so you can come back into harmony with your environment.

HOW CHAOS RESTORES HARMONY

"Purity is the perfect order of chaos." –James Daves

Change often looks and feels like chaos. It's not easy to understand why change must occur while you are in the throes of it, but once the chaos that change brings has subsided, the reason becomes clear.

Let's explore why chaos is connected to change and why it is a necessary function in restoring harmony.

Definitions of chaos:

1. Behavior so unpredictable as to appear random, owing to great sensitivity to small changes in conditions.
2. The formless matter that existed before the creation of the universe.

Chaos is the energy of the feminine, representing the mother of creation.

As I began writing this book, the world was in the midst of chaos due to the pandemic that began in 2020, along with outrageous political and social issues of injustice. The chaos we experienced is the result of a lack of harmony in the world. It may have appeared random, but there is a very good reason why we're here experiencing all of this right now. We've literally been forced to do life differently in many ways. Various aspects of everyday life (i.e., career and family) crashed together and maybe were even meeting for the first time. For the sake of our own health and sanity, and the health of the planet, we were being asked to integrate all the aspects of our lives to achieve harmony within ourselves and our environment.

Staying home not only positively impacted the natural environment, but many people began to question the way they had been living life and decided to make major changes. For so many, life does not look anything like it did before the pandemic began. I am not downplaying or trying to romanticize the negative aspects of the pandemic—all the lives lost, the economic struggles, the constant fear of becoming ill—it was painful. The point here is that change rarely comes without some element of chaos. From the perspective of society as a whole, when we make decisions that disrupt harmony, we will be forced to change direction, and that often means we will experience some level of chaos.

Since we are a part of the whole, our own personal integration work positively impacts the whole. We have no choice but to do this in cooperation with the natural world, which will course-correct as needed so it can reach its destination—and that is harmony.

The belief in separation has rocked the planet for millennia. We've been under the spell of materialism, the belief in lack, competition, and the need to control. Now, we find ourselves entering a period of great change. You've probably heard the saying "stress creates change." Well, more specifically, stress creates chaos, and chaos gives birth to change so we can achieve harmony. It may all seem random, but it's not. Random events only occur when there is no destination. It may not be immediately obvious, but there is always a destination in nature. It is divine law. Since we have not been living in harmony with the planet, we have found ourselves in a state of chaos. Nature works with all aspects of itself as it integrates by focusing on the needs of the whole. In chaos, we evolve.

Think about a caterpillar's metamorphosis. Caterpillars eat the leaves of the plant they live on, essentially destroying their environment, and then they move into a chrysalis, where they begin their transformation into a butterfly. What would happen if you cut open the cocoon? You would not see a butterfly. You would instead see what appears to be chaos —a blob of goo representing the end of the old and the beginning of the new. When it's time, the butterfly struggles for two solid days to break free, and it must do so in order to build its strength to fly.

HOW TO INTEGRATE LIKE A GODDESS

If some area of your life is making you miserable (your relationship, your job, your health), this is the area you want to give your full attention to, even if your focus on it initially creates some chaos in other areas. It is similar to when you clean out your closet. You have to first pull everything out of the closet to see what you have. Someone entering your space might only see a mess, but you are in fact creating order. You have a destination:

a clean closet. Once you've sorted through your stuff, you can begin to let go of things that no longer serve you and keep the things that are meaningful to you. When you're finished, the chaos disappears, and you have more space. It feels better because you have moved in the direction of harmony.

When you struggle in one area, it impacts everything else in your life. Focus on restoring harmony in areas where you currently struggle the most, and make changes to the areas that represent your highest pain point. Usually, these are areas that we like to leave for last because they are the most challenging and painful to deal with. However, when you are experiencing a major misalignment in one area, all other areas of your life will suffer. The universe will always work on your behalf to restore harmony, even if you resist. It's better to choose to be a conscious manifestor and do your part in the co-creation process to realign with harmony so you can get back into the flow. If you want a better romantic relationship, then focus on that—hire a relationship coach or spend more quality time with your partner to get clear on how to move forward together. If your job is making you miserable, then make changing that your focus—brainstorm with your boss or colleagues on ways to make your situation better and see if you can come to a resolution, or work on a strategy to find another way to make money, preferably in service to your purpose.

The elements of your life that are the most important to you might feel the most challenging to integrate. You can explore by trial and error and see what areas feel good to combine, even if you at first start small. Get some exercise while you work by having walking meetings. Give your kids a science, math, history, or English lesson by explaining to them what you're doing at work in real-time. Have family time by asking everyone to pitch in to make a healthy, gourmet lunch together. Host themed community gatherings that allow for both socializing and learning.

Maybe you're faced with a problem that is not easily solved. You can use your divinely-given imagination to explore ways to make certain aspects of your life work together, and you will find a solution that is much simpler than you expected. Do not allow fear to get in the way of solving your big problems because the energy of fear blocks your imagination from inspiring you.

If creating harmony means you must rearrange your life in some area, then you can expect some chaos as you leave the old for the new. Integration often requires you to step into the unknown and do something different than you've ever done before. Allow the space for chaos, practice patience, and give yourself a break while you're learning to move through the world in a new way.

❧ 22 ❧

EXPANSION

OUR EVER-EXPANDING UNIVERSE CREATES HARMONY THROUGH integration, which always creates new possibilities because the universe is always expanding. And since you are part of universal consciousness, you are also continually expanding. When your consciousness expands, your subconscious beliefs become altered. When you practice expansion intentionally, you are essentially integrating your conscious beliefs with your subconscious beliefs so they can merge into wholeness. When all of you is on board with what you say you want, you widen the realm of what is possible for you.

We explored the meaning of consciousness with the words of Marti Spiegelman and Todd Hoskins in Chapter 20, Efforting. In this chapter, we will explore how to expand your subconscious mind to accept new possibilities and see them as possible so you can manifest them.

Here are three definitions of consciousness:

1. The state of being awake and aware of one's surroundings.
2. The awareness or perception of something.
3. The fact of awareness by the mind of itself and the world.

The subconscious mind is the part of the mind that we are not consciously aware of, and it influences our thoughts, feelings, actions, and ultimately, our manifestations.

Neuroscientist Joe Dispenza explains that the conscious mind is made up of only about five percent of cognitive activity, while the subconscious is in charge of the rest. Human behavior depends on the subconscious mind, which is not attached to conscious awareness.

The conscious mind is always being influenced on some level by the subconscious mind. You can think of the subconscious mind as the lens you see your subjective reality through. You can use your conscious mind to tell yourself that certain things are possible, but if your subconscious mind does not believe that it is possible, then it is highly unlikely that the conscious mind will be able to find the possibilities that exist and then use them to change your reality. When you expand your subconscious mind, you change your perception, which changes how you interpret information. It dictates what is possible for you.

If your subconscious mind does not have proof that your desire is possible, you will not be able to co-create with the universe to make it happen. The goal of this chapter is to explain how to reprogram your subconscious mind by offering it proof that something is in fact possible to achieve despite the fact that your subconscious has not witnessed it personally.

The easiest way to reprogram your subconscious is to consciously put yourself in a state of joy and do something different (have a new experience). Here are three small, yet powerful steps you can take right now to reprogram your subconscious mind:

1. Give yourself permission to dream bigger.
2. Have new experiences.
3. Take action based on the new possibilities that emerge.

GIVE YOURSELF PERMISSION TO DREAM BIGGER

"There is nothing more important than developing your imagination to transform your life from the inside world of your thoughts and feelings to the outside world of your results and manifestations." –Neville Goddard

You've read in this book snippets here and there about the importance of imagination and allowing yourself to use the tools that Source gave you so you can manifest your own reality.

Your imagination is your divine gateway to manifesting. Nothing can be created until it is first imagined. As a child, you used your imagination constantly. As you were socialized, you began to understand the expectations that others had of you. If the collective belief in your social environment was that using your imagination was a waste of time, then it's possible that your imagination, along with your desires, became buried beneath the expectations of others.

Maybe your dream feels too big. Maybe it feels like you don't have enough time left to pursue your greatest passions. Maybe there are people relying on you to maintain the status quo, so you keep trudging through life doing things that have nothing to do with your purpose.

Unless you set your intentions from a place of wholeness, you will not be able to consciously manifest. Maybe you are wanting to manifest a promotion, but there is a part of you that would rather stay at home with your family or spend more time traveling, or have more time to pursue another passion instead of taking on more responsibility at work. If you have conflicting desires, you will knock yourself out trying to manifest a promotion that will probably never come. And if you do manifest it, you will soon see how what you manifested is not what you actually wanted. The universe makes this very clear in ways that are unique to your circumstances so you can learn from these outcomes. The lesson in this scenario is that you haven't allowed yourself to dream big enough.

You must allow yourself to dream so big that it scares you. This is how you flex the imagination muscle and make it strong. Without a strong imagination, you will struggle to figure out what you actually want. You want your desires to be super clear so you can help the universe manifest them for you and with you.

When I left the corporate world, I had to be willing to step into the unknown and expand my sense of awareness so I could create the space for something else to manifest. I began to imagine what it would be like to work for myself. I journaled about what I would offer in my business, who my clients were, and how I would support them. I imagined how it would feel to create this experience for myself and others, and then I took inspired action to make it a reality. The process looks like this: imagine what you want, allow yourself to feel what it would be like to have it, and then take inspired action in the world. If you just begin, the possibilities that open up for you become endless.

THE BIG QUESTION

If it's been a long time since you've allowed yourself to dream, it can feel scary to even try. I had to find the courage to keep asking myself this powerful question until I was able to honestly answer it:

"If I could have anything I wanted, what would it be?"

Give yourself permission to consider this question. Don't expect an answer immediately. Sit with the question for a period of time (however long it takes) and see what surfaces in your imagination. Pay attention to the ideas that excite you, and allow yourself to take them seriously. You don't have to have all the answers right now, and you don't need to worry about how you will achieve it. Just allow yourself to be honest with your answer.

You will periodically change the answer to this question, and that is OK. As you grow and expand, so will your answers. You will either achieve the outcome you really want or change your mind completely because your journey of self-awareness will bring up a new big answer to this big question.

You and only you get to choose what fulfills you.

You can begin exploring this question now, and when you have some answers to work with, you can begin to organize your life in such a way that supports them. Start with where you are and keep your big dreams in mind.

Imagine that you are already living out your desired experience. What would you be doing right now if you were living the lifestyle you've imagined? What types of relationships would you have? What passions would you invite into your life? Would you be changing the world in some way? Writing your answers down is a form of intention-setting. Then take those dreams with you into your own chrysalis and create some chaos.

EXPAND YOUR CIRCLE

No one on this planet has ever achieved anything alone. We are relational beings who are all connected to Source consciousness. We must tap into that consciousness in the manner that 3-D reality allows, which is making connections with others so we can know what is possible for us. If your subconscious mind does not believe your desires are possible, you will struggle with the creation process.

Let's say that you have a talent for acting, and you want to become a famous screen actor. If you have never met any famous actors or anyone in the industry, then you will find yourself struggling to reach your goal. You wouldn't even know where to begin to land acting gigs. But if you decide to move to Los Angeles, the likelihood of you meeting people in the acting business is exceptionally high. You would see that it is possible to achieve your dream because your subconscious mind will begin to understand that it is possible. If the person sitting across from you is getting acting gigs, then you can too. If you can't uproot yourself and move to L.A., you can begin networking in certain circles where there is a good chance that you will meet someone who knows the industry and may be able to give you some great advice or make an introduction. Once you make contact with people who are doing what you want to do, the process of getting there yourself feels more natural and normal, and that is because your subconscious mind is now on board.

Finding people who are living out the dreams that closely mirror yours is the way your subconscious mind will begin to understand that it is absolutely possible. If your subconscious mind does not know your dream is possible, you will not be able to manifest it. Once your subconscious mind gets the message, it will help you see possibilities that were previously hidden from you.

I know a young woman, whom I'll call Shelly, who wanted to become a doctor, but she didn't personally know anyone who had achieved this goal, so it was difficult for her to believe that she could achieve her dream. I told Shelly to ask everyone she knows if they know any doctors personally. Her friend mentioned that she had a friend whose aunt was a doctor. Shelly asked for an introduction and was able to have coffee with her friend's aunt, the doctor, and learned about how she was able to achieve her goal. Shelly recognized that they had some common life experiences of struggle. They also went to the same high school. This gave Shelly's subconscious mind the information it needed to believe that it was possible for her to become a doctor. Possibilities began to open up for her in the form of recommendations, financial aid, and guidance with the process, and she was able to realize her dream, which began to feel perfectly natural to her.

Think about how easy it would have been for Shelly to believe that she could achieve her dream if her mom or dad had been a doctor. She would have seen her goal as easily achievable—and we would expect her to achieve it simply because we know that she has been exposed to the possibility of it.

This is the power of the subconscious mind. We all know this truth but we rarely acknowledge it. If you are in a situation you don't like and it feels impossible to change it, then you have to step outside of what you already know and expand your circle by including people who have accomplished what you are desiring to accomplish.

To practice expansion, you don't actually need to personally know anyone right now to begin the process. Your subconscious mind can begin to understand that your desires are possible through information-gathering. Even just knowing that another human being is doing the thing you want to do helps your subconscious mind know that it is in fact possible. Dreaming in private will not get you to where you want to go. You have to throw the first stone to create a ripple and then watch it expand until it's time to take action.

"Just as ripples spread out when a single pebble is dropped into water, the actions of individuals can have far-reaching effects." –Dalai Lama

Find people who are doing what you want to do or living the life you want to live and do some research to find out how they got there. Learn as much as you can about each person you find that has achieved what you want. What life experiences, values, or interests do you share? Find the similarities between you. They can be people you know or people you don't know. Sometimes, we can feel "less than" when doing the work of expanding our circles because we haven't gotten to the place where "they" are. Remember that your path will never be exactly the same as anyone else's, but when you see something in someone that you admire, you can relax in the knowing that the world is your mirror, and that means you possess those qualities, too.

Taking it a step further, reach out to the people you've researched and ask them questions about their own path and progress. Doing this will give you important clues about next action steps to take in realizing your vision. Even speaking your desires aloud to those who are supportive of you will open opportunities. You may create a connection to someone who can provide you with information you need, connections to other people, or inspire you to think more broadly in terms of how to get where you want to go. This will allow your subconscious mind to begin making connections so it can get on board with helping you manifest. Practicing expansion will often lead you down a path you never considered before. This is why it is important in the intention-setting process to ask for "this or something better."

When I set intentions to manifest a desire that I've struggled to achieve in the past, I help my subconscious mind catch up to my conscious desire by researching people who have achieved similar outcomes. If it feels good, I will reach out and ask for thirty minutes of their time. I can't tell you how many introductory conversations I've had that have sparked a way forward that I could not have imagined before having that conversation, whether it was another introduction, a valuable piece of advice, or an idea that was better than what I had originally imagined. On several occasions, I've been introduced to exactly the right person who not only achieved the goal I wanted to achieve but also helped me get there by offering information, ideas, services, or another important introduction.

When I decided that I was going to coach people on how to discover their purpose in life, I had no idea how to begin. The only thing I knew was my own experiences of discovering my own purpose. I didn't even know if purpose coaching was a real thing! It turned out that I could find no purpose coaches to connect with. But what I was able to do is talk to people who specialized in some very specific areas related to what I wanted to offer. I connected with people who taught me how to integrate all of the tools that I learned over the years. I discovered a specific test that determines natural talents, gifts, and abilities and became certified to administer it. And I took a journey of self-exploration with the support of many other coaches and certain field experts who helped me further develop my abilities and learn certain skills that supported them. I believe the most important gift of all was the gift of self-love that helped me feel worthy of achieving my dream.

All of this didn't happen overnight, and I didn't do it alone. Instead, slow and steady progress helped me feel more comfortable with each day. I took small steps toward my big dream and practiced patience as I watched the path unfold. If it had happened quickly, I would not have been ready for such a big responsibility. It wasn't long before I began to feel like a coach and felt confident in leading clients toward their destinies.

As the action steps you take toward your goal begin to feel less out of the ordinary and more normal, know that your desire is on its way to being realized. Co-creating with the universe is a thrilling experience, but you have to participate in the creation process. The time will pass anyway, so you may as well try.

EXPANSION THROUGH INTEGRATING THE MASCULINE AND FEMININE

We explored Integration in Chapter 21, and here, we will further explore what it means to create expansion through integration. Manifesting like a Goddess requires integration of the masculine and the feminine polarities, which represent doing and being, respectively.

When you step into the unknown (which represents the feminine essence), possibilities will begin to unfold that you might have never imagined. Once those possibilities are realized, it's time to take action in the world (which represents the masculine essence). Integrating both masculine and feminine energies to manifest is not a skill that we are often encouraged to develop, so you may not have given much thought about what it actually means to integrate these two energies within.

Feminine energy represents constant motion. It is ever-changing and fluid, like the butterfly that flutters gently from one flower to another, fulfilling its purpose of pollinating so plants can grow. The feminine essence is life-giving and ethereal, and she dances with the energy of inspiration when it moves her. Masculine energy represents stillness and consistency. The goal of the masculine is to consistently work until the end goal is conquered.

This may seem counterintuitive, considering that the masculine essence is about taking action and the feminine essence is about simply being. Yet, the butterfly does nothing outside of her innate wisdom. Her movement represents her beingness. She doesn't build a strategy to pollinate flowers and then go off to conquer those flowers. She moves with the wind and allows inspiration to take her wherever it wants to go. The masculine uses thought to build strategy so it can use what it already knows to go out and conquer the world. If you are not expanding what you know, then you have nothing new to work with, and your efforts will not produce different results. Use your feminine energy to expand your consciousness, and use your masculine energy to take that new information and expand your circle through strategy and action based on what new information you learn. Essentially, you are stepping into the unknown and making it known so you can co-create with the universe.

Integrating polar energies can feel like being stretched. As with all integration, there are moments during the process when you may feel uneasy or off. The reason it feels uncomfortable is because of the uncertainty that comes with bringing the self into wholeness.

There will always be a part of you that craves what you know, because the known brings certainty. It feels safer to stay in the known and shrink your desires to fit in with what you already know is possible. But when you choose to expand your consciousness and make room for new possibilities, your life begins to transform in amazing ways. The uncomfortable stage of ups and downs will pass, and you will begin to feel empowered by what you are able to create for yourself, provided you stick with it. Allow your dreams and visions to inspire you, and then move into action with focus and determination.

The ego will try to convince you that so many things could go wrong as a result of taking action. When it comes to taking action, you want to rely on your masculine energy and feel the fear, and do it anyway. It's not the time to hold anything back. This is when you must change your focus from what could go wrong to what could go right. If you don't take a chance, you will never reach your destination.

If you can relate to this fear of taking action, the Solar Plexus Guided Meditation that is available in the *Manifest Like a Goddess Experience* can help you strengthen and align your masculine center. Developing your self-awareness will help you recognize when your ego is attempting to take over so that you can begin rising above egoic messages and moving in the direction of your desires.

❧ 23 ❧
BENDING TIME

"Time is the most unknown of all known things."–Aristotle

THE MOST COMMON CONCERN I HEAR FROM CLIENTS AS TO why they struggle to make changes in their lives is because they don't have enough time. And on some level, that's fair. They are busy people, and time is their most precious commodity. It's not like money. If you lose money, you can get it again. Once time is gone, it's gone. At least, that is the human experience of time.

What if I told you there is a way to create more time for yourself...by bending it?

The idea of bending time seems a bit like science fiction, doesn't it? We think of time as how we measure the past, present, and future and also as a tool to measure how long it takes to do things. We can easily look back on a time when we did this or that, and we can predict how much time something might take based on our past experiences. In our 3-D reality, we experience linear time, which means time appears to be on a continuum and therefore fixed. But time is actually fluid. If you did not live within the confines of 3-D reality, say if you were floating in empty space, you would not have any concept of linear time. You would instead be experiencing *now* all the time.

In Newtonian physics, length and time are considered absolute. In earlier chapters, you learned that Newtonian physics only explains part of the truth, while quantum physics explains our fundamental reality. Albert Einstein's theory of relativity and quantum mechanics supports the idea that time is relative, meaning the concepts of past, present, and future are an illusion, because time moves relative to the observer.

"Time and space are modes by which we think and not conditions in which we live." –Albert Einstein

The past, present, and future feel real to us, but in reality, all of it is happening at once. There is only now. This is a mind-bending concept, but it doesn't matter if you completely understand it. Just as you don't have to understand how a car starts in order to drive it, you don't have to be able to understand Einstein's explanation of time and space in order to bend time to manifest your desires.

And you actually already know how to bend time. We have all at one point said, "I don't have enough time to [fill in the blank]," but when we are up against an important deadline, somehow, the work tends to get done. If you have a week to turn in a project, you will probably take a week to do it. If you have one day, you will take a day to do it. When you have less time to complete something, you give it all of your attention and focus and complete it by the deadline.

It is your focus that creates the bend in time.

SPEEDING UP AND SLOWING DOWN TIME

We all have the ability to speed up or slow down time. We actually do it without even thinking about it. Linear, or clock time, exists outside of us, but non-linear time exists within us. So your experience of time is based upon your perception, and therefore the passing of time is subjective.

When you do something you've never done before, such as visit a new city, try a new hobby, take a different route to work, or even brush your teeth with your non-dominant hand, you are stepping into the unknown and firing new synapses in your brain that are creating new possibilities through memories. What do memories have to do with bending time, you ask?

Our sense of time passing is dictated by our memories. We experience time differently in the moment than what we do retrospectively. When you go on a fun vacation, it may seem like time just flies by, but when you reminisce about it, it feels like you were away having fun for a much longer period of time. This is because you have many memories of the event. The more memories you create for yourself, the longer your life will feel when you look back on it. Variety is not only the spice of life, it is the way to become present and slow down time. If you want to slow down time, simply fill your days with as many novel and memorable experiences as you can.

Unless you are doing things each day that you really love, repeating the same experiences actually speeds up time. When you are doing the same things day in and day out, boredom can set in, and time can seem to move much slower. But when you look back on a year of doing the same mundane things every single day, it seems that time has flown by. This is because you have not experienced anything new and therefore have no new memories to help you create a different perception of time.

It also feels like time passes faster as you get older. This is because we measure the passage of time differently as we get older. As children, we tend to live in the present moment most of the time. As adults, we tend to think more about the past or the future. In hindsight, we may feel like we have wasted time either by worrying or doing tasks that feel meaningless.

The perceived passage of time has everything to do with how much you are paying attention to it. When you are in the present moment, you're noticing everything. If you're having fun, your attention is focused on what you're doing and not on time. It goes by without you noticing because you are existing in the now.

Where your attention goes is where your energy flows.

HOW DO YOU BEND TIME?

The simple answer is to be in the present moment. Yet, the simple answer is often not easy.

Neuroscientist Joe Dispenza explains that when you are feeling stress, all of your energy becomes invested in your material reality, and then you have to play by the rules of Newtonian physics, which includes the illusion of linear time. In stress, it feels like you are on your own and separate from everything, so you begin forcing, competing, and trying to control outcomes. When you try to control and predict everything in your life, you narrow your focus to the material world. This is when you begin to experience the feeling of separation. Creating anything new is not possible in this state. Most people exist in a stress state the majority of their waking hours, and because daily stress has been so normalized in our society, they are not even aware of it. In that space, you can't help but be preoccupied with time because your focus is on the material reality of the third dimension where linear time appears to be real.

When you are experiencing the present moment, you are not limited by your perception of linear time because time ceases to exist. When you make it a priority to live in the present moment, you will naturally experience more joy, which is the organic state of the soul. The soul does not care about linear time. It only cares about now.

While you cannot achieve anything in the material world alone (as we covered in Chapter 22, Expansion), you actually don't need anything outside of you to create a bend in time. As you open your heart, you're also opening your creative center, becoming more energy and less matter, and less dependent on linear time.

You can practice focusing on your heart space in meditation by visualizing your energetic field growing and expanding out into infinity. This creates synchronization between your energetic field and the universal energetic field. The truth is, they are one and the same, so this practice simply allows for the recognition of your connectedness to All That Is. As the conscious mind and the subconscious mind become integrated, the heart space can lead in these moments, and the analytical mind can rest.

As you open your heart, the barriers to manifesting begin to disappear. You are able to access a deep knowing within and become inspired, and create from that space.

The Heart Chakra guided meditation I created for the *Manifest Like a Goddess Experience* helps you tap into your heart center and strengthen your ability to access the universal energetic field at will.

THE MAGIC OF THE PRESENT MOMENT

Zen Buddhists say to meditate for twenty minutes per day unless you're too busy, and then you will be best served to meditate for an hour a day. The reason for this is because you gain more time in your life to do what you want the longer you can stay in the present moment.

Your external reality will actually begin to shift to support your desires and create more space for you to do the things you love.

Meditation is not just for yogis or the highly spiritual. It provides every human being access to universal consciousness, which is where pure inspiration comes from. The more you meditate, the more neural pathways you create and the more connections are created in your brain's network. Integrating the conscious and subconscious mind becomes second nature, and you will naturally learn to function using both. This allows you to be in linear time and non-linear time simultaneously, and you will find that life becomes more effortless and rich.

I can recall so many past situations when I was feeling pressed for time, yet I wasn't feeling inspired to do the thing I thought I needed to do. I began practicing setting the intention to let go of worry and forget about time. I would instead choose to become present through meditation, a bike ride, or anything I felt like doing that would help me to just be in the present moment. If I found that I struggled to stay in the present moment no matter what I chose, I would take a nap. When I came back to the task, I often realized that either plans changed and the task was no longer necessary—or a brilliant idea arrived in my conscious awareness that allowed me to complete the task with less effort. Brilliant ideas are a product of inspiration and are accessed through your inner knowing. You can then act on these ideas using the analytical mind. This process can help you create outcomes that are much more amazing than you had originally planned.

The more in tune you are with the present moment, the better able you are to determine when to take inspired action. This gives you even more time to have more fun and create more memories, which results in a richer life that is more meaningful and actually feels longer.

When I decided to write this book, I set the intention to first create an outline that would support what I wanted to convey to those who want to discover their innate power and consciously manifest. I began tapping into my joy space by visualizing the perfect outcome of what I wanted to create. I set up my environment to support my complete focus. I lit some candles, burned some incense, and meditated for a while until I was able to relax into the present moment. Time no longer existed for me. I was ready to give my complete focus to beginning the book.

Time seemed to fly by each time I sat down to write and organize my thoughts. However, I finished the outline and very rough draft in just seven days. I had tapped into an expansive and creative space, and I was having fun. And I had stepped into the unknown by doing something I've never done before and discovered new possibilities around creating what I had imagined. I did all this by becoming present. I set the intention to offer my complete focus, and I finished the outline much faster than I predicted. When I think back on that process, it feels like I spent a lot longer than seven days pulling it all together.

If you have not yet developed a daily meditation practice, begin with just ten minutes per day. In a couple of weeks, you will see how better able you are to tap into the present moment with ease. Spending more time in the present moment allows you to give all of your attention to what you're doing. When you focus your energy, you will enter into a space where time ceases to exist.

Time will seem to fly. When you are finished creating, you will see that you have accomplished more in that particular amount of measurable time than you would have if you were trying to force your way through.

BENDING TIME TO MANIFEST

You wouldn't desire something if your multi-dimensional being wasn't already experiencing it on some level. Your desires are a divine urge within that is encouraging you to experience more of who you already are. Desiring from the energy of fulfillment is choosing to experience another part of who you are: your multi-dimensional self. This is how you collapse time and space—by having faith and being persistent in the idea that your manifestations already exist in your present energy. When you embody the energy of your desired reality, you create the inner experience of it happening right now within you. You experience it in the now by feeling and claiming it.

You become stuck when you believe that your manifestations are happening sometime in the future. You also become stuck when you translate your desires (which is divine energy) into thoughts and emotions of longing, which is the energy of lack that pulls you out of the present moment where all of life exists.

When you believe that the present moment is somehow not good enough, you perpetuate the lag in time. When you feel lack, you create more lack. Do not expect your manifestation sometime in the future. Instead, create the feeling within that what you want is already fulfilled. There is no longing, no craving, and no resisting. The feeling of lack occurs when you give your attention only to what is happening in your physical reality. Consider the things that you see in your physical reality as mere relics of your past manifestations.

Infinite reality is right now. This fact requires you to hold space for the things that are not yet seen in your material reality. And when your manifestation arrives, you will notice that it feels almost uneventful. This is when you know you've created a bend in time and space.

❧ 24 ❧

THE ART OF CREATION

EVERYTHING YOU ARE LEARNING IN THIS BOOK IS PREPARING you to awaken your inner Goddess and consciously manifest your desires, which is your divine right. The art of creation begins here, as you are the creator of your destiny.

Goddess consciousness is a universal energy that transcends the ego because it is connected to the compassionate wisdom of the heart. This connection is not solely reserved for women, because every human being can access this wisdom if they can open their hearts and trust in the infinite flow of life.

The feminine represents the wild, mystical, and life-giving force that is primal, untamed, and cannot be contained. The masculine is the protector of the feminine and a guiding force for action and completion. Even though these polarities appear separate, they are forever connected because creation cannot occur without the union of both the masculine and feminine essence. Ultimately, we are all being called to embrace our interconnectedness and recognize our shared humanity so we can heal together and create new possibilities for the future of humanity on the planet. We do this by integrating all the aspects of self, not only to realize Oneness, but to live in joy, which is the key to unlocking and manifesting your truest desires.

As I wrote this book, my own understanding of these concepts expanded. With every chapter, I found myself in a place where I had to walk my talk in ways that were not easy. I had to courageously let go of cleverness and comforts and embrace curiosity even more. I was nudged to lovingly release what was no longer my truth and step into the unknown in order to discover the possibilities before me. In that space, my life expanded.

The space was created for major shifts in my perception, and my life began to reflect this expansion. I found ways to offer even more value to those I work with. I found personal opportunities to heal relationships with important people in my life, and I found professional opportunities to expand my reach across the globe so I could serve others using my unique gifts. I know that as I continue to learn and grow, more will be required of me. We are on a journey of learning, and our growing is never over.

As mentioned in earlier chapters, every problem in the world is because of separation, and the solution is always connection. The teachings in Unitive Justice Theory and conflict resolution application transformed my life, and I believe it has the capability of literally changing the world. The teachings of unitive consciousness have become the foundation of all my work and are woven throughout this book; throughout the chapters on Emotional Mastery, Boundaries, Integration, Non-Attachment, Unconditional Self-love, Compassion, Authenticity, and many others.

If you're interested in learning more about conflict resolution coaching for world changers, visit my website for more information: https://saradaves.com/transcend-into-oneness/

When Sylvia and I teach unitive consciousness, we begin with theory. We do this in order to set the stage for the mindset shift that is necessary to put the practical application to use. It's the same for learning to manifest. You must understand the theory before you can put the practical applications to use. As you practice, your awareness of these truths also expands. Once you discover the truth of your inner Goddess power, you can't unknow it. And that is when you are equipped to use the tools to manifest in the material world.

There are many tools you can reference in the section, Tools for Manifesting Like a Goddess, located in the back of this book.

YOUR PROCESS IS UNIQUE TO YOU

As you have been anchoring in the information in this book, you have been shifting your mindset; you may be questioning some things you've assumed to be true, redefining your personal truths, and may be finally willing to let go of the beliefs that you realize no longer serve you. As you continue to explore and anchor in this new mindset, new awareness and possibilities that you never imagined will continually be revealed to you.

The tools you decide to use to manifest is up to you. There is no rush, and you cannot get it wrong. Once you finish this book, you can begin using it as an oracle. Leave it by your bedside, and before you go to sleep, flip through the pages and randomly choose a page or section to read. It will be exactly what you need to remember.

I often come back to my own work to remind myself of what I already know. I hope you will keep coming back to the information in this book when you find yourself slipping back into old patterns or when you find yourself being challenged by the ever-changing world around you.

I've also shared information about some tools I use to bring forth my own manifestations in Tools for Manifesting Like a Goddess in the back of this book.

EMBRACING CHANGE

A manifesting Goddess knows how to let go and trust that the universe is working for her.

As you continue on your manifesting journey, I want you to remember that change is inevitable. It is the only thing we can rely on to be a constant in our lives. Our human understanding of manifesting is seeing and having what we want in physical reality, which we experience through linear time. As we covered in Chapter 23, Bending Time, you are also working with non-linear time, which is divine timing. Co-creating with the universe is a lot easier and a lot more fun when you can remain in the flow, even when circumstances change. This requires patience and trust.

Unexpected change is a sign from the universe that it knows better than you about how you can best receive your desires. Trust it. Don't allow yourself to get stuck in commitment for the sake of commitment. If you have asked the universe to help you manifest something different from what you're currently experiencing, then expect change.

Going with the flow when the universe wants you to change direction requires checking in regularly with yourself for answers. You are a unique expression of Source consciousness, and therefore all the answers you are looking for are within. You not only have direct access, you are the direct access.

Whether you identify with and lead with the masculine or feminine essence, you can use the concepts you've learned to help you manifest your desires. We have covered the theory behind conscious manifesting, and there are tools explained in the back of this book that will help you with the manifesting process.

MESSAGE TO THE FEMININE

"Like a star, the moon, a flower, or the sunset, the Feminine attracts and enchants us, opening our hearts to beauty and love." –David Deida

To the feminine being who has nearly made it to the end of this book: I want to congratulate you for your commitment to raising your Goddess energy and choosing to serve as a beacon of love for us all. Learning to manifest like a Goddess not only increases joy a hundredfold in your own life, but you are also showing others by example how to step into their own power and live a conscious life based on truth and connection.

The sacred feminine is rising and will heal the Earth through us. We, the feminine essence, are the vessel for a massive healing process that has already begun. As the healing wave rushes over us, we are being called to practice unconditional love and trust. We're being asked to tap into our inner senses and be in service through our purpose. The Goddess embraces her feminine essence and lovingly integrates her masculine essence, celebrating the alchemical wedding within.

Goddesses choose divine joy unless there is pain present that has an important message that needs to be revealed. Since the feminine carries the wounds of the entire planet, we have both collective and personal wounds that need our attention from time to time. As they surface, she courageously embraces them with the curiosity and wonder of a child, because the only way out is through.

In your Goddessness, you lovingly set boundaries because you know it is one of the most caring acts of love that you can offer another. You give yourself what you need and ask for what you want, allowing yourself to want it and receive it unapologetically.

As a Goddess, you reserve your own energy so you can love your body, giving it the gift of movement, play, pleasure, and stillness. Your body is a temple, and you honor it as such. You own your sensual nature and honor yourself as a divine sensual being. You recognize your power, and you speak the truth with love and forgiveness—for yourself first, and then for others.

The Goddess essence understands the importance of purpose and will stop at nothing to live into it. She also understands that the purpose of the collective feminine includes supporting the divine masculine as he shines his light on the world. Living into his purpose supports healing on a collective scale.

Your inner strength allows you to stand beside the masculine and honor him as he raises his divine protective essence and leads you back into your own power—because you have surrendered to him—and not because you are beneath him. His divine responsibility is to protect you and bring focus, and yours is to nurture and bring flow as you open the secrets of the universe to him. One is nothing without the other.

Thank you, divinely powerful Goddess.

MESSAGE TO THE MASCULINE

To the masculine being who has nearly made it to the end of this book: I want to congratulate you for having the courage to practice vulnerability and open your heart to the power of Goddess consciousness. It is crucial that the masculine essence also align with their innate feminine essence in order to support the collective integration of the feminine and masculine polarities. Thank you for supporting the recognition of the power of feminine essence. This is how we will integrate and heal the collective wounds on the planet together.

The universe may have already been working in the background to teach you about the mystical wildness of the Goddess. Maybe you've witnessed this through a woman who pushes your buttons because she speaks uncomfortable truths.

A woman who has embraced her Goddess energy will see through facades, and her eyes will penetrate your being. You cannot hide from her. She will shift your perspective and ignite your soul and show you the only way to win the game is to stop playing.

She will give it to you straight, in a way that is expansive, vulnerable, loving, and forgiving. She will bear witness to your divinity and challenge you to walk through the depths of your own darkness until your heart breaks open and shines its light upon the world. She will gently press you to become your highest self.

If you've encountered a Goddess and you weren't ready for her, you may have run, and she let you. In your effort to escape the mysterious depths of the truth of her, you may have found yourself running from your own truth until there was nowhere to hide. The fact that you are reading this book means that you have already begun the awakening process and your role in the opening of your own heart and assuming your divine role as a guiding light. Your participation in this process at this time on the planet is crucial. I hope you find that the words on these pages offer you permission to practice surrendering to the mystical power of the wild feminine as you question everything in an effort to get to the truth.

As your heart begins to open, you will find it increasingly difficult to live the status quo. You will notice a primal hunger in the depths of your own being to embrace your purpose, and you will stop at nothing to fulfill it. And she will press you, challenge you, and love you as you attune to your calling, supporting your complete presence to both purpose and divine connection. And when you are clear on your purpose, you will be able to dive into the unknown depths of the mystical feminine and lead with your masculine essence to further open her heart so you can receive her love and so she can receive your light.

If you have not yet crossed paths with a Goddess, expect her to arrive soon. All the truths that you have uncovered in this book will help you recognize her and understand the collective and personal pain it took her to get where she is right now. And she will also honor your journey and what it took for you to arrive here.

DIVINE RELATIONSHIP

We may dream of beautiful homes, new cars, trips to beautiful places, and amazing adventures, but ultimately, it is our relationships that bring the most meaning to our lives. It is the people with whom you share your material items and experiences that make manifesting it all worthwhile. This is because we are relational beings. Even your purpose cannot fill you up in the way that the joy of loving another person can. And because purpose includes serving up your gifts, you cannot fully live into your purpose outside of relationship. As Bob Dylan said, "You gotta serve somebody."

The beauty of relationship rests in both the joy and the pain. It is the duality—the push and the pull between the masculine and feminine—that helps us get clear on who we are and where we're headed. We learn about ourselves and we heal, through relationship.

You may have heard the saying, "If your relationships are not right then nothing is right." This is true. The world is a reflection of us, made up of our beliefs, dreams, fears...everything. When we struggle in our relationships, it means we are also in an internal struggle because there is a wound present that needs healing, whether it is a wound unique to you or a collective wound we carry for our ancestors; it needs healing nonetheless.

When we can tune ourselves into the flow with the music of the masculine and the dance of feminine, we have integrated both polarities. This act of integration on the physical plane is the representation of divinity on Earth, and our souls shine in wholeness.

It has been my honor to support you in your manifesting journey.

My wish is for this book to serve as a guide to you along your path toward conscious manifestation as you uncover and clear fears and false beliefs that have held you back from manifesting the magnificent life that is meant for you. Keep reading to learn about the manifesting tools and rituals I use to consciously manifest.

Together, we've got this.
In love and light,

Sara

NEXT STEPS AFTER
READING THE BOOK

TOOLS FOR MANIFESTING
LIKE A GODDESS

After you've consumed everything in this book, you will want to have some tools on hand so you can begin your manifesting practice. My favorite manifesting components are my Goddess altar, setting intentions with the moon's phases, connecting to my amazing sisterhood for support, creating sigils for intention-setting, and also receiving guidance from the tarot and the runes.

Here you will also find the Feelings Inventory List and a By-You Feelings List that I refer to in Chapter 7, Emotional Mastery. You can review this chapter to help you learn how to properly use these lists.

CREATE YOUR GODDESS ALTAR

Some years ago, right before Christmas, I decided to set the intention to create a small, sacred space in my home just for me. I envisioned creating a Goddess altar as a Christmas present to myself. But holiday time gets hectic, and it seemed I never had the time to give any thought to where I would even put it, much less what it would contain. So, I set my intention to manifest a Goddess altar and held the space for it to unfold without expectation.

On Christmas Eve, I came home to a surprise—a gift bag on my porch. I checked the tag. It was from a dear friend of mine. In the bag was a miniature string of Om Mani Padme Hum prayer flags, colored candles for every chakra, incense, and crystals. It was more than enough to get my altar started.

Then, my mom gifted me a little antique table. I had everything I needed to create my altar. I added my mala beads, small Goddess relics, an angel candle holder that another dear friend of mine gifted to me when Trey crossed over, Palo Santo, a few large crystals, and my son's ceramic fish that he made in middle school. Everything that sits on my altar has special meaning to me, and I add more items when I feel inspired to do so.

My altar is my personal sacred space that I use for creation. It's where I set my intentions during certain moon cycles, chant my personal mantra, perform daily meditations, pray, and simply find peace.

When I need a reset, I come to my cushion at my altar and do whatever I feel like doing. Even if it's just to light a candle, burn some incense, or just simply close my eyes for a few minutes. In these little moments, I can feel my connection to Source consciousness. If this sounds like heaven to you, I highly recommend creating an altar for yourself.

Altars have been used for millennia in every religion and culture, and for me, my altar is an essential element in the manifesting process. Having a Goddess altar will help you create your ideal manifesting environment. It provides a sacred space that is just for you, where you can set your intentions, meditate or just find some quiet time to relax and recharge for a few moments. While your Goddess Altar does not need to follow any particular religion or culture, you can always create yours to reflect your own religious or spiritual beliefs, or simply create a safe space to call your own.

HOW TO WORK WITH THE MOON'S ENERGIES

Those who lead with the feminine essence have direct access to the moon's powerful energies. The collective feminine essence has an innate understanding of this connection. We are vibrationally aligned with the energy of the moon and can use the different phases for creation. It is not something you need to learn, it is instead what you need to remember, because this knowledge has been a part of the feminine's DNA memory since the earth was created. Using the basic principles of the moon's energies, you can manifest anything into being. Learning how to manifest with the moon will help you determine when to set intentions, take action in the physical world, practice patience, and reflect on and redesign your intentions as needed. You can use this guide to manifest anything you want—love, prosperity, abundance, peace, connection—and bring your own creations into reality.

I've provided a brief description of each moon phase.

DARK MOON PHASE

The dark moon represents the three days where the moon is not visible. This period begins during the last visible crescent of the waning moon, and the new moon occurs on the second day of this dark period.

The feminine are the keepers of the unseen, where the darkness resides. It is in the darkness, within the unseen matter, where all of creation occurs. In order to tap into this energy, carve out some time to rest your mind. This three-day period is an auspicious time to get rid of things you do not want—clutter, ideas, beliefs—anything that is not serving you. Create the physical and mental space for what you want to enter your reality, and allow yourself to rest.

NEW MOON PHASE

The new moon occurs on the second day of the dark moon phase. It symbolizes new beginnings in business, relationships, or in any area of your life that needs a reset. This is the time to set your intentions. Intentions are like seeds of energy that you plant deliberately to begin the manifesting process. You can set intentions to initiate change, increase financial abundance, bring in your dream job, start a business or project, attract a romantic partner, or simply allow more love and peace into your life. There are literally no limits to what you can set intentions for. Setting intentions is as simple as writing down your desires that you would like to see manifested in your physical reality—write them as if they have already happened, and then speak them into existence. I personally love doing sigil work during the dark moon phase. Sigils are described later in this section.

WAXING MOON PHASE

The waxing moon is beginning its journey back to fullness and gaining strength. This is the time to begin taking action in the physical world. It's also a good time for study, organization, connecting, or reconnecting with people. It is also a time of fertility, so this is a good time to conceive or begin a project.

It's also a good time to take action in your career, look for a job, ask for a promotion, start a business, or focus on receiving clarity on your purpose. This energy can spark sexual magic in an existing romantic partnership if you set that loving intention. Be playful and have fun with this energy. Sexual energy is the energy of creation.

FULL MOON PHASE

This phase represents the beginning of the moon's journey from light to dark. It marks the time for slowing down, letting go, and allowing things to come to completion. It also marks endings. It is an ideal time to break bad habits, lovingly end relationships, wrap up projects, resolve conflict, and close legal matters. Use this energy to finalize details, make corrections, and polish projects. It's also a wonderful time for releasing fear, anxiety, and depression, and even saying your goodbyes to an illness.

The full moon is the most powerful moon phase. This is most likely the time when you will see your seeds begin to sprout. It can also be a time of fulfillment of the intentions you set, or a time to revisit, build awareness around, or let go of patterns that no longer serve you, such as former relationship attachments and career decisions.

There are only two weeks between each new and full moon, which is not a lot of (linear) time for manifesting. But when you have cleared all the blocks and barriers that once kept you from receiving your desires, two weeks is usually all the time you need to see your seeds sprout, unless the universe has a different plan for you. You'll receive some confirmation of a different destined plan if that is the case.

If you do not see your seeds of intention sprouting at this time, then question your intentions and make sure they are based in love and not in fear. You may notice certain truths surface, which will help you to align with your own truth and get clear on the fine details of what you would like to manifest. Our personal truth changes as we evolve, and this particular moon phase helps to support your evolution by bringing you clarity that may cause you to choose to head in a different direction than you previously anticipated. The universe really wants you to have everything you've asked for, but it will not bring it to you if you're not ready, or if it's not in your highest good right now.

The full moon can also denote a time of fertility and heightened spirituality. You can more easily tap into higher guidance from your spiritual guides and hear their messages at this time. Asking for an increase in your psychic abilities is a wonderful use of this energy.

BUILDING A SISTERHOOD

Before I began my business, I attended a workshop in Monterey, California, with hundreds of women who were just beginning their spiritual-based business. I had not planned on attending this workshop, but I received an email from a spiritual-based business coach who was offering free admission to her workshop for a chosen few who could not afford to attend.

I felt that this was my chance to begin my new life. I had no idea how I would get there, but I accepted the invitation anyway, and three days later, I ended up getting a credit for a free flight from an airline due to a canceled flight a year prior.

The workshop was amazing. More than 400 women came together to learn how to begin building their businesses in ways that felt natural to the feminine essence, which looked nothing like the corporate world most of us came from. We discovered it was possible to build a thriving business with authenticity, collaboration, and love.

I had never been witness to so many spiritual entrepreneurs in one room, and they were all female! I made some lifelong friends that week. I will never forget one of the exercises we did, which affirmed my belief in the power of women coming together to love and support one another.

I did not always have nor want the support of women. Like so many other women I've worked with, I once believed that feminine connection was not valuable and could offer me nothing that I couldn't provide for myself.

My experience during that incredible week changed the way I saw other women. I finally recognized the value of having a group of amazing women to lift me up so I could confidently step into my own power. I also felt gratitude for being able to help to uplift them. Our energies combined created something that felt magical and incredibly powerful. Our compassion for one another fueled our personal passions for our own work.

We came together in small groups to share our stories with one another. We also spent some time sharing what our business aspirations were and why we were being called to serve in no particular way but our own.

It didn't matter that we had just met. We were there for each other in that moment, really hearing and seeing one another.

After we shared our stories, we were asked to describe each of the women in the group, in just one word. All seven women focused their attention on one woman at a time and began to say aloud the words that we felt described her. I heard everything they said about me, and I was in awe. When the exercise was over, we were given a notecard with all the words that were used to describe us personally. My card included these words: powerful, spiritual, open, honest, vulnerable, heroic, love. I was blown away. Just showing up as the real me, I made an impact on these women, and they saw me in ways that I could not see myself. I needed to hear this from a group of women who I barely knew, yet had so much respect for because of their own stories.

It was in this moment that I knew how I wanted to do business from now on—the feminine way.

Since then, I have met and connected and reconnected with so many amazing women whom I have a profound love and respect for, and we know that we can rely on one another when we are in need of love, support, advice, or just a boost of confidence.

There is great power in belonging to a sisterhood, one that is full of amazing women with big, beautiful hearts. Having the support of other women is one of the most powerful gifts a woman can receive. Building sacred relationships with other women also fuels our own radiance.

MANIFESTING THROUGH ART

Since the birth of humanity, we have created art to illustrate sacred universal feminine principles. Goddess consciousness can be found in artwork around the world, representing mysteries that the logical mind is not able to completely comprehend. Art represents the masculine aspect of creating that provides the gateway to the feminine—the "being" aspect of existence.

When you tap into your creativity with intention, you double your manifesting power and you have the ability to manifest rapidly. By creating a tangible representation of what you desire, you create an energetic output that can carry your intention all the way to fruition.

Consider painting, drawing, sculpting, writing—literally any artistic expression—as a tangible representation of the energy of your intention.

You can take this a step further by using other creative outlets to set intentions and sow the seeds of your desires. It doesn't matter what you choose: gardening, woodworking, dancing, playing music, or any other creative outlet so long as what you choose brings you joy. The alignment between intention and creation occurs when you visualize your desired outcome during the artistic process. As you begin creating your masterpiece, allow yourself to feel what it is like to have your desire manifested right before your eyes. Then, allow your creation to reflect this feeling in whatever unique way that feels good to you. When you're finished, you'll have a uniquely powerful masterpiece that holds the energetic vibration of your desire, and its energy will call forth your manifestation to you.

When creating through music or dance, we have the ability to build a powerful energetic field. This field not only aligns to the energetic frequency of your desire, but it also touches the emotional body, essentially doubling its manifesting power. In Chapter 13, Raise Your Frequency, we explored the magical power of sound. The combination of moving the body to sound can help you clear energetic blocks and replace them with the energy of your manifestation.

My friend Albert explained to me how dancing to shamanic drumming can shake trauma from the body.

He says the emotional body is the first layer right outside of the physical body, so it's what we have easiest access to. The next layer is the mental body, and the outer layer is the spiritual body. The strong emotions you've experienced in the past may still exist within the cells in your body. Dancing to shamanic drumming can release the stuck trauma from those cells.

You can also manifest by combining sound and dance. As you move, visualize the musical sounds as universal energy that is moving through your body and bringing you closer toward your desire. This builds the energy in the body and helps to raise your vibration so you can energetically align to your desires.

USING YOUR SENSUAL ENERGY TO MANIFEST

By far, the most powerful way to manifest is to harness your own sensual energy. Your sensual energy is raw, manifesting energy. It is the energy of creation.

The feminine has experienced a psychological split when it comes to sensuality. We have essentially been trained to create a split between the sensual self and the normal, everyday self, which means that we have replaced sensuality with neutral or masculine energy to get through everyday life. As a young woman, you may have received the message that your sensuality is not acceptable and that it is dangerous or inappropriate to express in public. The outcome of this conditioning is the shrinking of the sensual self in order to align with social expectations.

When I was a very little girl, I would tear off my clothes every chance I got, and I just danced. I really can't tell you why; I just felt an overwhelming desire to do it, so I did. Of course, I was told that is not what good little girls do, and my clothes were put back on me. During my sixth birthday party, I opened a gift box that had Superwoman Underoos in them. I immediately stripped off all my clothes and put them on, in front of all my friends. I remember that some of the boys (the brothers of my girlfriends) were a little embarrassed, and so were the adults, but I did it so fast that they couldn't catch me in the act. After all, it was my birthday.

When I look back at that innocent little girl who just wanted to be free and in her raw Goddess power, I feel for her, because this was the beginning of the social conditioning that set the tone for how I would show up in adulthood. I was told "cross your legs," and "don't wear that because it shows too much." And by the time I became a mother, nearly every ounce of sensual power had been drained from me. And forget about being a sensual Goddess and a new mom! Those two roles for the same woman just seemed gross to me. My Shakti became blocked because I was too afraid then to acknowledge the power of my inner Goddess. Shakti is considered the mother of all Goddesses, the essence of all Goddess power. "Shakti" means powerful divine feminine energy that is radiant, creative, authentic, intuitive, and sensual—and it flows throughout the universe. So many women have blocked themselves off from their Shakti energy, and as a result, have lost touch with their sensuality—and therefore their authenticity, radiance, and creative force. If your Shakti energy is blocked, it will be more of a challenge to manifest your desires. It wasn't until years later that I became comfortable enough in my own skin to embrace my sensuality. Now, I recognize it as the essence of my being.

I am not suggesting that you tear off your clothes in public or share your sexual energy freely. However, I am suggesting that you make it a regular practice to tap into your sensuality so you can experience the power and joy that it brings.

Sensuality is a confusing and sometimes difficult topic for women to delve into. There is so much shaming in cultures around the world for those who lead with their sensual energy. This cultural judgment is the biggest and most oppressive act because it cuts us off from our sexual energy, which is our creative force. Cultural judgment coupled with outrageous cultural standards of what beauty is supposed to look like can make it difficult for any woman to show up in her full sensual Goddess essence. The media tells us what sexy is supposed to look like (with Photoshopped pictures of models who are often dangerously thin), but somehow, we still believe that their backsides and breasts are a natural result of good genes. And if we do not look like them, then we are not beautiful. This belief could not be further from the truth.

There is also a fear of what could happen when leading with sensual energy. The National Sexual Violence Resource Center reported that one in five women in the United States alone has been sexually assaulted in their lifetime. For many women, leading with their sensual energy is associated with feelings of embarrassment, shame, or outright fear of attack, or the presence of all of these feelings at once. We need to get serious about healing our fears around sensuality because it is our divine right to experience it, and our raw power rests in this energy.

A powerful practice for embracing your sensuality is to wake up all your senses in ways that feel good. Through touch (a soft blanket), sound (beautiful music), smell (essential oils), sight (beautiful scenery), and taste (your favorite dessert). Get creative with this concept, and take it as far as you can. Goddess energy is wild and free and touches all five senses.

The sensual beingness of the feminine is powerful and magical. Allowing your sensual energy to move through you can actually help you mentally focus so you can manifest quickly. First, you must clear any shame, fear, and limiting beliefs about what it means to lead with your sensual energy. You can do this by spending time practicing self-care and spending more time in the nude. This will help you get more familiar with your own body and become more comfortable in your own skin. My coaching programs in the *Manifest Like a Goddess Experience* include ways you can tap into your sensual energy and activate your Sacral Chakra. I have witnessed with my own eyes how differently people approach me after I have spent time doing sacral activation work, which includes the powerful practice of sacral rocking that is done seated in a chair. I learned this technique from a powerful Goddess named Lois Kniss, the creator of Soul Gardening. This technique will not only change the way you interact with the world, you will also feel more beautiful, free, and capable.

Here, we shift our focus to physical applications and learn ways to initiate the manifesting process through igniting your inner Goddess in the physical body.

We human beings are powerful. Your body is a temple, and I encourage you to regard it as such. Many great yogis and mystics have used the power of the human body to manifest through movement—whether creating art through dance, painting, music, and through the seat of creation: our sexuality. Allowing the body to connect to and flow with this energy is not only a powerful way to move through the world but to bring your manifestations to fruition.

MANIFESTING THROUGH ORGASM

"Sexually awakened women, affirmed and recognized as such, would mean the complete collapse of the authoritarian ideology."
–Wilhelm Reich

This is the most taboo of all manifesting techniques listed here, but it is powerful. It has been said that the closest humans come to knowing God is through the act of sex. However, humans have created and perpetuated the belief that sex is somehow perverse. I am not suggesting that people should carelessly spread their sexual energy around. I strongly believe in sex being a holy act between two people who love each other, yet I do not hold any judgments regarding how people choose to have sex. I personally consider the sexual energy exchange between two loving partners to be extremely powerful and life-changing. During the act of sex, you are blending your divine energies together to co-create sacred energy that cannot be duplicated. I consider sexual energy as the creation of an energetic connection between lovers in the physical, mental, and emotional bodies, as well as the spirit.

The height of sexual connection happens through orgasm. We've been conditioned to believe that achieving an orgasm is the entire point in having sex. Not having a conscious partner shifts the goal of sex from bathing in ecstasy to achieving orgasm as quickly as possible. If you find yourself tensing up in order to build orgasmic energy, you might be in the habit of rushing to get there.

In order to really enjoy bathing in ecstasy, you will want to be able to maintain a relaxed state so you can lengthen your orgasms. You can practice being in a relaxed state by focusing on your breath so you can create and extend your sacred orgasmic experience with your partner, but when you're manifesting, I recommend doing the following technique solo. You want to be fully present with your partner during the act of sex. Being off in your head trying to manifest anything while you're having sex with someone who has no idea what you're up to is not only rude, but it is also pulling on their energy for your personal manifestation. And you don't want someone else's energy in your manifesting field unless you are both visualizing a shared intention together.

In an extended orgasm, an energetic alignment happens between the physical body and the spirit because your energy is hyper-focused, transforming it into a powerful, creative force. Learning to move sexual energy through your body and transmute it is incredibly empowering, and setting intentions from this space is a powerful way to manifest.

To manifest through orgasm, you want to get into a meditative state. Set the mood in your environment in such a way that you can fully relax.

Allow yourself some time to sit on your meditation cushion or lie down, relax your muscles, and clear your mind. You can also use guided meditations to help you. I recommend using the Sacral Chakra guided meditation created for the *Manifest Like a Goddess Experience*, described at the end of this book. Once you are relaxed and in the present moment, get clear on the intention you would like to set. Allow yourself to feel all of the feelings that come up with having your manifestation realized. As you begin experiencing pleasure, visualize your manifestation coming to fruition. You can imagine a color or a symbol to represent your manifested outcome if you need to. As you move into the orgasmic threshold, remain conscious of what is happening in your body. It is rather typical to contract muscles to build up sensation and then release it when it becomes too much. Instead, breathe slowly to regulate the flow of energy moving throughout your body. When you reach orgasm, maintain the image of your manifested intention in the forefront of your mind. This attaches your intentions to the energy of creation.

WORKING WITH RUNES

Reading runes is something I knew nothing about until I met my soul sister, Delanea Davis. She's the author of *Rune Reading Your Life*. Reading the runes has enhanced my manifesting practice in amazing ways. Runic practice is a powerful ancient art, and her book will help you learn all about the runes and how to use them in your daily life. I use them for daily clarity and insight, to strengthen my intuitive abilities, and for spiritual assistance in making difficult decisions. Rune work is a wonderful ancient magical practice that will help you in your Goddess work and strengthen your intuitive abilities. Do yourself a solid and get Delanea's book so you can learn how to use runes to assist you. The link to her book is located in the References section of this book.

CREATE SIGILS TO HELP YOU MANIFEST

Sigils are a powerful, ancient manifesting tool that have been used for centuries. They are a symbol of your intent. You can use them in your intention-setting rituals to manifest anything.

A good example of sigils in modern-day life are logos, and we see thousands of logos every day that are designed with the energy of intent—to bring in customers. Companies use their personal logos as visual representations of their brand. They are designed to evoke emotion, build trust, and invoke action. The world of marketing understands how very powerful logos are. The best company logos send a message about the company's mission, vision, and values that make customers want to buy their products and services. If you look closely, you will even notice rune symbols in some very well-known logos.

Sigils are energetically similar to logos. By creating a sigil, you are essentially expending your personal energy to create a meaningful symbol based on the energy of your intent to manifest your desire into your reality. You use it to place your order with the universe.

I often create sigils at the new moon to help me set intentions, especially when I'm feeling extra attached to the outcome. For me, sigils serve as an act of releasing my attachment to my desire. It helps me surrender and let go of controlling outcomes so I can relax into the co-creation process and get out of my own way so the universe can get to work on my behalf.

You want to make sure that you set a very clear intention when you are manifesting with sigils. You know by now that even written words have incredible power, and when spoken, they vibrate at their own unique frequency, so it's important to state exactly what you want. Write your intention down in present tense, as if it has already occurred, and say it out loud. Then, take what you've written and create an artistic symbol of it. Then, release it by setting fire to it, adding water, or burying it in the ground. Sigils will help you practice non-attachment regarding the outcome through the process of releasing your art to the universe as an offering of energy that is aligned with your desires. I have a very specific process for creating sigils that I teach in the *Manifest Like a Goddess Experience*.

GET IN TOUCH WITH YOUR FEELINGS

In Chapter 7, Emotional Mastery, you learned about the importance of emotions and how mastering them is an integral step on your journey of self-awareness. Learning to identify your feelings allows you to show up authentically and vulnerably, which is the first step in resolving the inner and outer conflicts that are blocking your manifestations. I've added two lists of words you can use to identify exactly what you are feeling. The first is the By-You Feelings Words List. The second is the Feelings Inventory List. By-You feelings are feelings that were created by someone "out there," and the Feelings Inventory List is comprised of words that describe true feelings.

When you find yourself in a fight, flight, or freeze response, it is common and seems completely normal in our society to blame others for how you're feeling. Sometimes it can feel impossible to get past blame in order to access the underlying feeling, so this is the time when you would begin with the By-You Feelings Words List. Choose a word that correlates with the By-You Feeling (a feeling that was created by another person). Once you have located the word or words that resonate with your emotional body, you can then search in the Feelings Inventory List to locate the underlying feeling behind the By-You feeling. This practice will pull you out of blame and victimhood and back into your own power. From there, you can begin to resolve conflict from a place of deeper self-understanding.

REAL WORK FOR REAL
GODDESSES

If you would like to take your manifesting practice even further and learn the intricacies of co-creation, I have something special for you. I created a powerful group coaching experience that will help guide you along your manifesting journey and learn to Manifest Like a Goddess.

The *Manifest Like a Goddess Experience* is organized into four programs that support the four elements: Earth, Water, Air, and Fire.

The Earth Element Program provides you with everything you need to become grounded in your truest and highest self. The Water Element Program helps you find your emotional equilibrium and manifest on purpose. The Air Element Program teaches you how to work with universal consciousness so you don't have to do it alone. The Fire Element Program preps you for taking clear, decisive action so you can begin to manifest like a Goddess.

If you're ready to take a deep dive into the tools and concepts described here, then I invite you to join the *Manifest Like a Goddess Experience*. It includes group coaching inside the four programs listed above, which are designed to help you begin your own unique manifesting journey. You can learn more about this experience at saradaves.com.

Programs Inside the *Manifest Like a Goddess Experience*:

EARTH ELEMENT TOPICS:

Blend the Inner Masculine and Feminine Energies
Understand the Goddess Archetypes
The Self-Awareness Path
Reframe Limiting Beliefs
Release, Allow and Receive
Step Into Your Authenticity

You will learn how to:

Use both masculine and feminine energies in healthy ways that serve you.
Discover your Goddess archetype and utilize this energy when you need it.
Gain the self-awareness necessary to begin consciously manifesting.
Identify and eliminate limiting beliefs that are keeping you stuck.
Lovingly release what no longer serves you.
Discover and own your superpowers.
Create space and allow your manifestations to enter your life.
Courageously receive what is meant for you.
Stand firmly in your authenticity and be unapologetically you.

WATER ELEMENT TOPICS:

Emotional Mastery Techniques
Harness the Power of Compassion
Heal Your Inner Child
Unconditional Self-Love Practice
Radical Gratitude Practice
Understand and Eliminate Inner Resistance

You will learn how to:

Master your emotions while feeling what you need to feel.
Access your passions through acts of compassion for yourself and others.

Heal the wounds of your Inner Child and free yourself from those limitations.

Grow your self-love and increase your self-worth.

Practice radical gratitude and create momentum in the manifesting process.

Understand and release internal resistance and come into wholeness.

AIR ELEMENT TOPICS:

Raise Your Vibration
Ignite Your Intuition
Embody Oneness and Understand Your Connection to Source
The Art of Non-attachment
Manifest Signs and Synchronicities
Gain Clarity of Your Purpose

You will learn how to:

Increase your vibration and clean up your auric field.

Become a master at differentiating between your soul's voice and your shadow's voice.

Develop a personal, intimate relationship with the universe (Source consciousness).

Discover freedom and be free of suffering with the practice of non-attachment.

Work with the universal energies within you and all around you.

Manifest and recognize synchronicities from universal consciousness.

Develop a personal vision to lead you to your purpose and help you make decisions quickly.

FIRE ELEMENT TOPICS:

Lovingly Set and Enforce Boundaries
Effort Less to Gain More
Integration for Wholeness
The Art of Expansion
Bending Time to Your Will

The Art of Creation in the Manifestation Process

You will learn how to:

Activate your throat chakra so you can speak your desires into existence.
Create, set and enforce boundaries in a healthy way.
Do less while manifesting more.
Integrate all the parts of your life so they flow in unison.
Create collaborative relationships that will support your desires.
Reprogram your subconscious to help you manifest.
Make both linear and non-linear time work for you.
Use art and your sensuality to speed up the manifestation process.
Activate your Sacral Chakra and step into your Goddess essence at will.
Develop a deeper understanding of the tools of manifesting, (runes, sigil-making, moon phases, and more).

Here's what else you'll get:

- Comprehensive and experiential exercises and journal prompts that will help you move deeper into the practice of manifesting.
- Access to guided meditations that are specifically designed for the *Manifest Like a Goddess Experience*. They include Theta waves in Binaural beats with specific chakra frequency notes (with singing bowls in the specific keys of each chakra) to assist in alignment and healing. There are many other guided meditations that will help you resolve inner conflict, outer conflict, and heal Inner Child wounds, and help you tap into your authenticity, Goddess power, and your soul's guidance. All these guided meditations will assist you in releasing old blocks and reprogramming your subconscious mind. These meditations will help you dive straight to the heart of common self-worth issues so you can rewrite your story and begin manifesting everything you want (love, money, relationships, peace, and overall abundance).

- Supportive group coaching with other Goddesses, specifically designed to help you anchor into your inner Goddess power and build your sisterhood.
- Monthly Mastermind Sessions to explore your unique, personal challenges and help you become a master in the art of manifesting.

By-You Feelings Word List

abandoned

abused

accused

assaulted

attacked

avoided

backstabbed

badgered

banned

beaten down

belittled

berated

betrayed

blacklisted

blackmailed

blamed

bossed-around

bothered

boxed-in

brushed-off

bugged

bullied

burdened

caged in

cheated

cheated on

coerced

commanded

compared

condescended

conned

controlled

convicted

cornered

corralled

criticized

crowded

crushed

cut-down

cut-off

damaged

damned

deceived

defamed

defeated

degraded

dehumanized

demeaned

demoralized

depraved

deprived

deserted

destroyed

devalued

discriminated

disempowered

disenchanted

disgraced

disowned

disregarded

disrespected

dominated

double-crossed

doubted

dumped

dumped on

duped
emasculated
evaded
excluded
exploited
exposed
guilt-tripped
hassled
humiliated
hurried
ignored
imposed-upon
imprisoned
indoctrinated
insulted
interrogated
interrupted
intimidated
invalidated
jerked around
judged
kept apart
kept away
kept in
kept out
kept quiet
labeled
left out
let down
made fun of
manipulated
mistreated
mistrusted

mocked
nagged
objectified
obligated
obstructed
offended
oppressed
over-protected
overwhelmed
pressured
provoked
punished
pushed away
put down
rejected
resented
ridiculed
scarred
screwed over
shamed
singled-out
smothered
shamed
singled-out
smothered
snapped at
stereotyped
suffocated
tricked

Feelings Inventory

The following list is made up of words we use when we want to express our emotional state. This list is neither exhaustive nor definitive. It is meant as a starting place to support you in embracing the process of self-discovery and facilitating greater understanding and connection.

There are two parts to this list: feelings we may have when our needs are being met and feelings we may have when our needs are not being met.

Feelings when your needs are satisfied:

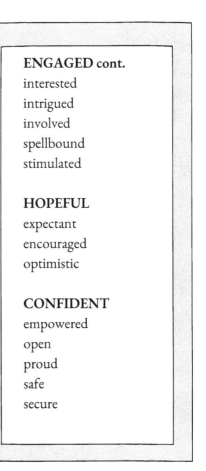

AFFECTIONATE
compassionate
friendly
loving
open hearted
sympathetic
 tender
warm
optimistic

ENGAGED
absorbed
alert
curious
engrossed
enchanted
entranced
fascinated

ENGAGED cont.
interested
intrigued
involved
spellbound
stimulated

HOPEFUL
expectant
encouraged
optimistic

CONFIDENT
empowered
open
proud
safe
secure

EXCITED
amazed
animated
ardent
aroused
astonished
dazzled
eager
energetic
enthusiastic
giddy
invigorated
lively
passionate
surprised
vibrant

EXHILARATED
blissful
ecstatic
elated
enthralled
exuberant
radiant
rapturous
thrilled

GRATEFUL
appreciative
moved
thankful
touched

INSPIRED
amazed
awed
wonder

JOYFUL
amused
delighted
glad
happy
jubilant
pleased
tickled

PEACEFUL

calm
clear headed
comfortable
centered
content
equanimous
fulfilled
mellow
quiet
relaxed
relieved
satisfied
serene
still
tranquil
trusting

REFRESHED

enlivened
rejuvenated
renewed
rested
restored
revived

Feelings when your needs are not satisfied:

AFRAID
apprehensive
dread
foreboding
frightened
mistrustful
panicked
petrified
scared
suspicious
terrified
wary
worried

ANNOYED
aggravated
dismayed
disgruntled
displeased
exasperated
frustrated
impatient
irritated
irked

ANGRY
enraged
furious
incensed
indignant
irate
livid
outraged
resentful

AVERSION
animosity
appalled
contempt
disgusted
dislike
hate
horrified
hostile
repulsed

CONFUSED

ambivalent
baffled
bewildered
dazed
hesitant
lost
mystified
perplexed
puzzled
torn

DISCONNECTED

alienated
aloof
apathetic
bored
cold
detached
distant
distracted
indifferent
numb
removed
uninterested
withdrawn

DISQUIET

agitated
alarmed
discombobulated
disconcerted
disturbed
perturbed
rattled
restless
shocked
startled
surprised
troubled
turbulent
turmoil
uncomfortable
uneasy
unnerved
unsettled
upset

EMBARRASSED

ashamed
chagrined
flustered
guilty
mortified
self-conscious

FATIGUE

beat
burnt out
depleted
exhausted
lethargic
listless
sleepy
tired
weary
worn out

PAIN

agony
anguished
bereaved
devastated
grief
heartbroken
hurt
lonely
miserable
regretful
remorseful

SAD

depressed
dejected
despair
despondent
disappointed
discouraged
disheartened
forlorn
gloomy
heavy hearted
hopeless
melancholy
unhappy
wretched

TENSE
anxious
cranky
distressed
distraught
edgy
fidgety
frazzled
irritable
jittery
nervous
overwhelmed restless
stressed out

VULNERABLE
fragile
guarded
helpless
insecure
leery
reserved
sensitive
shaky

YEARNING
envious
jealous
longing
nostalgic
pining
wistful

TESTIMONIALS FOR THE MANIFEST LIKE A GODDESS EXPERIENCE

"I started my Manifesting Like a Goddess journey in 2019. With Sara's guidance, motivation and endless patience, this journey is bearing fruits in abundance. Sara is the perfect guide on this journey; she will gently coach you into understanding your authenticity to live your life's purpose purposefully." —Louisa D.

"I had some fears about the future and I wasn't sure what I wanted to do next. Joining the *Manifest Like a Goddess Experience* taught me how to be still, be present, release my fears and love myself. And now I'm looking forward to the future, and also writing my book. Thank you Sara! You're amazing!" —Honesty L.

"I am loving the *Manifest Like a Goddess Experience*! All of it; the journaling, meditations, guidance and the supportive community. I appreciate Sara's combination of spiritual and practical approaches, using tarot, astrology, leading meditations, conflict resolution and what she teaches about individual purpose. I feel more grounded, more centered and confident that I have the power to manifest the life I want." —Bergen N.

"The *Manifest Like a Goddess Experience* is interesting, informative and empowering. I've gained more awareness and a deeper understanding of the manifesting process. It takes honest, consistent work and you need to be aware and present every day in order to successfully manifest what you ask for. It's exciting work!" —Jessica M.

"Working with Sara is like being sprinkled with fairy dust. No matter if we are just having a conversation or working on something, you always walk away feeling like you are dancing in the moonlight. She has a way of grounding you and making you feel like all is right with the world." —Margaret L.

"I wanted to learn about the power of manifesting, and the *Manifest Like a Goddess Experience* gave me a new framework to work with. Sara embodies pure Goddess energy! She is so genuine; so real. She helped me get comfortable in dealing with the unknown and how to dance within the realm of possibilities." —Jessica M.

"Due to emotional barriers and limiting beliefs from childhood, I felt I could not manifest the life I wanted. The *Manifest Like a Goddess Experience* gives a clear step-by-step process to create the life of your dreams. Sara really knows her stuff. This program is unlike any other I've seen. Her meditations are amazing at helping to connect with your inner self and move past blockages." —Megan A.

"I knew what I wanted but I didn't know how I could get there. The *Manifest Like a Goddess Experience* requires a lot of self-reflection and deep introspection. Through the modules, I learned to trust my intuition and recognize when I was straying from my purpose. I was surprised by how open and available Sara is to all of our questions. I feel like she really took the time to get to know all of us. Finding clarity is the best way I can describe how Sara has helped me!" —Sheela M.

ACKNOWLEDGMENTS

I would like to thank everyone who either helped me write this book or taught me what I needed to learn so I could. Thank you, Kim Eley, my enthusiastic editor and publisher, for your superb guidance, humor, and patience; Delanea Davis for planting the seed of the Goddess essence into my conscious awareness; Sylvia Clute for being my mentor and friend, and helping me to shift my consciousness from punitive to unitive so I could embody my life's purpose; my mom for helping me articulate the Goddess essence; Lois Kniss for teaching me how to embody my feminine essence; and Sophia, Goddess of Truth, for guiding me along my spiritual journey.

I also want to thank my parents and my brothers, and also my friends for supporting me through the toughest years of my life—which included the passing of my son, his father, and my own dad. I would not have made it through in one piece without you. Thank you, Gregg Archibald, for always believing in me, Albert Moore for being the shining light on my path, and Denise Dolan for connecting me to Trey in spirit, which has brought all sorts of wonderful magic into my life!

Thank you, my dearest Treybird, for always being here with me and showing me your unending love through daily synchronicities. And thank you, Dad, Grandma, and Grandpa for your continuous guidance and love, even from the afterworld. I see you.

REFERENCES

Chapter 1:

Bruce Lipton, Gaia Series, Inner Evolution: gaia.com

The Empowered Wife, by Laura Doyle: https://lauradoyle.org/the-empowered-wife/

Choose Her Everyday or Leave Her, by Bryan Reeves: https://bryanreeves.com/choose-her-everyday-or-leave-her/

Chapter 2:

https://deborahking.com/isis-goddess-of-healing/

http://www.sistersofearthsong.com/SOPHIA/SOPHIA.html

http://www.lowchensaustralia.com/names/african-goddesses.htm

https://kashgar.com.au/blogs/gods-goddesses/kali-a-most-misunderstood-goddess

https://norse-mythology.org/gods-and-creatures/the-vanir-gods-and-goddesses/freya/

http://rootedsun.com/persephone/

www.goddessgift.com

https://www.santuariolunar.com.br/en/goddess-gwenhwyfar/

Waldherr, Kris. The Barefoot Book of Goddesses. Barefoot Book, Ltd. 1995.

Chapter 7:

"The New Rules of Retail by Robin Lewis and Michael Dart" https://us.macmillan.com/books/9781137480897/thenewrulesofretail

Chapter 10:

The Five Love Languages, by Gary Chapman: https://www.5lovelanguages.com/

Chapter 13:

Map of Consciousness, by Dr. David Hawkins: https://veritaspub.com/product/map-of-consciousness-dr-david-hawkins/

Hindustan Times: https://www.hindustantimes.com/columns/cosmic-vibration-of-om/story-s7mFAHCv7JoSMzXYHkASQK.html

Sand moving to music: https://youtu.be/wvJAgrUBF4w

Chapter 14:

Albert Moore, author of *Eyes In The Mirror: Everything Changed When He Met His Soul*: https://www.iuniverse.com/BookStore/BookDetails/765806-Eyes-in-the-Mirror

Rune Reading Your Life, By Delanea Davis: https://www.penguinran-domhouse.com/books/616800/rune-reading-your-life-by-delanea-davis/

Francis P Cholle, founder of the Human Company: www.psychologyto day.com/us/contributors/francis-p-cholle

Chapters 4, 8, 13, 15 and 24:

Sylvia Clute, president of The Alliance for Unitive Justice and author of *Unitive Justice: Bending the Arc of Justice Toward Love*, her work is mentioned throughout the book.

Chapter 16:

Description of Gabor Mate's research on the top three risk factors for chronic illness: https://www.youtube.com/watch?v=ajo3xkhTbfo

An Uncommon Bond, by Jeff Brown, Enrealment Press, 2015.

Deepak Chopra's work: https://iamfearlesssoul.com/deepak-chopra-you-suffer-because-you-dont-know-who-you-are-amazing-speech/

Chapter 17:

Denise Dolan, CEO and Cofounder of LOVE. LIFE. WISDOM. https://lovelifewisdom.com/ and The Bridging Loss Healing Project: https://bridgingloss.com/index.html

Chapter 18:

Levi Strauss *The Case Study: Child Labor in Bangladesh* in 2017: https://www.levistrauss.com/wp-content/uploads/2019/03/Case-Study_Child-Labor-in-Bangladesh.pdf

Chapter 19:

The Boundaries Program, by Bryan Reeves and Silvy Khoucasian: https://bryanreeves.com/boundaries/

Chapter 20:

Marti Spiegelman: https://www.martispiegelman.org/

Todd Hoskins http://canopygap.com/
Oneness Summit Interview with Todd Hoskins and Marti Spiegelman: https://www.youtube.com/watch?v=GUEwnupSR4Q&t=255s

Chapters 22 and 23:

Joe Dispenza: https://drjoedispenza.com/

References from Tools for Manifesting Like a Goddess

GET IN TOUCH WITH YOUR FEELINGS

Feelings Inventory List, Center for Nonviolent Communication: www.c-nvc.org

USING YOUR SENSUAL ENERGY TO MANIFEST

National Sexual Violence Resource Center: https://www.nsvrc.org/Lois Kniss, Soul Gardening: https://soul-gardening.com/

NOTES

INTRODUCTION

1. The Bloom of Consciousness illustration located inside the front cover of this book explains the various vibrational levels that we can embody. This concept is explained in Chapter 13, Raise Your Frequency.
2. I have chosen to use the word "manifestor" instead of "manifester" as words ending in "or" such as "creator" indicate a person. https://www.goodvibeblog.com/manifestor-vs-manifester/

17. SYNCHRONICITY

1. From https://www.guru99.com/alpha-beta-testing-demystified.html.

ABOUT THE AUTHOR

Sara Daves is an intuitive purpose coach and conflict resolution expert. For more than two decades, she's learned about the power of manifesting—the hard way. Her life fell apart after Trey, her beautiful son, crossed over into the spirit world. Through her grieving process, and by making lots (and lots) of mistakes, she learned how to bring joy back into her life, even when she saw nothing left to live for. Sara shifted her focus from a place of lack to one of abundant possibilities and taught herself how to consciously manifest the life experiences she wanted—the recognition of her connection to Source and serving through her purpose, and to empower others to manifest a magnificent life for themselves—the life they were meant to live.

Sara offers group manifesting coaching programs, conflict resolution facilitator training, private purpose coaching, and retreats.

Website: saradaves.com

 facebook.com/sara.daves
 instagram.com/saradaves